100 YEARS OF LYNCHINGS
RALPH GINZBURG

Black Classic Press
P.O. Box 13414
Baltimore, MD 21203

Black Classic Press
P.O. Box 13414
Baltimore, MD 21203

ISBN-13 978-0-933121-18-8
ISBN-10 0-933121-18-0

FOREWORD

What lies at the root of race hatred? After spending several years with the subject, I hold with psychologists that it is unconscious guilt feelings on the part of the race-hater. The person who hates Negroes usually hates other people beside Negroes. He's almost a professional hater. If he's poor, he hates the rich. If he's rich he hates the poor. If he's a Democrat, he hates the Republicans. If he's a Protestant or a Jew, he hates the Catholics. The reason is that the race-hater is inwardly a man who hates himself. He finds it necessary to shift to others his own unconscious feelings of guilt. Hence he chooses as his victim a member of a minority group who is less able to defend himself than the average person. To his victim he unconsciously shifts his own shortcomings and guilt-laden desires. Jews, he says, are deceitful and money-mad; Negroes, he says, are slothful and sex-mad. A perfect example of such "projection," to use the psychological term, is found in the New York Herald Tribune dispatch of February 9, 1936, contained in this book, which tells of the mob hanging of a Negro, allegedly for attempted rape. The leader of the mob, it later turns out, is convicted for the very same offense he ascribed to the Negro.

I shall not discourse upon the horror of the white man's treatment of the black man in American history. The facts in this book speak too eloquently for themselves. I shall only say that I hope the publication of this book, in this Centennial of the Civil War, will give pause to segregationists everywhere to reflect upon their continued persecution of the black man.

A few technical points: Many of the press accounts contained in this book appear verbatim as originally published. Others have been drastically rewritten for the sake of clarity or conciseness. In a number of cases where two or more newspapers contained conflicting reports of a given incident, the several reports have been reprinted. In cases where two or more newspapers contained different—but not conflicting—information, the information from all sources has been synthesized into one story and attributed to the newspaper which provided most of the facts. In no case have facts, as reported in the press, been altered.

Ralph Ginzburg

There's a great time coming
And it's not far off,
Been long, long, long on the way.

—from the song "Wake Nicodemus"
written during the Civil War
by the Negro Composer Henry Clay Work.

NEW YORK TRUTH SEEKER
April 17, 1880

FIRST NEGRO AT WEST POINT KNIFED BY FELLOW CADETS

WEST POINT, N.Y., Apr. 15—James Webster Smith, the first colored cadet in the history of West Point, was recently taken from his bed, gagged, bound, and severely beaten, and then his ears were slit. He says that he cannot identify his assailants. The other cadets claim that he did it himself.

CHICAGO TRIBUNE
November 22, 1895

TEXANS LYNCH WRONG NEGRO

MADISONVILLE, Tex., Nov. 21—News has been received here of the lynching of a Negro in this part of Madison County on Tuesday night. He was accused of riding his horse over a little white girl and injuring her. On Wednesday it was discovered that the wrong Negro had been gotten hold of by the mob. The guilty one made his escape.

EDITORIAL FROM THE SPRINGFIELD (MASSACHUSETTS) WEEKLY REPUBLICAN
January 19, 1896

WHITE SUPERIORITY IN FLORIDA

The noble and valiant Anglo-Saxons of Manatee county, Fla., are engaged just now in demonstrating the superiority of the race. Some days ago the son of the county sheriff and the son of a poor negro quarreled and the black was the victor in a boys' fight. Thereupon the sheriff and a number of brave whites, fully armed, went

9

to the negro's cabin at night and demanded that the boy be handed over to them. Knowing what would be his probable fate, the negro refused to surrender his son. On the contrary he seized a gun and when the white mob fired upon the house he returned the fire and killed the sheriff. Then the whites in a rage picked up a log and rushed upon the cabin door to batter it in, and another shot from the negro's gun killed another white man and fatally wounded a third. The mob retreated for reinforcements, and the negro took his boy and gun and made off for the swamps. At last accounts he had not been captured and tortured to death, but in lieu of this the noble and manly whites were going about the country firing into the cabins of innocent and defenseless blacks, burning up the homes of some, killing others, and ordering a general exodus of negroes, threatening a boycott on employers of labor who would not discharge their negro help.

KISSIMMEE VALLEY (FLORIDA) GAZETTE
April 28, 1899

SAM HOLT BURNED AT STAKE

Sam Holt, the negro who is thought to have murdered Alfred Cranford and assailed Cranford's wife, was burned at the stake one mile and a quarter from Newnan, Ga., Sunday afternoon, July 23rd, at 2:30 o'clock Fully 2,000 people surrounded the small sapling to which he was fastened and watched the flames eat away his flesh, saw his body mutilated by knives and witnessed the contortions of his body in his extreme agony.

Two counties, Campbell and Coweta, directly interested in the crimes of the negro, and the entire state have waited with impatience for the moment when the negro would pay the penalty for his fiendish deeds. Such suffering has seldom been witnessed, and through it all the negro uttered hardly a cry. Those who witnessed the affair saw the negro meet his death and saw him tortured before the flames with unfeigning satisfaction.

For sickening sights, harrowing details and blood-curdling incidents, the burning of Holt is unsurpassed by any occurrence of a like kind ever heard of in the history of Georgia. A few smouldering ashes scattered about the place, a blackened stake, are all that was left to tell the story. Not even the bones of the negro were left in peace, but were eagerly snatched by a crowd of people drawn from all directions, who almost fought over the burning body of the man, carving it with their knives and seeking souvenirs of the occurrence.

Holt went to the stake with as much courage as any one could possibly have possessed on such an occasion, and the only murmur that issued from his lips was when angry knives plunged into his flesh and his life's blood sizzled in the fire before his eyes.

Then he cried, "Oh, my God! Oh, Jesus."

The crowd that burned Holt believed it had made no mistake of his guilt or identity. After the first flames licked at his feet, he was temporarily removed from the sapling at which time he is said to have admitted his guilt.

One of the strangest features of the entire affair is the part played in the execution by a northern man. This man, whose name would not be divulged by those who knew him, announced that he was from the north, while he calmly saturated Holt's clothing with kerosene oil.

Mrs. Cranford, the rape victim, was not permitted to identify the negro. She is ill and it was thought the shock would be too great for her. The crowd was satisfied with the identification of Holt by Mrs. Cranford's mother who did not, however, actually see Holt commit the crime.

Masks played no part of the lynching. There was no secrecy; no effort to prevent anyone seeing who lighted the fire, who cut off the ears or who took the head. On the trunk of a tree nearby was pinned the following placard:

"We Must Protect Our Southern Women."

SPRINGFIELD (MASSACHUSETTS)
WEEKLY REPUBLICAN
April 28, 1899

NEGRO BURNED ALIVE IN FLORIDA; SECOND NEGRO THEN HANGED

NEWMAN, Ga., Apr. 23—Sam Holt, the murderer of Alfred Cranford and the ravisher of the latter's wife, was burned at the stake, near Newnan, Ga., this afternoon, in the presence of 2000 people. The black man was first tortured before being covered with oil and burned. An ex-governor of Georgia made a personal appeal to his townspeople to let the law take its course, but without the slightest avail.

Before the torch was applied to the pyre, the negro was deprived of his ears, fingers and genital parts of his body. He pleaded pitifully for his life while the mutilation was going on, but stood the ordeal of fire with surprising fortitude. Before the body was cool, it was cut to pieces, the bones were crushed into small bits, and even the tree upon which the wretch met his fate was torn up and disposed of as "souvenirs." The negro's heart was cut into several pieces, as was also his liver. Those unable to obtain the ghastly relics direct paid their more fortunate possessors extravagant sums for them. Small pieces of bones went for 25 cents, and a bit of the liver crisply cooked sold for 10 cents. As soon as the negro was seen to be dead there was a tremendous struggle among the crowd, which had witnessed his tragic end, to secure the souvenirs. A rush was made for the stake, and those near the body were forced against it and had to fight for their freedom. Knives were quickly produced and soon the body was dismembered.

One of the men who lifted the can of kerosene to the negro's head is said to be a native of Pennsylvania. His name is known to those who were with him, but they refuse to divulge it. The mob was composed of citizens of Newnan, Griffin, Palmetto and other little towns in the country round about Newnan, and of all the farmers who had received word that the burning was to take place.

W. Y. Atkinson, a former governor of Georgia, met the

mob as he was returning from church and he appealed to them to let the law take its course. In addressing the mob he used these words: "Some of you are known to me and when this affair is finally settled in the courts, you may depend upon it that I will testify against you." A member of the mob was seen to draw a revolver and level it at Mr. Atkinson, but his arm was seized and the pistol taken from him. The mob was frantic with delays and would hear to nothing but burning at the stake.

Before being put to death, the negro is said to have confessed to killing Cranford, stating that he had been paid $20 by "Lige" Strickland, a negro preacher at Palmetto, for the deed.

Holt was located in the little cabin of his mother on the farm of the Jones brothers between Macon and Columbus and brought to jail.

Word was sent to Mrs. Cranford at Palmetto that it was believed Holt was under arrest and that her presence was necessary in Newnan to make sure of his identification. In some way the news of the arrest leaked out, and as the town has been on the alert for nearly two weeks, the intelligence spread rapidly.

From every house in the little city came its occupants, and a good-sized crowd had soon gathered about the jail. Sheriff Brown was importuned to give up the prisoner, and finally in order to avoid an assault on the jail and possible bloodshed, he turned the negro over to the waiting crowd.

A procession was quickly formed and the doomed negro was marched at the head of a yelling, shouting crowd through several streets of the town. Soon the public square was reached. Here ex-Gov. Atkinson of Georgia, who lives in Newnan, came hurriedly upon the scene, and standing up in a buggy importuned the crowd to let the law take its course.

Gov Atkinson said: "My fellow citizens and friends: I beseech you to let this affair go no further. You are hurrying this negro on to death without an identification. Mrs Cranford, whom he is said to have assaulted and whose husband he is said to have killed, is sick in bed and unable to be here to say whether this is her assailant. Let this negro be returned to jail. The law will take its course, and I promise you it will do so quickly

13

and effectually. Do not stain the honor of the state with a crime such as you are about to perform." Judge A. D. Freeman of Newnan spoke in a similar strain and prayed the mob to return the prisoner to the custody of the sheriff and go home. The assemblage heard the words of the two speakers in silence, but the instant their voices had died away shouts of "On to Palmetto, burn him, think of his crime," arose, and the march was resumed.

Mrs Cranford's mother and sister are residents of Newnan. The mob was headed in the direction of their house and in a short time reached the McElroy home. The negro was marched through the gate and Mrs McElroy was called to the front door. She identified the African, and her verdict was agreed to by her daughter, who had often seen Holt about the Cranford place. "To the stake," was again the cry and several men wanted to burn the negro in Mrs McElroy's yard. To this she objected strenuously, and the mob, complying with her wish, started for Palmetto. Just as they were leaving Newnan news was brought that the 1 o'clock train from Atlanta would bring 1000 people from Atlanta. This was taken to be a regiment of soldiers, and the mob decided to burn the prisoner at the first favorable place rather than be compelled to shoot him when the militia put in an appearance.

Leaving the little town, whose Sunday quiet had been so rudely disturbed, the mob, which now numbered nearly 1500 people, started on the road to Palmetto. A line of buggies and vehicles of all kinds, their drivers fighting for position in line, followed the procession, at the head of which, closely guarded, marched the negro. One and a half miles out of Newnan, a place believed to be favorable to the burning, was reached. A little to the side of the road was a strong pine tree. Up to this the negro was marched, his back placed to the tree and his face to the crowd, which jostled closely about him.

The clothes were torn from the negro in an instant. A heavy chain was produced and wound around his body. He said not a word to this proceeding, but at the sight of three or four knives slashing in the hands of several members of the crowd about him, which seemed to forecast the terrible ordeal he was about to be put to, he sent

14

up a yell which could be heard for a mile. Instantly a hand grasping a knife shot out and one of the negro's ears dropped into a hand ready to receive it. He pleaded pitifully for mercy and begged his tormentors let him die. His cries went unheeded.

PALMETTO, Ga., Apr. 24—The body of "Lije" Strickland, a negro preacher, who was implicated in the Cranford murder by "Sam" Holt, was found swinging to the limb of a persimmon tree within a mile and a quarter of Palmetto, Ga., early today. Before death was allowed to end the sufferings of the negro, his ears were cut off and the small finger of his left hand was severed at the second joint. These trophies were in Palmetto yesterday. On the chest of the negro was a piece of bloodstained paper, attached by an ordinary pin. On one side of this paper was written:—

—We must protect our ladies.

The other side of the paper contained a warning to the negroes of the neighborhood. It read as follows:—

Beware all darkies! You will be treated the same way.

Before being lynched, Strickland was given a chance to confess to the misdeeds of which the mob supposed him to be guilty, but he protested his innocence to the last. Three times the noose was placed around his neck and the negro was drawn up off the ground; three times he was let down with a warning that death was in store for him, should he fail to confess his complicity in the Cranford murder. Three times Strickland proclaimed his innocence, until weary of useless torturing, the mob pulled on the rope and tied the end around the slender trunk of the persimmon tree. Not a shot was fired. Strickland was strangled to death.

The lynching of "Lije" Strickland was not accomplished without a desperate effort on the part of his employer to save his life. The man who pleaded for him is Maj W. W. Thomas, an ex-state senator, and one of the most distinguished citizens of Coweta county. He did all in his power to prevent the lynching of the negro and did not discontinue his efforts until he had been assured by the leaders of the mob that the negro would be taken to jail at Fairburn. One mile from the spot where this promise was made, Strickland was hanged. The negro was a tenant on the plantation of Maj Thomas. When "Sam" Holt, the murderer of Alfred Cranford and the assailant of his wife, made his confession immediately prior to his burning, he implicated "Lije" Strickland, Holt contending that he had been offered money by Strickland to kill Cranford. It was known positively, however, that Holt had made false statements in his last confession, and many of those who aided in his burning were disposed to disregard his statement in regard to Strickland.

About 15 men went to the plantation of Maj Thomas late Sunday night and took Strickland from his little cabin in the wood, and left his wife and five children to wait and weep over the fate they knew was in store for the negro. Their cries aroused Maj Thomas, and that sturdy old man followed the lynchers in his buggy, accompanied by his son, William Thomas, determined to save, if possible, the life of his plantation darkey. They overtook the lynchers with their victim at Palmetto, and then ensued, with only the moonlight to brighten the faces of these grim men, a weird and dramatic scene. Lije Strickland was halted directly opposite the telegraph office. The noose was adjusted around his neck and the end of the rope was thrown over a tree. Strickland was told he had a chance before dying to confess his complicity in the crime. He replied: "I have told you all I know, gentlemen. You can kill me if you wish, but I know nothing to tell."

The negro's life might have been ended then, but for the arrival of Maj Thomas, who leaped from his buggy and asked for a hearing. He asked the crowd to give the negro a chance for his life, and said: "Gentleman, this negro is innocent. Holt said Lije had promised to give him $20 to kill Alfred Cranford, and I don't believe Lije had $20 since he has been on my place. He has never done any of you any harm; I want you to promise me that you will turn him over to the bailiff of this town that he may be given a hearing. I do not ask you to liberate him. Hold him for the courts." The mob replied that Strickland had inflamed the negroes in the neighborhood and had a bad reputation, having run away from Eastpoint several years ago. Maj Thomas reminded the mob that the negro had voluntarily told of having seen Holt on the night of the murder. One of the mob replied

16

that Strickland had done this in the cunningness of his guilt to establish his own innocence.

There were some, however, who agreed with Maj Thomas, and after a discussion, a vote was taken, which was supposed to mean life or death to Lije Strickland. The vote to let him live was unanimous. Maj Thomas then retired some distance, and the mob was preparing to send Strickland in a wagon to Newnan, when a member of the mob cried out: "We have got him here, let's keep him." This aroused the mob and a messenger was sent to advise Maj Thomas to leave Palmetto for his own good, but the old man was not frightened. He drew himself up and said emphatically: "I have never before been ordered to leave a town, and I am not going to leave this one." And then the major, uplifting his hand to give his words force, said to the messenger: "Tell them the muscles in my legs are not trained to running; tell them I have stood the fire and heard the whistle of minis from a thousand Yankee rifles, and I am not frightened by this crowd." Maj Thomas was not molested. Then, with the understanding that Lije Strickland was to be delivered to the jailer at Fairburn, Maj Thomas saw the negro he had pleaded for led off to his death.

The mob took the negro to a grove near the home of Marshall Givens of Palmetto, and again the noose was adjusted. He was hauled off the ground, but was let down to allow him to confess. He refused to do so, and the lynchers were about to haul him up again when the son of Marshall Givens came upon the scene, and asked that the lynching should not occur near his father's home. The negro was then taken to the yard in the rear of Dr W. S. Zeller's home, and tied up to a persimmon tree and left hanging. A coroner's jury held an inquest over the body Monday afternoon and returned the usual verdict— death at the hands of parties unknown. Another mob is hunting the county for Albert Sewell, who has made himself obnoxious by remarks concerning the treatment given the negros by the whites. There is not much prospect of his capture however, as he has had a day's start of his pursuers.

ATLANTA, Ga., Apr. 24—The Atlanta Constitution said this morning: "The terrible expiation which Sam

17

Holt was forced to pay for his crime will arouse a flood of discussion carried on by those who know the facts in the near side and those who do not care for facts on the other. But while the form of this criminal's punishment cannot be upheld, let those who are disposed to criticise it look into the facts, and by these facts temper the judgment they may render.

"An unassuming, industrious and hard working farmer, after his day's toil, sat at his evening meal. Around him sat wife and children, happy in the presence of the man who was fulfilling to them every duty imposed by nature. At peace with the world, serving God and loyal to humanity, they looked forward to the coming day. Noiselessly the murderer with uplifted ax advanced from the rear and sank it to the hilt in the brain of the unsuspecting victim. Tearing the child from the mother's breast, he flung it into the pool of blood oozing from its father's wound. Then began the culmination, which has dethroned the reason of the people of western Georgia during the past week. As critics will howl about the lynching, the Constitution will be pardoned for stating the plain facts. The wife was seized, choked, thrown upon the floor, where her clothing lay in the blood of her husband, and ravished.

"Remember the fact. Remember the dark night in the country home. Remember the slain husband, and, above all, remember that shocking degradation which was inflicted by the black beast, his victim, swimming in her husband's warm blood as the brute held her to the floor. Keep the facts in mind. When the picture is painted of the ravisher in flames, go back and view that darker picture of Mrs Cranford outraged in the blood of her murdered husband."

ATLANTA, Ga., Apr. 24—Gov Candler of Georgia Sunday night gave the Associated Press the following statement on the burning of Sam Holt, near Newman: "The whole thing is deplorable, and Holt's crime, the horrible details of which have been published and are too horrible for publication, is the most diabolical in the annals of crime. The negroes of the community lost the best opportunity they will ever have to elevate themselves in the estimation of their white neighbors.

18

"But they lost the opportunity, and it is a deplorable fact that, while scores of intelligent negroes, leaders of their race, have talked to me about the Palmetto lynching, not one of them has ever in the remotest way alluded to the diabolical crime of Holt which provoked the lynching. I do not believe these men sympathized with Holt but they can see but one side of the question and are blinded by race prejudices."

EDITORIAL FROM THE SPRINGFIELD (MASSACHUSETTS) WEEKLY REPUBLICAN
April 28, 1899

THE GEORGIA EXHIBITION

The annals of the savage will be searched in vain for anything worse than the exhibition given to the world by the white civilization of the state of Georgia. The best that the devilish ingenuity of man has ever been able to do, in any age or among any people, to make the ordeal of death as excruciating and awful as it could possibly be made, was equaled in the torture and mutilation and burning of the negro Holt; and if any large company of human beings at any stage in the development of the race ever gave greater evidences of joy, in such a spectacle or rushed with greater eagerness to secure mementoes of the fearful tragedy in the form of pieces of the burned flesh and bits of the charred bones, history makes no record of the fact.

The nation and the whole civilized world must stand aghast at the revelation. A civilized community numbering thousands, at the drop of a hat, throws off the restraints and effects of many centuries of progress and stands forth in the naked savagery of the primitive man. Men and women cheer and express feelings of triumph and joy as the victim is hurried on to the stake to make a Sunday holiday in one of the most orthodox religious communities in the United States. They cut off his ears, his fingers and other members of the body, and strip him and pour oil upon him while the spectators crowd desperately for positions of advantage in the great work of

19

torture and death. As the flames rise about the victim the people watch the quiverings of the flesh and the writhings of the frame, and shout back descriptions to the jostling, cheering hundreds on the outskirts of the ring. The negro raises a cry of agony that can be heard far away, and in a supreme effort loosens the upper part of his body from the chain which binds it to the tree. The fire is deadened while he is being chained back, and the awful agony prolonged to the evident relish of the spectators. Then more oil and fire, and death at last comes to the man's release.

Meantime the news has spread of what is going on and hundreds leave Atlanta and other places by special train to see the fun. There is a rush upon what is left of the body and spectators cut off bits of the flesh, the liver and the bones as precious souvenirs of the day. The mob is now only fairly started on the hunt for vengeance and amusement. The victim, in the midst of the torture, gives the name of one alleged to be implicated in his crime. It may have been the suggestion of truth, or it may have been the false prompting of a desperate desire to save himself. Quite likely the latter. But the mob sets off after the negro Strickland. He is seized in the dead of night. His white employer says he believes the man is innocent. No matter, the appetite for blood is up and has not been satisfied. The negro is "tried" by mob oratory and condemned. He is strung up and let down once or twice by way of extorting a confession, and through it all he protests his innocence. His ears and fingers are cut off and the body is finally left dangling from a tree limb. The mob next sets out for a negro who had been heard to say his race should be avenged, and at last accounts it was still spreading terror and death among the blacks, while a similar mob in South Carolina has inaugurated a like campaign.

And this, fellow-citizens, is the quality of the civilization of which you and we boast. This is of the white civilization we would carry to the Orient and shoot into the hearts of the Malays if we cannot get it there otherwise. Is there to be found in the story of the Malay, treacherous and bloody as he is said to be in a state of nature, anything more savage and cowardly and devilish than this exhibition in one of the original states of the American Union? It is impossible that there could be! A braggart civilization is revealed which needs to look to itself and its home problems before venturing further on a world crusade.

BANGOR (MAINE) COMMERCIAL
September 5, 1899

VISITING SOUTHERN REPORTER DESCRIBES LYNCHINGS SEEN

A veteran reporter on one of the Southern newspapers, who is now visiting this city, gives an interesting account of his experiences in "covering" lynching parties. "The news that there is to be a lynching," he begins, "spreads very rapidly in the south, especially in the small cities and towns. To the reporter it is a very disagreeable business to attend these lynchings, for he is usually not overcome by frenzy like the mob made up from the immediate neighborhood, and so cannot sympathize with its method of procedure. I have attended in my capacity as a reporter at least 12 lynchings, and on each of two of these occasions I have seen as many as three negroes lynched.

"The first time I saw a triple lynching I felt no doubt as to the victims' guilt. When arrested they confessed their crime and were placed upon a pile of railroad ties which had been put along the railroad track under the shade of some tall trees, and when the rope was ready the crowd pulled the ties out from under them. Before the victims were dead they were riddled with bullets from the pistols, which are always to be found with southern men on such occasions.

"This lynching did not impress me as half so horrible as one a short time afterwards in which an innocent man named John Peterson was the victim. He was charged with the usual crime at a place near Denmark, S. C.

"He hastily made his way to Columbia, S. C., as soon as he heard he was suspected, and surrendered himself to the penitentiary authorities there, saying that he was innocent and wanted their protection. When a warrant

21

for Peterson came from the authorities of Barnwell county, the governor surrendered him. It was known that the people in the neighborhood of Denmark were so excited that there would be little chance of the poor fellow's getting a fair trial. If he had been kept in the state penitentiary until things cooled off, the outcome would clearly have been different.

"Peterson was, however, taken back to Denmark by several officers, and the party was accompanied by representatives of all the newspapers. On arriving at the small village, we found a crowd of several hundred men and boys had assembled, and organized a mock court. It must be acknowledged that some of the leading men in the county were there. Testimony of various kinds was offered against the negro. None of it was very damaging except that of a woman of low character, who testified that she had seen Peterson quite near the place where the crime had been committed, and at the time.

"The crowd then took the prisoner to the home of the man whose daughter had been assaulted. She declined to identify him positively, saying that he looked like the man, but that she was not sure of him. After the crowd went back to town and placed Peterson in the lock-up, the father of the girl began to blame her severely for not fixing the crime upon the poor fellow. This man was so excited that he wanted to have the crime avenged at once, and was not particular as to who should pay the penalty. The girl was finally brought over to the point of saying that she felt sure Peterson was the guilty man. This was sufficient.

"The townspeople and those who had gathered to see the affair decided to lynch Peterson that night. The work was done so quickly after this conclusion was reached that most of the newspaper men did not know anything was going to happen until they heard the hammering of the axes on the door of the wooden lock-up. Peterson was seized and taken to a patch of pine woods not far from the home of the young woman.

It so happened that two railroad lines crossed near this point. On one of them a train bound for Augusta Ga., was due in a few minutes, and a goodly number of the men present wanted to board that train to go to their homes. There was also a great demand on the part of the reporters to have the job done before the arrival of the train. The telegraph facilities in the little town were insufficient to accommodate all the newspapers, and the reporters preferred to take the train and go to their home offices and there write the story. The result was that one or two of the reporters took matters into their own hands and hurried them along as a piece of newspaper enterprise. The crowd was too slow. The reporters showed them how they ought to work. The execution took place in the regular way, hanging and shooting, and just at the moment the train arrived Peterson was dead and most of the crowd boarded the train. This was regarded as a well-arranged affair.

"I had opposed lynching, and with another man had freely expressed my opinion of the victim's innocence. We were waited on by an excited group who cautioned us to say nothing of that kind or short work would be made of us. On our way back that night on the train, for we took a second train on the line crossing the one first mentioned, we continued to express our opinions freely, with nothing more resulting than an exchange of threats. Some of the crowd returning from the lynching threatened to kill us and we threatened to kill them. The powder was finally saved on both sides. It was afterwards discovered that Peterson was entirely innocent. The guilty man was found in Georgia. He confessed his crime there, and was taken in charge of by a mob in that state."

KANSAS CITY (MISSOURI) STAR
October 31, 1899

NEGRO SUSPECTED OF SLAYING BARTENDER IS HUNG BY MOB

WEIR CITY, Kas., Oct. 31—A lynching followed a murder here last night. Gus McArdle, a bartender in Berry Janes's joint, was shot and killed at half past 10 o'clock and a few hours later his supposed murderer, George Wells, a negro miner from Scammon, was swinging from the nearest telephone pole. A mob took him from jail.

Earlier in the evening McArdle and Wells had a quar-

23

rel in the saloon, after which the negro left. Shortly afterwards a shot was fired from across the street. The bullet passed through the wood of the frame of a screen door and struck McArdle squarely in the forehead. He died in half an hour.

A few minutes later Wells came up in the crowd which had collected and inquired what was the trouble. A spectator of the previous quarrel pointed him out to an officer, who arrested him on suspicion and put him in jail. Another spectator shortly afterwards identified him as the negro who had quarreled with McArdle and the report quickly spread that he was identified as the man who did the killing.

It was not until 2:55 that the mob appeared at the jail. Overpowering the marshal and night man it broke the locks to the jail, took the negro to a telephone pole at a corner of the city hall, where he was hanged.

It is reported that Wells, just before he was lynched, denied doing the shooting.

NEW YORK WORLD
December 7, 1899

ROASTED ALIVE

MAYSVILLE, Ky., Dec. 6—Richard Coleman, a twenty-year-old colored boy was burned at the stake at noon today within the limits of this city, in the presence of thousands of men and hundreds of women and children.

Tortures almost unbelievable were inflicted upon the wretched negro. In all the vast crowd that witnessed the agonies of the man, not one hand was raised in humanity's behalf, nor a single voice heard in the interest of mercy. Instead, when some new torture was inflicted upon the shrieking, burning boy, the crowd cheered and cheered, the shrill voices of women and the piping tones of children sounding high above the roar of men.

Not one person in the crowd wore a mask. The leaders of the mob disdained the semblance of any disguise. Every act was done in the open. There was no secrecy. The population of the whole city and country for miles around, church men and church women, professional and

24

business men of eminence, people of distinguished ancestry, formed the mob, and not a single regret for the horrible tragedy can be heard to-night from one end of the town to the other.

Coleman was to have been tried here this morning for a crime peculiarly brutal. He had confessed to assaulting and barbarously murdering a beautiful young woman, the wife of his employer, James Lashbrook, a wealthy farmer. There was not a particle of doubt that he would have been executed according to law.

It was two months ago to-day, that Coleman killed Mrs. Lashbrook. He was taken to Covington and kept in jail there for safe-keeping. Had he been imprisoned here, he would have been lynched without delay. The authorities hoped that the public indignation would die out. Instead it ramified, hardened and became as fixed in the minds of thousands as any human determination could be.

For weeks members of the Lashbrook family had been silently on guard in Covington. They heard last night that Coleman was to be sent to Maysville. The news was telegraphed and spread everywhere. The Maysville jailer asked that the journey be delayed until this morning.

Sheriff Perrine started from Covington for Maysville with Coleman and several assistants on the 7:30 A. M. train. The World's correspondent accompanied them. Coleman begged to be allowed to remain in Covington. He knew what he had to expect. He told the Sheriff he would be horribly killed. Pleadingly he said he didn't want any trial; that he was willing to be hanged without a trial. He was so frightened he could not walk and had to be practically lifted into the patrol wagon which carried him to the station.

The members of the Lashbrook family telegraphed word of the coming and went on the same train. They kept in the background as much as possible, but rode in the smoker, where Coleman sat handcuffed to the Sheriff, and never took their eyes from him. They feared some trick by the authorities and were determined to track him to any hiding place that the Sheriff might have in view.

Coleman saw and recognized the Lashbrooks in the car and their quiet, determined manner paralyzed him with fear.

25

Deputy Sheriff Robinson tried to make him talk, but when asked questions he simply shook his head. Once asked his age, he said:

" 'Bout fourteen, I guess."

Robinson said:

"You told me twenty."

"Maybe I did; I don't know," was the reply.

Sheriff Perrine while en route was informed that a mob was awaiting the arrival of the train at the depot here and he hastily prepared for the swearing in of deputy sheriffs. As the train pulled slowly into the old station the mob formed on both sides.

Armed men stationed themselves at the platforms of all the cars and warned the frightened passengers to remain quiet and not to interfere. The sheriff and his assistants were strongly armed and there was some resistance as the leaders of the mob jostled roughly against them and demands were uttered from the outer fringes of the crowds for the prisoner.

Sheriff Perrine made a bold movement and started walking swiftly but with no indications of panic from the car. A step behind him followed the officers with Coleman seeking to conceal himself behind the forms of his protector.

As the officers proceeded the number of the mob were constantly swelled by new arrivals, and through the downtown business streets to the Court House they were closely followed.

Hundreds of stones and other missiles were thrown, and revolvers and rifles were freely displayed. The prisoner was frequently struck, and he presented a frightful appearance, blood streaming from wounds on his face and head.

At the Court-House a mob of 2,000 men headed by James Lashbrook, the husband, had been hastily formed. The demand for the prisoner was made, accompanied by threats from the leaders.

There was a brief struggle in which weapons were hastily drawn by the officers and then the Sheriff and his assistants were overcome by force of numbers and the prisoner was pulled from them.

Up through the main street of the town the mob marched, the prisoner being held by the vanguard and dragged along with the aid of ropes loosely attached to his body. He was the target of hundreds of missiles and several times he sank half conscious to the ground while the crowd pressed forward striking at him with clubs, sticks and whips until his head and body were scarcely recognizable.

More dead than alive, he was dragged along and forced to his feet. Scores of women joined the men. High above the noise the wretch could be heard pleading for his life.

The place of execution had been selected weeks ago, in accordance with all the other arranged details of the programme mapped out by the leaders of the mob. The prisoner was dragged to the sapling and strapped against the tree, facing the husband of the victim.

Large quantities of dry brush and larger bits of wood were piled around him, and oil was poured on the mass while he was praying loudly for speedy death.

James Lashbrook, the husband of the victim, applied the first match to the brushwood. A brother of the victim struck the second match.

Some one with a knife slashed at the prisoner's chest. By a sort of cruel concurrence of action on the part of the mob not a single shot was fired.

The purpose seemed to be to give the wretch the greatest possible amount and duration of torture. The lower part of his clothing was torn away leaving him bare.

As the flames grew, Coleman's horror increased, and he struggled terribly to withdraw his limbs from the encroaching fire.

The shrieks of the burning negro nerved the crowd to greater deeds of horror. One man had in his hand the same pepper-box which Coleman had used to throw pepper in the eyes of Mrs. Lashbrook when he first attacked her.

This man had filled the box with cayenne pepper. He stepped close to the shrieking wretch, whose eyes were almost bursting from his head with pain and calmly threw the pepper into the eyes of the negro, again and again. The boy writhed and strained at the stout ropes, and his face became horribly distorted with the awfulness of the pain, but the man with the pepper-box kept on deliberately shaking more pepper into his victim's

eyes. At least twice, he stopped to press down the eye-
lids of the negro to make sure that the pepper did its
work of agony.

Scores of men had pistols in their hands. The men
who came in from the country had their trousers stuffed
into their boots and the handles of revolvers projected
outside their bootlegs. In an ecstacy of rage one
countryman, a neighbor of Mrs. Lashbrook, pulled his
revolver from his bootleg as if to shoot the negro. A
dozen men pounced upon him and made him promise not
to use the weapon. They did not want the negro to die
that way. It would have been too quick.

Eager hands kept feeding the flames and soon the blazing mass reached the waist of the negro. The ropes which
held the upper part of his body burned away and he top-
pled into the flames. Long poles were used to push him
back and hold him in an upright position. Men burned
themselves to catch him with their hands and hold him
up, and the crowd cheered them again and again.

It was thought the negro was dead, but as he sank to
a sitting position in the flames he cried out faintly:

"If you take the fire away, I want to say something.
Oh! give me water!"

Those were the last words he uttered. The next minute
he was probably dead, as his head fell forward on his
chest.

But the crowd was not satisfied. They kept on feeding
the flames. Lashbrook, the husband of the murdered
woman, stood all the time directly in front of the burning
negro and he did not leave until the body was almost completely incinerated.

Long after most of the mob went away little children
from six to ten years of age carried dried grass and
kindling wood and kept the fire burning all during the
afternoon.

Relic-hunters visited the scene and carried away pieces
of flesh and the negro's teeth. Others got pieces of
fingers and toes and proudly exhibit the ghastly souvenirs
to-night.

With tears in his eyes James Lashbrook said to The
World correspondent this afternoon:

"I touched the match to the fire that sent Coleman to

his doom. I did as I thought right, and I will stand for all that may follow."

Judge Wadsworth said:

"I am a police Judge, but for once perhaps I forgot the duties of the office. Lashbrook has my sympathy. He left my office fifteen minutes before train time. We expected Coleman last night and we waited all night for him."

The Coroner held an inquest this evening, and rendered a verdict that Coleman came by his death at the hands of unknown persons.

What was left of the body had not been removed up to this evening and was still smouldering. All that was visible was the charred skull.

Several of the women who witnessed the burning said to The World correspondent to-night that they now feel as if they could walk the loneliest country road at midnight without being molested by a black man.

The crime for which Coleman was burned was an awful one. He murdered the woman who had befriended him.

Coleman was not only employed on the Lashbrook farm, but he had been installed as a house servant and was trusted implicitly by Mr. Lashbrook and his wife.

On the day of the murder Mr. Lashbrook was at work some distance from the house, of which Coleman was left in charge. Mrs. Lashbrook had driven to Maysville and returned, when Coleman asked her to enter the cabin to look at some work on which he had been engaged.

The negro locked the door on the inside. Mrs. Lashbrook became frightened and screamed. Coleman threw pepper in her eyes, struck her on the head and knocked her down, but did not stop her cries. He then seized a razor, cut her throat and assaulted her. He then left the room, but returning and hearing her groaning, he struck her repeatedly on the head with an axe until he was sure she was dead.

Without any show of alarm or remorse the negro washed the blood from his hands and clothing and went to where Mr. Lashbrook was at work in the field and told him that he had better come to the house, as some one had killed his wife. Mr. Lashbrook did not take the matter seriously until Coleman insisted that his wife was dead.

Even then, so great was the confidence of Mr. Lashbrook in Coleman that no thought occurred that he was the murderer. It was not until after the officers arrived that suspicion was directed against Coleman. Blood spots had been found on his clothing, but he accounted for them by saying that he had been killing chickens.

That night, however, at Maysville, a partial confession was obtained, and knowing the result if the fact should become known, the officers quietly took him to Covington, Ky., for safekeeping.

Never before to-day was there a man burned alive by a mob in Kentucky.

WASHINGTON TIMES
February 18, 1900

NEGRO LYNCHED TO AVENGE ASSAULT ON WHITE WOMAN

COLUMBIA, S. C., Feb. 17—Will Burts, a negro, nineteen years old, was lynched this morning in Aiken county. Three days ago he attempted to outrage Mrs. C. L. Weeks and failed.

A crowd of 250 tracked the negro fifty miles across Aiken, Edgefield, and Greenwood counties. He was caught last evening by a farmer, who received $100 from the posse. The party returned to Greenwood, and at daylight this morning the lynching occurred. Some wished to hold the man till tonight and make a public demonstration of it, but this was outvoted.

A clothesline was obtained, one end swung over an oak limb, and the other fastened to Burts' neck. He was then ordered to climb the tree and get out on the limb. This the negro did without hesitation. He was then shot from the limb. The rope broke, and, as Burts was not dead, he was again hoisted up and then shot to pieces.

NEW ORLEANS TIMES-DEMOCRAT
March 24, 1900

LYNCH NEGRO WHO TESTIFIED FOR ANOTHER NEGRO

RIPLEY, Tenn., March 23—This morning, in the heart of the city, the body of a negro, Louis Rice, was found dangling from a limb of a tree. The lynching grew out of a trial in the Circuit Court of Lauderdale county, during the course of which Rice testified in favor of one of his color who was charged with the murder of a white man named Goodrich.

NEW YORK TIMES
June 11, 1900

AN INNOCENT MAN LYNCHED

NEW ORLEANS, June 10—A mob willfully and knowingly hanged and burned an innocent man, as well as another who was probably innocent, near Mississippi City, Miss., between midnight and 1 o'clock this morning. The lynching was the result of impatience on the part of the people of Biloxi, a nearby town, over the failure of the officers of the law to produce the man who a week ago murdered Christina Winterstein, a schoolgirl who was returning to her home near Biloxi after attending the commencement exercises of her school.

The crime was an unusually atrocious one even for outrages of this nature, and naturally suspicion pointed to some unknown negro as the perpetrator. Many arrests were made, and two of the suspects, Askew and Russ, were placed in the Mississippi City jail for safe keeping. The proof against neither was more than remotely circumstantial. In the case of Askew the District Attorney made an examination and practically declared the man innocent.

The next night Askew was taken from the jail by a mob and tortured with fire to extort a confession. After the terrible ordeal the mob virtually declared the man guiltless, as they returned him to jail.

Yesterday the District Attorney, at a public meeting at Biloxi, obtained a pledge from the citizens not to molest the prisoners if they were returned for examination. It is stated on good authority that he thought the men could prove their innocence, and the citizens were aware of his views. Some refused to pledge themselves, and yesterday afternoon it was openly asserted that it was out of the question to think of postponing the matter any longer, as the crime merited a lynching.

Last night a crowd went to the jail, secured Askew and Russ, hanged them, fired into the bodies, and then built a fire under them.

HOUSTON POST
June 11, 1900

TWO BLACKS STRUNG UP; GRAVE DOUBT OF THEIR GUILT

BILOXI, Miss., June 10—Lynch law ran rampant in this section last night. Two negro men were lynched, possibly for one man's crime, early this morning at Mississippi City, and it is not absolutely certain that either victim of mob law was guilty. Henry Askew and Ed Russ, held as suspects, were taken out and strung up to a tree in a thicket, just behind the railway station at Mississippi City.

Attorney White had promised that they would be brought to trial on Monday and yesterday at a mass meeting held in this city urged the people to support the laws and see that justice was done through the proper legal channels.

Early last night Sheriff Ramsey, in order to protect Askew and Russ from mob violence, moved them to a bath house. After midnight the mob assembled near the bath house and afterward overpowered a deputy sheriff with whom the sheriff thought to protect his prisoners, and dragged the two negroes away. The crowd, which was supposed to know nothing of the negroes' hiding place, did not stop at the jail, but went straight to the bath house. The negroes were tied back to back and swung up to the same tree. Their bodies were riddled with bullets, and after death ensued, were set on fire. The nauseating smell of the burning flesh could be smelt for miles around.

Sheriff Ramsey and Marshal Moseley saw the members of the mob, but it is stated "were unable to recognize them on account of the trees casting shadows on their faces."

About 100 men gathered near the scene of the crime, waiting for the appearance of the posse with their prisoners, but were disappointed. The mob was impatient and did its work when the first tree was reached.

On June 2 Christina Winterstein, a 13-year-old schoolgirl, was outraged and murdered about two miles. from Biloxi while on her way home from school exercises. Askew and Russ, both of whom had been in the vicinity of the place where the outrage was committed that day, were charged with the crime.

SNEADS, Fla., June 10—Ernest Hardwick, a white farmer, was set upon by a gang of negroes several days ago and beaten so badly that he died in a few hours. Only one of the negroes was caught and sent to jail. Two nights after the murder a mob went to the house of John Sanders, a supposed accessory to the crime, and shot him to death. Another negro, innocent of the murder, was also killed. Both bodies were literally shot to pieces.

BALTIMORE AMERICAN
July 24, 1900

MILITIA ARRIVES TOO LATE

HUNTSVILLE, Ala., July 23—Elijah Clark, the negro who yesterday assaulted Susan Priest, a thirteen-year-old girl, was taken from the jail in this city this evening and lynched near the spot where his crime was committed. His body was riddled with bullets. Sheriff Fulgham defended his prisoner to the last, but a dense smoke, from a combination of tar, feathers and oil, fired by the crazed mob, was too much for him, and he was dragged from the jail and placed under a physician's care. William Vining, an employe of the street railway company, who attempted to rush through the crowd and up the jail steps to assist the sheriff was shot and dangerously wounded. A crowd of one hundred and fifty men, principally employes of the big cotton mills at Dallas, a suburb of this city searched the woods all night for Clark, who was identified at the time he assaulted Miss Priest by her little sister.

No success attended their efforts, and early this morning Sheriff Fulgham started out with a posse, and before nine o'clock had captured Clark on Beaverdam Creek, ten miles from Huntsville. He was soon landed in jail, and by one o'clock the news of the prisoner's capture was heralded to all parts of the city. A mob—composed of mill operatives and men of all callings—was soon formed and marched to the jail, where they stood for a time, apparently waiting for a leader. Sheriff Fulgham, quickly seeing that he had a desperate crowd to combat, wired Governor Johnson the facts in the case. The governor responded to the effect that he had ordered the militia at Birmingham, Montgomery and Decatur to proceed with all haste to the scene. The sheriff then telephoned Judge S. M. Stewart, and asked for an immediate trial of the negro, and the judge replied soon after that he had arranged for a special session of court at three o'clock before Judge H. C. Speake.

The mob by this time had assumed alarming proportions, and the sheriff, thinking to quiet the storm, appeared at a window and announced that a special trial had been arranged for the prisoner, and that he would be brought before the court at three o'clock in the afternoon. This was greeted with jeers by the crowd of citizens and the cry "Revenge!" went up.

The outer door to the jail, a wooden barrier, was soon battered down, and the mob gained entrance to the first floor. Here they encountered the sheriff's wife, who pleaded with them to refrain from violence, and let the law take its course. Sheriff Fulgham, however, on hearing the door being forced, retired with his prisoner to the third floor, where he locked himself in with Clark. A large amount of tar, feathers and oil was secured and

34

piled upon the cement floor of the jail, and a match applied. A suffocating smoke arose, and spread quickly throughout the jail. The sheriff again retreated to the corner farthest from the fire, taking his prisoner with him. More tar and feathers were brought in and ignited. Fulgham was finally dragged from the jail in a semi-conscious condition, and taken to the city hall, and doctors summoned.

The sheriff's departure was the signal for the mob to proceed to their work, and they quickly took complete possession of the stronghold. Fully an hour was consumed in breaking the lock to the cell in which the culprit was confined, but as soon as this was accomplished two men secured Clark and quickly appeared with him on the front steps of the jail. A plow line was placed around his neck, and guarded by twenty heavy-armed men in fours, he was dragged out of the jail yard. The mob was followed by fully 1,500 people. The doomed man was taken before his victim and positively identified. The identification complete, the wretch collapsed, and had to be taken up and borne on the shoulders of his captors. The rope around Clark's neck was thrown over the limb of an immense tree by Miss Priest's brother. The negro was thrown across the back of a horse and the animal was led out from under. him. The body was riddled with bullets.

Just as the work was finished the Decatur militia arrived at Huntsville.

NEW YORK HERALD
July 24, 1900

LYNCHED BEFORE TRIAL

HUNTSVILLE, Ala., July 23—Elijah Clark, a negro, twenty years old, was lynched at two o'clock this afternoon by an immense mob of citizens of Huntsville and the surrounding country. Clark was about to be removed from the Madison county jail to the court house for a preliminary hearing, when the mob compelled the officers to give him up, took him to the scene of his crime, hanged him and riddled the body with bullets.

35

NEW YORK WORLD
December 30, 1900

HARVARD PROFESSOR FAVORS LEGALIZING LYNCHINGS

DETROIT, Dec. 29—Professor Albert Bushnell Hart, of Harvard College, speaking before the American Historical Association in convention here to-day, said that if the people of certain States are determined to burn colored men at the stake, those States would better legalize the practice.

CHICAGO RECORD
January 4, 1901

NEGRO FREED, THEN LYNCHED

ROME, Ga., Jan. 3—George Reed, a negro charged with attempting to assault Mrs. J. M. Locklear of this city last night, was hanged to-day to a tree. His body was then riddled with bullets by a mob of 150 men. Reed protested his innocence.

After his arrest this morning the negro was taken before Mrs. Locklear, but she failed to identify him and he was returned to jail. However, the mob which had been seeking the prisoner's life was not satisfied. The demonstrations were so pronounced that Judge Henry of the Superior court, not seeing any reason for holding Reed, ordered the sheriff to release him. The mob learning of the release, formed within the city limits and marched to the house of Lila Gover in North Rome, where it found Reed. He was taken three miles from this place and lynched.

CHICAGO RECORD
February 27, 1901

HOOSIERS HANG NEGRO KILLER

TERRE HAUTE, Ind., Feb. 26—George Ward, the negro who murdered Miss Ida Finkelstein, the school teacher, last evening, was placed in jail at 11 o'clock this morning, and shortly before 1 o'clock was taken out by a mob, dragged face downward to the banks of the Wabash, only two squares away, at the wagon bridge at the foot of the main street of the city, thence to the draw, and hanged from a beam more dead than alive. Then his body was cut down and tumbled off the bridge on the west bank of the river and a fire built, on which he was burned. For two hours the crowd came and went in thousands, while a few hundred gathered close to the fire and renewed it as it died down with oil and crates from a near-by poultry house. The hat was passed around several times for money to buy oil. Some of the bridge weatherboarding was torn off for fuel. No effort was made by the authorities to stop the inhuman conduct, and so far as appearances went it was simply a big bonfire, watched idly by a great number of people.

When the crowd near the fire tired of renewing it after two hours, it was seen that the victim's feet were not burned. Some one called an offer of a dollar for one of the toes, and a boy quickly took out his knife and cut off a toe. The offer was followed by others, and the horrible traffic was continued, youths holding up toes and asking for bids.

Nothing has been done by the authorities as yet looking to the punishment of the lynchers. They were not disguised and there would be no difficulty in identifying them. Policemen stood on the river bank and watched the men and boys about the fire for an hour or more. Outside the jail a number of policemen tried to persuade the crowd to disperse, but when a man would not move on no further effort was made.

CHICAGO RECORD
March 14, 1901

CORONER'S JURY COMMENDS MOB FOR CREMATING NEGRO

CORSICANA, Tex., Mar. 13—John Henderson, the negro accused of murdering Mrs. Younger, was burned at the stake by a mob of 5,000 persons in this city to-day. He purportedly had confessed his guilt. Subsequently the coroner held an inquest over his remains and the jury returned a verdict commending the mob for its act of horror.

NEW YORK TRIBUNE
March 17, 1901

NEGRO SUSPECT ELUDES MOB; SISTER LYNCHED INSTEAD

NASHVILLE, Tenn., Mar. 16—Ballie Crutchfield, a colored woman, met death at the hands of a mob at Rome about midnight last night. The mob surrounded her home and took her to a bridge over Round Lick Creek, near the town. Her hands were tied behind her, and after being shot through the head her lifeless body was thrown into the creek. The body was recovered to-day, and the jury of inquest returned a verdict that she met death at the hands of unknown persons.

The lynching was the result of a suspicion that the negress was in some way connected with the theft of the contents of a pocketbook containing $120, which was lost by Walter Sampson last week. The purse was found on the ground by a negro boy, who was on his way to return it to the owner, when he was met by William Crutchfield, a brother of the dead woman, who induced the boy to give him the pocketbook upon the representation that the contents were of no value. Mr. Sampson had Crutchfield arrested, and he was taken to the house of Squire Bains for safe keeping.

That night a mob visited the house of Squire Bains and took Crutchfield from the custody of the Sheriff. The mob had started with Crutchfield to the place selected for execution, when he broke from them and succeeded in effecting his escape in the dark. This so enraged the mob that they suspected Crutchfield's sister Ballie of being implicated in the theft, and last night's work was the culmination of that suspicion.

CHICAGO RECORD-HERALD
May 12, 1901

BELIEVES WRONG MAN LYNCHED

BIRMINGHAM, Ala., May 11—A negro supposed to be James Brown, accused of assaulting Miss Della Garrett of Springville, was shot and killed by a number of white men near Leeds, near here, to-day. The coroner is of the opinion that the wrong man has been killed.

CHICAGO RECORD-HERALD
June 20, 1901

LYNCH TWO IN LOUISIANA

SHREVEPORT, La., June 19—Two of the negroes implicated in the murder of John Gray Foster were lynched by a mob at Benton to-night. One was Frank, commonly known as "Prophet" Smith, who, at the head of the "Church of God" movement in that section, was blamed as being responsible for the sentiment against the whites which led to the death of Foster. The other was F. D. McLand.

At 6 o'clock men began quietly to obtain horses and ride eastward, crossing the river there in twos and threes and ostensibly unarmed. They were all bound for Benton, and had a prearranged plan for meeting with a similar crowd from Bossier to form the lynching party.

The mob appeared before the Benton jail about 9 o'clock and made a demand on Sheriff Thompson for the prisoners. That official at first maintained his attitude of the last few days, but was overpowered by the lynchers.

Having secured the prisoners, the mob went out on the Arkansas road about a mile and a half from the jail and strung them up. Both negroes made statements before they died denying that they had anything to do with the killing of Foster. While Smith died praying, McLand was silent as he was hanged.

There were about 200 armed men in the mob. The lynchers declare that the death of these negroes was necessary to the preservation of the lives of the white men in that section.

CHICAGO RECORD-HERALD
August 8, 1901

NEGRO BURNED AT STAKE

BIRMINGHAM, Ala., Aug. 7—Uttering alternate curses and prayers and shrieking as the flames encircled his writhing body, John Pennington, a negro, died at the stake near Enterprise to-day, a victim of the vengeance of a mob of 500 whites.

Though the suffering wretch pleaded for mercy and frantically endeavored to break the chains that tightly bound him, not a trace of sympathy was shown on the faces that peered at him through the flames. Pennington had committed a brutal assault upon Mrs. J. C. Davis, the wife of one of the best known farmers of Coffee County and confessed his guilt.

The attack was made yesterday when Mrs. Davis, who was alone at home, was in her garden. Leaving his victim unconscious, the negro fled into the woods about the place. As soon as she regained her senses Mrs. Davis crawled to the house and gave the alarm.

A large posse was quickly organized with bloodhounds and the negro was chased until early this morning, when he was captured in a swamp. Pennington was bound hand and foot and taken back to the Davis home for identification.

Mrs. Davis immediately recognized him, and the negro broke down and wept. He admitted the crime and pleaded for mercy, but deaf to his cries of terror, the leader dragged the trembling man from the house.

Several members of the crowd had already driven an iron pipe into the ground, and as the men approached with Pennington both whites and blacks were piling brushwood around the stake.

The negro saw his doom and with a scream of terror, fell to the ground in a faint. He was quickly revived and dragged to the stake, while the crowd stood silent. The frightened man was limp and had to be held up while the chains were fastened around his neck and body.

When all was ready the cry was given and the crowd stood back. A match was applied to the pile and, with oil to feed upon the tiny flame soon burst into a roaring fire. The terrified negro again pleaded for mercy in the most agonizing tones and prayed that those around him might perish. He then called upon the Maker for forgiveness, and as the flames leaped up and encircled his neck an unearthly shriek was heard and the man's eyes had almost bulged out of the sockets.

By this time the fire had gained such headway that nothing could be seen excepting a wriggling motion in the center of the circle of fire. A deathly silence followed and in a few minutes the flames had subsided sufficiently to disclose Pennington's head, fallen forward and hanging limp over the iron chain.

The body was quickly consumed, after which the crowd quietly dispersed.

CHICAGO RECORD-HERALD
August 20, 1901

SHOOTING AT LYNCHED BLACK, MOB KILLS BOY BYSTANDER

PIERCE CITY, Mo., Aug. 19—Eugene Carter and another negro named Godley were taken from jail to-night and lynched on the charge of assaulting and murdering Miss Casselle Wilds on her way home from Sunday school yesterday. When Godley was strung up there was much shooting at the body and a boy was killed and several persons wounded by the indiscriminate firing.

41

Just before his death Carter confessed that the real culprit was Joe Clark, a Pullman car porter, and the mob has arranged to meet him when he returns from his run and lynch him.

The feeling against the negroes is intense and twenty-five armed men are now raiding the colored quarter, shooting at every black they can find.

The murder of Miss Wilds was most atrocious. She was met near a railroad bridge, dragged into the woods, assaulted and her throat cut with a razor. A farmer working in a near by field witnessed the assault, but hearing no outcry did not go to her relief. When he saw the negroes running away he gave the alarm. The body of the girl was found at noon to-day, and the negroes were captured shortly afterward.

CHICAGO RECORD-HERALD
August 21, 1901

PIERCE CITY MOB DRIVES
NEGROES OUT, BURNS HOMES

PIERCE CITY, Mo., Aug. 20—With the exception of a few car porters, who are known to be respectable, there is not a negro in this town. For fifteen hours an armed and furious mob coursed through the streets chasing away every negro. The homes of five negroes were burned, and in one of them Peter Hampton, aged 71 and feeble, was cremated, as he was unable to escape.

Beginning Sunday afternoon, when the mangled remains of Miss Gazelle Wild were discovered in a ravine, where she had been murdered while struggling with a negro assailant, this community has been in a terrible fever. Yesterday Will Godley, a suspect, was arrested and last night he was lynched. His grandfather, French Godley was shot to death. Eugene Carter, alias Barrett, also a suspect, was strung up until he confessed, and may die of his injuries. A boy was fatally injured by a stray bullet during the raid upon the negro quarters last night, and the mob is thirsting to get its hands upon two other negroes suspected of complicity in the murder. If caught they will surely be lynched.

After the lynching of Godley last night it was thought the excitement would die down, but instead it became more intense, inasmuch as the impression grew that Godley was not the real culprit. Early this morning the mob broke into the arsenal of the local militia company, secured the rifles and ammunition and started out to clear Pierce City of all negroes. The work was thoroughly done. The terrified blacks, bullets whistling about their ears and in some instances finding lodgment in their bodies, fled to the woods and near-by towns, where they are being hidden by friends.

This afternoon partial quiet was restored, but this fact is due to the lack of negroes to shoot upon. Citizens, mindful of several hideous crimes against women hereabouts in recent years, have decreed that no negro can hereafter live in Pierce City or pass through the place on pain of death. This may necessitate a complete change in the car porter system of four railroads centering near here.

New elements in the murder of Miss Wild developed to-day. It appears she started home from church alone, her brother lingering behind. About one mile from town the brother found her with her throat cut, lying lifeless near a culvert, under which her assailant had attempted to drag her. Evidence of a terrible struggle was shown.

A copper-colored negro was seen sitting on the bridge a short time before the tragedy occurred. It is supposed that the negro sprang upon her when she was passing and attempted to force her beneath the bridge. She fought with such desperation that he could not accomplish his purpose and cut her throat in the struggle. Her body was not violated.

Monday bloodhounds were taken to the scene and the girl's bloody handkerchief was laid before them. They immediately caught the trail and ran at full speed to the home of Joe Lark, where on being admitted rushed into his bedroom and sprang upon the bed. It is believed that the man under arrest at Tulsa, I. T., who boarded with Lark, the Springfield suspect, slept upon this bed.

43

CHICAGO RECORD-HERALD
October 9, 1901

MOB SCARES WOMAN TO DEATH

SHELBYVILLE, Ky., Oct. 8—Mrs. Ben C. Perkins, wife of the jailer at this place, died to-day as the result of shock and fright suffered Wednesday morning when a mob attacked the jail and lynched two negroes. At that time Mrs. Perkins was ill with a nervous attack, and Dr. W. F. Baird, her physician, declares that the raid of the lynchers is responsible for the woman's death.

CHICAGO RECORD-HERALD
March 31, 1902

LYNCH MOB MAY HAVE ERRED

SAVANNAH, Ga., Mar. 30—It is possible that in the search for Richard Young, the negro wanted for the murder of Dower Fountain in the southern part of this county, a negro now unknown has been caught by a posse and burned in error.

A bright bonfire was seen in the swamp in the direction a posse went Friday night and the members of the posse returned stating that they were satisfied with the night's work. It now developes, however, that their victim may not have been Richard Young, for whom the officers of the law are still searching.

The remains of the burned negro were brought before the mother of Richard Young who says that they resemble her son in no particular.

CHICAGO RECORD-HERALD
April 2, 1902

MOB VICTIM PLEADS INNOCENCE; PRAYS CULPRIT WILL BE FOUND

ROME, Ga., April 1—Walter Allen, a negro, charged with assaulting Miss Blossom Adamson, a 15-year-old girl, in this city yesterday afternoon, was taken from the jail to-night by 4,000 persons, who battered down the prison doors and hanged him to an electric light pole in the principal portion of the city. A volley was fired afterward, and fully a thousand bullets entered the negro's body. The sheriff tried to save Allen from the mob and refused to deliver the keys, but the crowd forced the jail door with sledge hammers. Allen was allowed to make a statement, in which he declared that he was innocent and prayed that the guilty party would be found.

CHICAGO RECORD-HERALD
May 23, 1902

NEGRO TORTURED TO DEATH BY MOB OF 4,000

LANSING, Tex., May 22—Dudley Morgan, a negro accused of assailing Mrs. McKay, wife of a Section Foreman McKay, was burned to death at an iron stake here to-day. A crowd of 4,000 men, most of whom were armed, snatched him from the officers on the arrival of the train.

Morgan was taken to a large field on the edge of town. An iron stake was driven into the ground and to this he was bound until he could only move his head. Heaps of inflammable material was then piled about him and he was given a few moments for prayer.

It was 12:12 when all arrangements were completed. The crowd by this time numbered at least 5,000. The husband of the woman Morgan was accused of abusing applied the match and the pyre was soon ablaze. Then began the torture of the negro. Burning pieces of pine were thrust into his eyes. Then burning timbers were held to his neck, and after his clothes were burned off to other parts of his body. He was tortured in a horrible manner. The crowd clamored continuously for a slow death. The negro, writhing and groaning at the stake, begged piteously to be shot. Mrs. McKay was brought to the field in a carriage with four other women, and an unsuccessful effort was made to get her near enough to see the mob's victim.

The negro's head finally dropped, and in thirty minutes only the trunk of the body remained. As the fire died down relic hunters started their search for souvenirs. Parts of the skull and body were carried away.

The men who captured Morgan were then held above the heads of the mob while their pictures were taken.

The last words of the doomed man other than the incoherent mutterings made in prayer were:

"Tell my wife good-by."

CHICAGO RECORD-HERALD
September 29, 1902

BURN A NEGRO BY SYSTEM

CORINTH, Miss., Sept. 28—In the most methodical and deliberate manner possible Corinth devoted Sunday afternoon to burning a negro to death. Even the victim, Tom Clark, seemed to enter into the spirit of the affair and walked unhesitatingly to the stake where he was to meet death. Eying the pile of fuel critically he said:

"I am guilty. I am a miserable wretch. I deserve the punishment that is about to be inflicted on me."

Five minutes later Clark was dead.

The execution was carried out in accordance with a revised plan which involved a strange mockery of mercy. Clark had confessed on Saturday, and it was decided to hang him to a telegraph pole on that afternoon. Clark, however, asked that the execution be delayed until today so that he could have a farewell interview with his mother and brother, who live in Memphis. The request was granted, much to the dismay of the newspaper correspondents who had bulletined the city papers that the execution was sure to take place that afternoon.

Meanwhile the news of the negro's arrest and confession spread rapidly over the surrounding country and today's incoming trains brought hundreds of people into the city to witness the execution.

At noon today it was found that the negro's relatives could not be located, and then, as if to make the execution as spectacular as possible for the benefit of the visitors, it was decided to burn Clark. The main street of the town was ordered cleared, and it was announced that it had been decided to burn the negro at 3:30 o'clock. This statement was met with cheers and the crowd shifted to the place selected for the enactment of the tragedy.

The committee of twelve and many of the representative citizens of Corinth vigorously opposed burning the negro and argued that he should be hanged. J. B. Henning of Birmingham, Ala., brother of Mrs. Whitfield, would not consent to this proposition and insisted that Clark should be burned.

At 2 o'clock pine faggots and larger pieces of wood were laid about an iron rod, which was driven deep into the ground, and half an hour later it was announced that "all was in readiness."

At 3 o'clock the prisoner, heavily manacled, was taken from the jail by a posse of armed men and led to the east gate of the negro cemetery, in the western part of the city.

Clark made a statement, saying he deserved his fate, then asked that a letter be delivered to his mother and brother. He appealed to his brother to raise his children properly, admonishing them to beware of evil company.

The word was given to fire the funeral pile. The husband and brother of Clark's victim stepped forward. They applied torches, and in a moment the flames leaped upward, enveloping the negro in smoke and fire. Soon the man's head fell forward and life became extinct. The flames were fed by the crowd until the body was burned to a crisp. Then the executioners and the crowd dispersed.

The crime for which Clark was executed was the murder of Mrs. Carey Whitfield on Aug. 10 last. Mrs. Whitfield, the wife of a well known citizen, was found dead in her home, her head practically severed from her body.

Diligent search failed to disclose the murderers. Two Chicago detectives were employed, but their efforts were fruitless. Several suspects were arrested, but in each case an alibi was proven.

Finally a committee of twelve citizens were named to continue the search for the murderer. Last Monday it became known that Clark had quarreled with his wife and she threatened to disclose the secret of a crime. Members of the committee visited the woman and she told enough

47

to warrant belief that Clark had murdered Mrs. Whitfield.

Clark was arrested and yesterday was taken before the committee of twelve. To the surprise of all the negro confessed to the murder and also told of other crimes he had committed.

He stated that several years ago he stole $1,500 from a physician at French Camp, Miss.

NEW YORK TIMES
April 27, 1903

TWO WHITE GIRLS WHIPPED

BLOOMINGTON, Ind., Apr. 26—Thirty-eight unmasked men broke into a house here early to-day and whipped Misses Rebecca and Ida Stephens, white, aged thirteen and sixteen years, and also whipped Joe Shively, a negro, aged fifty years. The Stephens girls live with their mother. Shively has a room in the house. The negro was whipped with a barbed wire and was hit in the eye with brass knuckles. The older girl was whipped with barbed wire and the younger one with apple switches but neither is dangerously injured.

Many of the assailants were recognized, and warrants will be sworn out for their arrest. Motive for the whipping appears to be local objection to a colored boarder living with a white family.

NEW YORK HERALD
June 8, 1903

NEGRO DRAGGED FROM CELL AND TORTURED TO DEATH

BELLEVILLE, Ill., Sunday—With the dawn of Sunday the full import of a wild night's work done by a mob of fully two thousand citizens stood revealed to-day. David Wyatt, a negro schoolteacher, who made an attempt to assassinate Charles Hertel, County Superintendent, in his office last evening, had been taken from a supposedly impregnable jail, hanged to a telegraph pole in the centre of the public square and his body burned.

Two hundred men, armed with sledge hammers, marched up to the jail in the night and attacked the rear doors with vigor. In half an hour the doors gave way to repeated hammer blows. Wyatt was confined in the lower section of a double tier of cells. The chilled steel bars were cut away with chisels, and when the door swung open a mighty shout informed the waiting crowd that the negro was in the hands of his pursuers.

Wyatt was six feet three inches tall and of powerful build. He tried to defend himself but he was doomed to quick death. His head was mashed almost to a pulp before he was dragged out of the cell.

A rope was placed about his neck and the dying negro was dragged down stairs and into the street. Hundreds of men jumped upon him and literally kicked and tore the bleeding form to shreds. Two men climbed the telegraph pole. Willing hands tossed up the loose end of the rope and the battered body of the negro quickly swung free in the air. Yelling like mad men, the mob surged around the victim. Knives were drawn and the body was slashed right and left.

Volunteer runners appeared with cans of benzine and gasolene. Signs and pickets from neighboring fences were tossed into a pyre and flames shooting as high as the improvised gallows soon enveloped the negro.

All this was done while the mob knew that the negro's victim was alive and had a fair chance to recover. The excuse given is that the lawless element among the negroes has been doing all sorts of deviltry, and that it was determined to teach the negroes a wholesome lesson.

Wyatt's crime was provoked by the refusal of Superintendent Hertel to renew his teaching certificate. The negro demanded favorable action, and on its refusal fired one shot at the superintendent while he was sitting at his desk.

NEW YORK HERALD
June 9, 1903

BELLEVILLE IS COMPLACENT OVER HORRIBLE LYNCHING

BELLEVILLE, Ill., Monday—Although the men who lynched David S. Wyatt; the negro teacher who shot Charles Hertel, County Superintendent of Schools, on Saturday night, worked without masks for six hours, in view of hundreds, including all the city and county officials, and although the few men who did the actual killing are known to scores, it is unlikely their prosecutions will follow.

State Attorney Farmer said to-day he had not been able to find anybody who would identify any of the lynchers.

At the inquest to-day no testimony which would tend to implicate any one in the lynching could be elicited from the witnesses examined. The Coroner's jury declined to wait for the arrival of all the witnesses, and after hearing ten men, including Mayor Kern, a verdict that Wyatt met his death at the hands of parties unknown was returned.

In the main, Belleville views the lynching and its attendant horrors with complacency. There were strong expressions of condemnation in all the churches yesterday, but many who are accounted leading citizens express approval of the lynching. The men who took part in the disorder believe they are safe.

Those who condemn the lynching urge that it could easily have been prevented. Not more than fifteen men did the actual work of breaking into the jail and lynching the negro. No attempt was made to defend the jail. Not a shot was fired. The authorities took no stand.

Mayor Kern is understood to have given orders that no shots be fired. State Attorney Farmer resented the suggestion that the mob could have been dispersed by the use of firearms.

It is doubtful if a lynching has ever been attended by such remarkable circumstances. The lynchers did not constitute a real mob. The mob spirit was entirely lacking. The attack on the jail was made by a comparatively small number of men, predisposed to disorder, who seized upon the opportunity which public indignation gave them to indulge their penchant for violence without incurring the usual risk. Actively aiding them was a somewhat larger number of youths. The rest of the crowd was made up of men of respectability, well dressed women—many leaning on the arms of escorts—and boys and girls. The sentiment of the crowd was as remarkable as its composition. It was as if all had turned out for a frolic. They had gathered for a spectacle, and they made merry over the prospect. Loud laughter greeted jokes with violent death as their theme. Demands for blood were cheered. Women were in front of the jail with baby carriages.

Mayor Kern, State's Attorney Farmer and former Judge Schaefer consulted and agreed that to oppose the crowd with force would not be good policy.

A suggestion was made that the fire department turn water on the crowd. Mayor Kern opposed this on the ground that it would make the people angry. Somebody rang the fire bell, however, and a hose cart dashed down the street through the crowd, reeling off hose by way of polite intimation of what it was proposed to do. The crowd calmly separated the hose into sections of convenient length and tied these into knots. The firemen went back to their house with all the hose the crowd would let them have.

For an hour and a half after the assailants got inside the jail the sounds of heavy blows were heard through the windows, which had been shattered by boys. Youths appeared frequently at the windows and shouted information meant to be humorous. The crowd was none too exacting as to the quality of humor offered and each sally about the progress made toward "the nigger" was greeted with cheers and laughter.

It was twenty minutes to twelve o'clock when the self-appointed announcers rushed to the windows and shouted gleefully, "We've got him!"

"They're taking him to the square," somebody shouted a few minutes later, and the well dressed throng moved, with many a jest, toward the square to see "the big show."

The crowd in the jail had broken into Wyatt's cell. He had fought fiercely for his life. A blow from a sledge hammer felled him. A rope was tied around his neck. He was dragged out into the corridor, down the stairs and into the jail yard, then into Spring street, up to Main street and to the centre of the square.

A man riding on a white horse led the way to an electric light pole in the square. The end of the rope was thrown over it. The body was drawn up above the heads of the crowd, who cheered and waved hats. Men on the pole kicked Wyatt in the face. The swaying form was stabbed repeatedly. Mutilations followed.

Kerosene was bought and poured over the body and it was set on fire, while the crowd cheered. The rope burned through and the body fell. More kerosene was poured on the body as the flames slowly consumed it.

Mayor Kern telephoned to the police station half an hour later and ordered that an undertaker be directed to remove what remained of the body. This was done.

Police and other officials say they could have held the jail if they had used their revolvers, but they did not do so because they were "afraid somebody would be hurt." Sheriff Thompson was out of the city.

Mr. Hertel's condition is improving. His recovery is expected. He greatly regrets the lynching.

NEW YORK TIMES
June 23, 1903

NEGRO MURDER SUSPECT BURNED

WILMINGTON, Del., June 22—A mob of 2,000 persons to-night took George White, the negro suspected of murdering seventeen-year-old Helen S. Bishop last Monday, from the Workhouse, burned him at the stake and riddled his body with bullets. Guards attempting to repulse the crowd inadvertently shot a man and a boy.

FIERY SERMON BY PASTOR

WILMINGTON, Del., June 23—A fiery sermon by a pastor was blamed today for the lynching last night of George White, negro, accused ravisher and murderer of Miss Helen S. Bishop.

The Rev. Robert A. Elwood, pastor of the Olivet Presbyterian church, preached a sensational sermon on the probable lynching of White last Sunday evening. The text of the sermon was widely distributed and this was believed today to have had much influence in the lynching of White which followed.

Rev. Elwood took his text from Corinthians V., 13: "Therefore put away from among ourselves that wicked person." In referring to the urgency for a speedy trial for the negro, Rev. Elwood said:

"I call your special attention to that part of my text found in the constitution which says: 'In all criminal prosecutions the accused shall enjoy the right to a speedy and public trial.'

"On the day of this terrible crime the officials arrested a man supposed to be guilty. He was taken before a magistrate and held without bail. Tonight he is in jail, with armed guards parading about for his protection, waiting until the middle of September. Is that speedy? Is that even constitutional?

"O, honorable judges, call the court, establish a precedent, and the girls of this state, the wives of our homes and the mothers of our fireside and our beloved sisters will not be sorry and neither will you.

"And honorable judges, if you do not hear and heed these appeals, and that prisoner should be taken out and lynched, then let me say to you with a full realization of the responsibility of my words, even as Nathan said to King David of old, after his soldiers had killed Uriah, 'Thou art the man,' so I would say to you. The responsibility for lynching would be yours for delaying the execution of the law.

"If the judges insist that the trial of the murderer of Miss Bishop be delayed until September, then should he be lynched? I say, Yes."

The father of the murder victim is also a minister. Prior to the lynching the Rev. E. R. Bishop, had issued a letter begging the people to permit the law to take its course. Rev. Bishop's letter said:

"Dear Friends: Mrs. Bishop and our children join me in this expression of the deepest gratitude for your Christian sympathy and tender ministrations in our agonizing grief. Though comparatively strangers, you have been as dear friends whose hearts had been proved by years of acquaintance. You have helped us bear our sorrow, made hundredfold more intense by the most revolting crime. Our cup of bitterness is full and we ask you to join us in our appeal to all citizens of our commonwealth to refrain from violence. The officers believe they have all the evidence necessary to convict the prisoner, and without doubt as soon as the court can reach his case he will receive his sentence and pay the full penalty for his atrocious crime. If he can be legally tried this will be so. By all means let justice be swift, but if not, then let us wait calmly until the law in its majesty may remove the vile wretch from society.

"In the meanwhile the culprit is shut up with his guilty conscience, a hell of itself, and knows he must meet the demands of law and justice with his life. Any other course of procedure would bring a kind of glory for those of his class, would intensify the suffering of the afflicted family, possibly endanger the life of a delicate woman, and certainly would dishonor the laws of our commonwealth. Let us not try to atone for one crime, no matter how hellish, by committing another. Sincerely yours,

"E. A. Bishop."

Mrs. Bishop, mother of the murdered girl is in a state of extreme nervousness. White was put to death within a few hundred yards of the Bishop home, and the glare of the fire and howls of the mob could be plainly seen and heard at the house.

Prior to the lynching, White was incarcerated in the Newcastle County workhouse. A crowd of several hundred whites advanced into the reception hall and demanded admittance to the jail. Their demand was refused by the guards and they were deluged by a stream of water by the fire fighting equipment of the institution. This did not lessen the eagerness of the besiegers, who immediately began an assault upon the iron doors. Chief of Police Black shouted to the crowd:

"The first man that comes into this corridor will be killed."

The leader of the mob grasped one of the heavy sledgehammers and as he attacked the steel grating he cried: "Then you had better kill me for the first one."

Another man shot out the cluster of incandescent lights in the vestibule. The mob and guards exchanged shots, but did not aim at each other.

Peter Smith, a 12 year old boy, and another youth, name not known, were wounded during the fusillade. Smith was shot in the back. The bullet which struck him evidently came from a pistol in the crowd, as it is claimed by the prison warden that his guards fired over the heads of the lynchers. Smith is not expected to live. The other injured youth was shot in the nose and is expected to live.

While about 300 men and boys were storming the front of the jail several thousand sympathizers were lined up outside, and, while they took no active part in the attack, were plainly in favor of lynching White.

After forcing their way into the lower corridor on the west wing the crowd surged up to the front row of cells on the third floor. The leaders, who had the sledges and rivet cutting appliances, were calm and determined and cut straight to the cell of the man they were after. That no other doors were demolished is due to the leaders, who told Chief Black and Warden Meserve that they intended to get the negro if they had to break every steel door in the place, and argued that it was a useless expense to the county to have unnecessary damage done to property. The officials saw the strength of this argument and informed the leaders that White was in cell No. 13 on the front row, third story. This was enough and the door to this row of cells was at once attacked. "This is the only door between us and our man,"

55

shouted one of the mob, "and if you will stand back we will cut it open in an hour."

It was just 22 minutes of 12 o'cleck when the mob with yells, curses, and cheers rushed into the corridor past the cell doors of the frightened prisoners to the cell occupied by White. Here more trouble was encountered, for in smashing the lever box the mechanism was damaged and the door to the cell of White could not be opened.

Warden Meserve then rushed into the cell corridor to prevent the mob taking the wrong man. He saw that the men with hammers were about to demolish the cell door and told them how to disconnect the door so it could be operated. As soon as the door to White's cell slid open there was a deafening cheer, and cries of "Don't hurt him; hang him; don't hit him; burn him at the stake. Take him to the place where he murdered Miss Bishop, for we have driven a stake there and will burn him."

White fought desperately for his life, and knocked down the first man who approached him. One of the leaders of the mob threw his arms around the negro, thus protecting him. At this time the narrow corridor was so tightly packed by the mob that it was impossible to get the prisoner out.

A rope was tied around his legs and he was lowered to the mob below, who dragged him to a previously selected site at Price's Corner.

When he found that his case was hopeless the negro confessed to having committed the deed, and did not spare himself in telling of it. He prayed fervently to God and seemed anxious to do as much talking as possible in the few minutes he had to live.

Another strong rope was brought and the negro was wrapped in its coils from shoulders to feet. His lips were moving while this was going on, and he seemed to be trying to finish his statement. The crowd was in a hurry to get through with its work, and called out for the executioners to hasten. After the rope had been adjusted the negro was fastened to the stake and the torch was applied to the straw.

The flames leaped up and licked the man's bare hands. He was held erect by one of the lynchers until his clothing was burning fairly, when he was pushed into the bed of the fire. He rolled about and his contortions were terrible, but he made no sound. Suddenly the ropes on his legs parted and he sprang from the fire and started to run. A man struck him in the head with a piece of fence rail and knocked him down. Willing hands threw him again into the flames. He rolled out several times, but was promptly returned. While this was going on shouts, cheers, and gibes went up from the crowd.

When the negro had ceased to show signs of life the body was placed on its back and fuel was piled up on it, and a roaring fire was soon consuming it.

The Rev. C. H. Thomas of Belleville, Ill., speaking at Quinn chapel last night, expressed grave doubts of White's guilt.

"The only evidence against White," he said, "was the testimony of a woman that a knife found near the spot where the crime was committed had belonged to him. That is no evidence."

CHICAGO RECORD-HERALD
June 29, 1903

WHITES ARE CALLED DEMONS

WILMINGTON, Del., June 28—The lynching of the negro, George F. White, was the chief topic in two churches here today. In the negro church some violent sentiments were expressed by a negro pastor, and in a white church the utterances of a week ago by the white pastor were indorsed by the congregation.

In the first African Methodist Episcopal church the Rev. Montrose W. Thornton said:

"The white man, in face of his boasted civilization, stands before my eyes tonight the demon of the world's races, a monster incarnate, and in so far as the negro race is concerned seems to give no quarter. The white is a heathen, a fiend, a monstrosity before God, and is equal to any act in the calendar of crime. I would sooner trust myself in a den of a hyena as in his arms.

"With a court, law, and officers of law in his hands the despised negro can expect no mercy, justice, nor protection. The negro is unsafe anywhere in this country. He is the open prey at all times of barbarians who know no restraint and will not be restrained.

"There is but one part left for the persecuted negro when charged with crime and when innocent. Be a law unto yourself. You are taught by this lesson of outrage to save yourself from torture at the hands of the blood seeking public. Save your race from insult and shame. Be your own sheriff, court, and jury, as was the outlaw Tracy. Die in your tracks, perhaps drinking the blood of your pursuers. Booker T. Washington's charity, humanity, advice of forgiveness, love, industry, and so on will never be reciprocated by white men."

The Rev. Robert A. Elwood, the Presbyterian minister who has come in for much criticism for his sermon of last Sunday night, in which he suggested lynching in case the negro escaped speedy punishment at the hands of the law, did not refer to the lynching or the criticisms today. These criticisms were answered by his congregation today when resolutions were read during the services expressing firm belief in the pastor's honesty, integrity, and Christian character.

Thousands of persons visited today the scene where White was burned. They came from all the small towns in this vicinity, and hundreds journeyed from Chester, Pa., and Philadelphia.

The burning took place in a freshly plowed field, about fifty feet from the roadway, which was hidden by high bushes. The field has been tramped almost as smooth and hard as asphalt by the thousands of persons that have visited the farm. The only evidence that remains of the work of the mob are three cobblestones, on one of which this inscription has been placed in indelible ink: "Here is all that remains of White."

The bushes behind which the murder was committed have been cut down for a distance of several yards and carried away by relic hunters. Many of those who visited the scene today, among them a large number of young men, carried away a sprig or a branch of the bushes.

NEW YORK TIMES
June 26, 1903

NEGROES ASK $100,000,000 TO RETURN TO AFRICA

MONTGOMERY, Ala., June 25—The National Colored Immigration and Commercial Association, meeting here in convention, today adopted a petition to President Roosevelt and the National Congress requesting an appropriation of $100,000,000 to secure transportation of members of their race who desire to settle in Liberia. Wrongs which the colored race was said to suffer from in the United States was cited as the reason for this request.

CHICAGO RECORD-HERALD
July 2, 1903

ONE NEGRO LYNCHED; 4 BEATEN

NORWAY, S.C., July 1—Charles Evans, colored, suspected of the murder of John L. Phillips, was taken from the jail here last night and lynched by an unmasked mob. Four other negroes who were confined in the jail were also taken by the mob and beaten into insensibility. Evans was charged with murdering John T. Phillips, a one armed confederate soldier.

CHICAGO RECORD-HERALD
July 2, 1903

MOB LYNCHES NEGRO MAN, FLOGS THREE NEGRO WOMEN

COLUMBIA, S.C., July 1—A dispatch just received here from Piedmont, Anderson county, says that Ruben Elrod, a respectable old negro, was shot and killed at his house last night by a mob of fifty men. Three women who lived in the house were taken out, stripped, and flogged severely, and then warned to leave the county. No reason for the attack was given.

CHICAGO RECORD-HERALD
July 15, 1903

RAPE VICTIM WITNESSES LYNCHING OF ATTACKER

EASTMAN, Ga., July 14—Ed Claus, a negro, was lynched near here tonight, while his victim, Miss Susie Johnson, was looking on. Claus was captured after being chased through seven counties by fifty farmers.

Claus attacked Miss Johnson last Thursday as she was returning from a small school which she teaches. The negro kept her prisoner for several hours, and she was found next morning by a searching party. A posse was organized and the negro was trailed from here almost to Savannah before he was overtaken.

He was brought here tonight by his captors and taken to the home of Miss Johnson. The young woman identified him, and when asked what she wanted done with him, she said:

"He ought to be killed."

The negro was then tied to a tree and the members of the mob fired at him until he was literally cut to pieces.

CHICAGO RECORD-HERALD
July 27, 1903

WRONG MAN LYNCHED AS RAPIST

SAVANNAH, Ga., July 26—Several days ago a negro, supposed to be Ed Claus, was lynched near Eastman, Ga., for assaulting Miss Susie Johnson, a young school teacher. The negro protested he was not Claus and asked for time to prove his statement. But the mob was merciless. It now transpires that the negro was not Claus and had never seen Miss Johnson. Claus, who assaulted the girl, has been located near Darien, Ga., and officers passed through here tonight to secure him. It is believed Claus will be taken from the officers and lynched.

CHICAGO RECORD-HERALD
July 27, 1903

WOMAN PLEADING INNOCENCE LYNCHED AS CHILD POISONER

SHREVEPORT, La., July 26—Jennie Steers, a negro woman, who, it was charged, gave 16 year old Elizabeth Dolan a glass of poisoned lemonade, causing her death, was lynched on the Beard plantation near here last night. The mob took her to a tree, placed a rope around her neck and demanded a confession. The woman refused and was hanged.

CHICAGO RECORD-HERALD
August 13, 1903

MOB TERRORIZES NEGROES AFTER POLICE SPOIL LYNCHING

WHITESBORO, Tex., Aug. 12—An attempted attack today on Mrs. Hart caused the arrest of eight negroes, seven of whom were released. The other was held for identification. About 8 o'clock tonight a mob took possession of him and hanged him to the limb of a tree. He had not been unconscious when officers arrived from Sherman, and, making their way through the mob with a rush, cut the negro down. He is being hurried to Sherman tonight, but there is talk of going there to take him from jail.

After the negro had been forcibly taken from the mob its members began terrifying the colored residents of the town. Guns were fired promiscuously in the negro section and the terror stricken negroes were ordered to leave town at once. As a result outgoing trains on all roads were filled with negroes.

NEW YORK PRESS
February 8, 1904

NEGRO AND WIFE BURNED

DODDSVILLE, Miss., Feb. 7—Luther Holbert and his wife, negroes, were burned at the stake here to-day by a mob of more than 1,000 persons for the killing of James Eastland, a prominent white planter, and John Carr, a negro, on Wednesday, at the Eastland plantation, two miles from this city.

The burning of Holbert and his wife closes a tragedy which has cost eight lives, has engaged 200 men and two packs of bloodhounds in a four days' chase across four Counties, and has stirred this section of Mississippi almost to frenzy.

Following are the dead: Luther Holbert and wife, negroes, burned at the stake by mob; James Eastland, white, planter, killed by Holbert; John Carr, a negro, killed by Holbert; John Winters, negro, killed by Eastland, three unknown negroes, killed by posses. The killing of Eastland, Carr and Winters occurred Wednesday at Eastland's plantation. Holbert and Winters were in Carr's cabin when Eastland entered and ordered Holbert to leave the plantation. A difficulty ensued, in which it is alleged that Holbert opened fire on Eastland, fatally wounding him and killing Carr. Eastland returned the fire and killed Winters.

When news of the tragedy reached Doddsville a posse was formed and left immediately for Eastland's plantation. Arriving there further shooting occurred, and an unknown negro was killed. Holbert and his wife had fled. Posses were formed at Greenville, Ittaben, Cleveland and other points and the pursuit of Holbert and his wife was begun with horses and bloodhounds. The chase, which was begun Wednesday morning, was continued until last night, when Holbert and wife, worn out from traveling over 100 miles on foot through canebrakes and swamps, were found asleep in a heavy belt of timber three miles east of Sheppardstown and captured. The two negroes were brought to Doddsville and this afternoon were burned at the stake by a large mob in the shadow of the negro church here.

Yesterday two negroes were killed by a posse near Belzoni, Yazoo County. One of the negroes bore a striking resemblance to Holbert, and was mistaken for him by members of the posse.

Eastland was a member of a wealthy Mississippi family, and a reward of $1,200 was offered by relatives for the capture of his slayers. Two brothers of Eastland participated in the chase and capture of the Holberts and both were present when Holbert and his wife were burned.

The dead couple leave a young son.

VICKSBURG (MISSISSIPPI) EVENING POST
February 8, 1904

LYNCHED NEGRO AND WIFE WERE FIRST MUTILATED

An eye-witness to the lynching of Luther Holbert and his wife, negroes, which took place in Doddsville yesterday, today gave the Evening Post the following details concerning retribution exacted from the couple prior to their cremation yesterday:

"When the two Negroes were captured, they were tied to trees and while the funeral pyres were being prepared, they were forced to hold out their hands while one finger at a time was chopped off. The fingers were distributed as souvenirs. The ears of the murderers were cut off. Holbert was beaten severely, his skull was fractured and one of his eyes, knocked out with a stick, hung by a shred from the socket.

"Some of the mob used a large corkscrew to bore into the flesh of the man and woman. It was applied to their arms, legs and body, then pulled out, the spirals tearing out big pieces of raw, quivering flesh every time it was withdrawn."

NEW YORK TRIBUNE
February 29, 1904

BOOKER T. WASHINGTON LETTER

BIRMINGHAM, Ala., Feb. 28—"The Age Herald" tomorrow will publish the following letter from Booker T. Washington:

"Within the last fortnight three members of my race have been burned at the stake; of these one was a woman. Not one of the three was charged with any crime even remotely connected with the abuse of a white woman. In every case murder was the sole accusation. All of these burnings took place in broad daylight, and two of them occurred on Sunday afternoon, in sight of a Christian church.

"In the midst of the nation's busy and prosperous life, few, I fear, take time to consider whither these brutal and inhuman practices are leading. The custom of burning human beings has become so common as scarcely to excite interest or attract unusual attention. I have always been among those who condemn in the strongest terms crimes of whatsoever character committed by members of my race, and I condemn them now with equal severity, but I maintain that the only protection of our civilization is a fair and calm trial of all people charged with crime and in their legal punishment, if proved guilty. There is no shadow of excuse for deviation from legal methods in the cases of individuals accused of murder. The laws are, as a rule, made by the white people, and their execution is by the hands of the white people; so that there is little probability of any guilty colored man escaping.

These burnings without trial are in the deepest sense unjust to my race. But it is not this injustice alone which stirs my heart. These barbarous scenes are more disgraceful and degrading to the people who inflict the punishment than to those who receive it. If the law is disregarded when a negro is concerned, it will soon be disregarded when a white man is concerned, and, besides, the rule of the mob destroys the friendly relations which should exist between the races, and injures and interferes with the material prosperity of the communities concerned.

Worst of all, these outrages take place in communities where there are Christian churches; in the midst of people who have their Sunday schools, their Christian Endeavor societies and Young Men's Christian Associations; where collections are taken up for sending missionaries to Africa and China and the rest of the so-called heathen world. Is it not possible for pulpit and press to speak out against these burnings in a manner that shall arouse a public sentiment that will compel the mob to cease insulting our courts, our Governors and our legal authority; to cease bringing shame and ridicule upon our Christian civilization?"

NEW YORK HERALD
March 9, 1904

NEGRO HATERS FIRE TOWN

SPRINGFIELD, Ohio, Wednesday—As a result of the murder of a white policeman and the subsequent lynching of Richard Dickerson, a negro, a serious race war is on to-night.

One entire square in the levee district inhabited by negroes is in flames and seven companies of the Ohio National Guard are on the scene, holding a crowd of five thousand excited people in check.

All yesterday mutterings were heard by the negroes, who, in their determination to revenge the lynching of Dickerson, threatened to kill all the policemen in the city. On the other hand the whites openly announced that they would burn the district during the night.

Alarmed by preparation for hostilities Mayor C. J. Bowlus, Sheriff Routzahn and several prominent citizens called on Governor Herrick for troops. The Governor quickly responded and five companies were ordered to assist the two local companies in preserving peace.

In the mean time crowds gathered in the street, and at night fall five hundred young men organized at the post office and started for the levee, shouting, "Burn the niggers."

Each man was armed with a rifle or shot gun and firing at random or command.

By half-past nine o'clock a crowd of about two thousand men had assembled along the Big Four railroad tracks, almost blockading Washington street. Two hundred negroes were clustered together just west of Fountain avenue, in the levee district near the place called "Honky Tonk."

The negroes were unusually quiet and seemed to be waiting for a start to be made by the white men. The other crowd was boisterous and there were frequent yells and several pistol shots heard, although no one has been reported injured so far.

Mayor Bowlus, Sheriff Routzahn, and the other officials were stationed in the Mayor's office. It was announced by the Mayor that the militia was coming as quickly as the cars could bring them.

No effort was made to use Company A, Ninth Battalion, composed of negroes, because of fear of race prejudice.

At midnight the crowd, realizing that the troops were about to arrive, applied a torch to the saloon occupied by "Les" Thomas.

Preceding the firing of the building the mob, at a distance of a hundred feet, shot at the front of the building for half an hour, but it is not known whether any of the occupants had remained in the building, and if they did whether any fatalities resulted from the shooting.

The fire spread both ways from Thomas' place and the mob would not tolerate any effort of the department to put out the fire in the levee district, but offered no resistance in the attempts to confine the fire to the buildings along Washington street, known as the levee. These buildings are dilapidated frame structures, ranging from one to three stories in height. They are for the most part saloons, dwelling and small rooming houses of negroes.

The militia had not yet arrived in sufficient numbers to attempt to quell the mob.

At midnight one whole square was in flames. The militia had been re-inforced by the Urbana company and a crowd of five thousand, under military check, were viewing the destruction of the levee resorts with great satisfaction. Half a block away cheers were heard as the buildings fell in.

While the eastern portion of the levee is doomed it is thought that the department will be able to confine the conflagration to the region east of Spring street. Members of the mob openly declare that when their work in the eastern levee district is completed they will transfer their efforts to that portion west of the Big Four station and the Arcade Hotel. This portion of West Washington street is also known as the levee and the buildings are similar to those in the eastern portion.

The arrival of the additional militia alone can save these places, and a trainload of troops from several towns between here and Cincinnati are anxiously awaited. Apparently the negroes all over the city are becoming intimidated and their boasts made earlier in the evening are no longer heard.

The Coroner held an inquest to-day over the body of Dickerson, but none was blamed for the lynching, which took place in the centre of the city last night before a mob of two thousand persons. The Coroner rendered this verdict:—

"After having heard the evidence and examined the body I find that the deceased came to his death at the hands of a mob which forcibly broke into the county jail, overpowering the authorities, and lynched the said Richard Dickerson. I am unable to determine the direct cause of death, but found him hanging by the neck to a pole at the southeast corner of Main street and Fountain avenue, in Springfield, with a number of bullet holes in his body. I have been creditably informed that he was placed there about a quarter after eleven o'clock P. M., March 7, 1904. I am unable to fix the responsibility for his death."

NEW YORK SUN
March 22, 1904

CONFEDERATE VETERANS DEPLORE LYNCHING EXCEPT FOR RAPE

NEW ORLEANS, March 21—The Confederate veterans of Mississippi are determined to give their assistance to try to stop lynching by burning. The W. R. Barksdale Camp of Confederate Veterans of Mississippi has adopted resolutions calling for the strict enforcement of law and order and denouncing mob violence as antagonistic to liberty and leading ultimately to anarchy, desolation and ruin. The resolutions say:

"As Confederate veterans and law abiding citizens of Mississippi and of the United States we are violently, vehemently and eternally opposed to the practice of burning a human being for any crime whatsoever. We appeal to all Confederate veterans, their wives and daughters, and to that great and glorious organization the Daughters of the Confederacy, one and all, to arise in their might and by precept and example, voice and pen, moral force and influence, help put a stop to this diabolical barbaric, unlawful, inhuman and ungodly crime of burning human beings. We are unalterably opposed to the lynching of a human being, except perhaps for the one unmentionable crime."

NEW YORK TRIBUNE
March 18, 1906

IS LYNCHED BY "ORDERLY" MOB; SUSPECTED OF COW KILLING

PLANQUEMINES, La., March 17—William Carr, Negro, was lynched without ceremony here today by an orderly party of thirty masked men who hurried him to a railroad trestle and hanged him. He had been accused of killing a white man's cow.

NEW YORK TRIBUNE
March 20, 1906

LYNCHED AFTER RECEIVING SUPREME COURT REPRIEVE

KNOXVILLE, Tenn., Mar. 19—A message from Chattanooga to "The Journal and Tribune" says that Ed

Johnson, the negro convicted of rape, in whose case the United States Supreme Court granted an appeal to-day, was removed from jail at 11 o'clock tonight and lynched.

CHICAGO TRIBUNE
March 26, 1910

INTER-RACIAL COUPLE'S 'CONDUCT' RESULTS IN LYNCHING OF MAN

PINE BLUFF, Ark., Mar. 25—Resenting alleged improper conduct on the part of Judge Jones, a Negro, and a young white woman, a mob of forty men gathered at the county jail here tonight, overpowered the jailer and his deputies and hanged the Negro.

NEW YORK PRESS
March 26, 1904

9 LYNCHINGS IN ONE WEEK

LITTLE ROCK, Ark., Mar. 25—A special from Dewitt says five negroes have been taken from the guards at St. Charles, this county, and shot to death by a mob.

This makes nine negroes who have been killed in the last week in the vicinity of St. Charles on account of race troubles.

MONTGOMERY ADVERTISER
August 1, 1910

15 NEGROES ARE SHOT DOWN

PALESTINE, Tex., July 31—At least fifteen and perhaps as many as twenty negroes, all of them probably unarmed, were hunted down and killed by a mob of 200 or 300 men in the Slocum and Denison Springs neighborhood of Palestine last night and yesterday. Sheriff Black said today that the negroes were killed "without any real cause at all."

69

After returning from a 24-hour investigation in the Southeastern part of Anderson County, Sheriff Black made the following statement this morning:

"Strong race feeling prevails in that part of the county. Men were going about and killing negroes as fast as they could find them, and so far as I have been able to ascertain, without any real cause at all. These negroes had never done anything that I could discover. There was just a hot-headed gang hunting them down and killing them.

"We found eleven dead bodies, but from what I have heard the dead must number fifteen or twenty. We came across four bodies in one house. We won't know the final number killed until the locations of all bodies are revealed to us by the buzzards.

"I don't know how many there were in the mob, but I think there must have been two or three hundred. A misunderstanding over a promissory note is said to have been the cause of the trouble."

EDITORIAL FROM THE LITERARY DIGEST (NEW YORK)
August 13, 1910

THE PALESTINE HORROR

We wish to publish, without comment, segments of editorials from two Southern newspapers on the recent outbreak of lynchings near Palestine, Texas. The first is from the Houston *Chronicle* which cries out against "indiscriminate butchery of negroes because of some crime committed by an individual member of the race" and says:

"It would puzzle Satan to find a satisfactory excuse for such an outbreak . . . With all the faults of the individuals, the negro race is not a bad race. Fidelity, loyalty, and courage are not uncommon traits. And the negro is the satellite of the white man. You could not drive him away from the white man, in whose shadow he flourishes, and the white race is not yet ready to dispense with the negro; certainly it can not afford to dispense with him by the assassination route, and to shoot down unarmed negroes in their cabins, to kill poor barefooted fugitives who, with their clothes bundled up to flee the country, are overtaken on country roads and shot down and left to welter and to thrash out their lives in the white dust of the roadway (as happened near Palestine) is nothing short of hell-inspired murder, and is just as demoniac, just as bloody, just as damnable a crime as if it had been committed by Turks on Armenians, by Kurds and Caucasians, or by red Sioux warriors on white men."

The second is merely a clause from an editorial in the Memphis *Commercial Appeal* which advises northerners to "remember their own troubles, and not be too severe in the condemnation of the Texas tragedy."

BIRMINGHAM NEWS
August 4, 1910

NEGROES FLEEING FOR LIVES

PENSACOLA, Fla., Aug. 1—Telephone wires to the vicinity of Dady, Fla., were cut to-night and negroes were reported to be fleeing for their lives from that section.

Business was reported suspended late to-day while farmers left their fields to join posses bent on carrying forward vengeance for the murder of the little school girl, Bessie Morrison, who was slain last Friday.

To-day it was reported that a negro had loaned an amulet for good luck to one of the colored men alleged to have slain the child. This negro, whose name has not been learned here, was captured, a rope placed around his neck and as he swung from the limb of a tree, his body was shot almost to pieces.

According to information here he is the fourth negro lynched for this murder. The cutting of the telephone wires made it impossible to learn the cause of the hunt for negroes said to be in progress to-night.

71

MONTGOMERY ADVERTISER
October 13, 1910

ANGRY MINERS LYNCH NEGRO

CENTREVILLE, Ala., Oct. 12—Grant Richardson, a negro, who lived near Braehead was lynched last night by unknown parties while Deputy Sheriff Cam Riley was on his way to jail with the prisoner. Riley was overpowered and the negro shot to pieces.

A white woman named Mrs. Crow gave birth some months ago to a child which was thought by many to be of doubtful color, but the woman strenuously denied the charge, till a few days ago when she declared that Richardson had assaulted her and that he was the father of the child. The miners and others living near Braehead, which is a mining camp about five miles from Blocton, were so incensed over the affair that they decided to inflict summary vengeance on the negro as soon as it was known that the sheriff had apprehended him.

Chief Deputy Charles Oakley left for the scene of the lynching early this morning as soon as the news reached him of the affair, but everything had quieted down, and it is not thought he will be able to get any clues to the members of the mob. It is supposed that a coroner's inquest will be ordered as soon as a special coroner is appointed.

It is not known here whether or not any charges have been preferred against the woman. This is the first lynching that has occurred in Bibb county, and the affair is deeply deplored by the best citizenship of the county. Grant Richardson has lived near Blocton for many years, and heretofore has borne a fair reputation, it is said.

MONTGOMERY ADVERTISER
August 5, 1911

THWARTED MOB LYNCHES BROTHER OF INTENDED VICTIM

DEMOPOLIS, Ala., Aug. 4—A lynch mob unable to locate Richard Verge, negro, wanted in connection with the slaying of Vernon Tutt, a prominent planter of these parts, today lynched Verge's brother, Sam, instead.

MONTGOMERY ADVERTISER
August 15, 1911

DESPERADO BURNED TO CRISP

COATESVILLE, Pa., Aug. 14—Zachariah Walker, a negro desperado, was carried on a cot from the hospital here last night and burned to a crisp by a frenzied mob of men and boys on a fire which they ignited about a half mile from town.

Walker had been cornered in a cherry tree yesterday by a sheriff's posse which suspected him of the murder of Edgar Rice, a special policeman at the Worth Iron Mills.

When he was cornered, Walker shot himself in the mouth, falling from the tree. The posse then brought him to the hospital.

News of the murder of Rice, who was very popular among the people here, spread rapidly. There had been no other crimes committed in this neighborhood that had been blamed on negroes and talk of lynching fell on willing ears. The main street of Coatesville is usually filled with people from the surrounding towns Sunday nights and a crowd soon gathered at the hospital. As the crowd increased the talk of lynching spread and finally a masked man mounted the steps of the hospital and shouted:

"Men of Coatesville, will you let a drunken negro do up such a white man as Rice?"

The orderly crowd was instantly transformed into a

73

riotous mob. The attack on the hospital was then made. There were only the superintendent, four nurses and a policeman in the institution at the time and a defense of the negro was impossible. The crowd swarmed into the place through smashed doors and windows and before most of the mob knew it, the wounded and frightened negro was being taken out of the building screaming piteously. Still lying on the cot, he was carried through the streets and out of the city to the Newland farm. He had been tied to the bed with ropes and as the crowd tore fence rails and gathered wood and other inflammables, Walker writhed on his cot and tugged at his bonds, but could not free himself.

All the leaders in the crowd wore masks made of handkerchiefs tied around their faces up to the eyes. They carried on their work quickly and after piling up the rubbish placed the cot, with its shuddering victim on it, over the pile. A dozen matches, it seemed, were simultaneously applied to the pyre and in an instant the negro was enveloped in the flames. The fire burned the ropes that held him and he made a dash for liberty. Walker reached a fence and was about to climb it when stalwart hands seized him and dragged him back to his funeral pyre.

As he was thrust back into the flames, he shrieked, "Don't give me a crooked deal because I ain't white."

Only vile oaths greeted his plea.

BIRMINGHAM NEWS
November 13, 1911

GOVERNOR COMMENDS LYNCHERS

AUGUSTA, Ga., Nov. 11—A special from Anderson, S.C., says:

What was unquestionably the most sensational gubernatorial address ever delivered by a man holding that office in South Carolina, came from Gov. Cole L. Blease, who spoke here to-day to a thousand people in compliance with an invitation.

Gov. Blease devoted considerable time to the recent lynching of a negro at Honea Path, when the mob was led by Representative Josh Ashley, and was rather commendatory in his expressions. He said he had been informed by a telegram from the sheriff of the situation and had in turn wired the sheriff instructions, sending two telegrams.

"The telegram to Sheriff King," said the Governor, "said: 'Keep in touch with the Honea Path affair and send me a report to-morrow morning telling me what is going on.'

"Sheriff King received that telegram, and he understood its meaning. Next morning I received his report, and it was exactly what I expected. As a matter of fact, if it had been any different I would have been greatly disappointed."

The Governor went on to say that rather than use the power of his office in deterring white men from "punishing that nigger brute" he would have "resigned the office and come to Honea Path and led the mob myself."

MONTGOMERY ADVERTISER
January 23, 1912

4 NEGROES LYNCHED AT ONCE

HAMILTON, Ga., Jan. 23—A mob of 100 men tonight broke into the Harris County jail, overpowered Jailor E. M. Robinson and took four negroes, three men and one woman out and hung them to trees one mile from town.

They then riddled the bodies with bullets. It is estimated that 300 shots were fired.

Last Sunday, while Norman Hadley, a well-to-do young married farmer, was sitting in his home, a shot was fired through the window and he fell dead. That afternoon four negro tenants, Belle Hathaway, John Moore, Eugene Hamming and "Dusty" Cruthfield, were arrested, charged with the crime.

Sheriff Hadley, who is an uncle of the dead man, feared no lynching and tonight he is in Columbus. Public sentiment, however, had been crystalizing here all day today and by nightfall there were a great many country people in Hamilton. Their number was constantly augmented and by 9 o'clock fully 100 men had congregated in front of the court house in which the jail is located. Despite the pleas of Jailer Robinson they advanced on the calaboose and, throwing him to one side, broke the doors down. The terrified negroes were hustled out at the point of guns and marched outside the town. There they were quickly strung up.

Immediately their writhing bodies became silhouetted against the sky, revolvers and rifles blazed forth and fully 300 shots were fired before the mob dispersed.

The negroes protested their innocence to the last, but the mob would have none of it.

MONTGOMERY ADVERTISER
April 10, 1912

LYNCHED AFTER ACQUITTAL

SHREVEPORT, La., Apr. 9—Tom Miles, a negro, aged 29, was hanged to a tree here and his body filled with bullets early today. He had been tried in police court yesterday on a charge of writing insulting notes to a white girl, employed in a department store, but was acquitted for lack of proof.

EDITORIAL FROM THE SAVANNAH TRIBUNE
May 4, 1912

AFRICAN RECRUITER LYNCHING

The account of the death of the Negro near Jackson, Ga., last Friday night who was lynched because he undertook to secure recruits for a proposed African colony shows with how little secrecy the whites of certain rural districts take the life of a Negro. We do not know the circumstances surrounding the death of this Negro other than the one fact that he was working among his own people endeavoring to get a sufficient number of them to go to Africa. The likelihood is that he was succeeding in his project and because of this apparent success the white farmers in the community, who were depending on these Negroes to gather their crops, became angered

76

and decided to nip the movement in the bud by lynching the leader and holding to their laborers whose services they were getting for little or nothing. This they did and the pitiful part about it is that this lynching, as all others, will go unnoticed by the state and government authorities. Nothing was brought against this Negro's character by the people who took part in the lynching. He was not charged with the "usual crime" or termed an "unruly, disrespectful black brute." In fact, nothing whatever was given out against him other than the fact that he was securing recruits for Africa. The time was whenever a Negro was lynched some heinous charge was brought up but of late years lynchings have become so common that not the slightest effort has been made by the law to apprehend the guilty parties so that they have not had to resort to this form of procedure in endeavoring to justify their actions. Truly has it come to a lamentable state when a Negro's life is to be snatched out for no cause whatever other than to satisfy the unquenchable thirst of certain white people for the blood of a black man.

MONTGOMERY ADVERTISER
September 12, 1912

LYNCHED "FOR BEING BLACK"

United States District Attorney O. D. Street, of Birmingham, today made public a letter which he is forwarding to Governor O'Neal. The letter is from C. P. Lunsford of Hackleburg, and reads as follows:

On last Wednesday there was a negro man chased and hounded down and murdered while going peacefully along the railroad. There was not anything against him, but a party of men got after him because his skin was black and murdered him. The grand jury was in session at the time, and has not paid any attention to the murder, not even so much as to put the parties under arrest. The negro who was murdered was Willis Perkins of Sheffield, and I am reliably informed that he was of an excellent character.

"I write you to know if there is any law in the United

States to protect its citizens against such outrage and the wholesale slaughter of human beings. This is the second negro that has been killed in this county in the last twelve months, and the State authorities seem to pay no attention to it whatever. The parties who murdered the negro are Walt Miller, Tom Mason, C. L. Baker, Jack Purser, George Stidham and others. I would be glad if you would send a detective over here and see if we can't stop this mob violence."

U.S. Attorney Street says that he is forwarding the letter to Governor O'Neal as he is powerless in the matter.

HARRISBURG (PENNSYLVANIA) ADVOCATE VERDICT

September 13, 1912

WRONG MAN BELIEVED LYNCHED

PRINCETON, W.Va., Sept. 7—That a mistake was made in lynching Walter Johnston, a colored man last night, is now believed by the authorities. A statement was issued today by Mayor Bennington, Sheriff Ellison, Judge Maynard and Prosecuting Attorney J. O. Pendleton stating that there is plenty of evidence that Walter Johnston did not commit the crime for which he was lynched.

A mob lynched Johnston last night, allegedly for attacking Nite White, 14-year-old daughter of a railroad man. Today's statement said that Johnston fell far short in dress and physical appearance of the man described by the girl.

MONTGOMERY ADVERTISER

November 11, 1912

BUGGY COLLISION INCITES MOB TO LYNCH ALA. NEGRO

WETUMPKA, Ala., Nov. 10—One negro is killed and a posse of infuriated citizens in the neighborhood of Floyd,

78

Elmore County, are hunting a second negro with the aid of the State penitentiary dogs tonight. The two negroes earlier in the day killed John Chrisitzberg, an Elmore County farmer, and later one of them, Berney, killed Claude Kidd, one of his pursuers.

It is learned here that Mr. Chrisitzberg's two daughters were on their way to church when they met the two negroes, driving in an opposite direction. The young women drove as far to the side of the road as possible, but the wheels of the vehicle driven by the negroes locked those of the Misses Chrisitzberg's buggy, causing the horse to run away.

A party of young men passing by, repaired the harness, and took the two young women to church, and returned to punish the two negroes. They informed Mr. Chrisitzberg, who joined them in the pursuit of the negroes.

Overtaking two negroes in advance of his party, Mr. Chrisitzberg attempted to horse whip both, when one of them shot Mr. Chrisitzberg through the body, inflicting serious, if not fatal, wounds. After the shooting the negroes took to the woods, and it was necessary to get the penitentiary dogs to follow.

A large number of the citizens joined in the man hunt. The occupants of a negro cabin stated that the parties sought were not there. Believing the negroes to be secreted about the cabin some of them went inside and noticed a loft overhead. Claude Kidd, one of the pursuers, mounted a rickety table, while some of his companions held it, and with a pole pushed up one of the planks of the loft. As he did so, a pistol shot from the loft rang out and Mr. Kidd fell to the table dead, the ball striking him in the top of the head, coming out under the lower jaw. Those in the house came out and made the negro owner of the cabin bring Mr. Kidd's body out. They told the negro to go back and tell the negro that did the shooting to come out or they would burn the house. The negro refused to come out, threatening to kill the owner of the premises if he came back.

The crowd proceeded to set fire to the cabin, the negro seeing that he would be burned, made a dash for liberty, shooting at the crowd as he ran. Fortunately no one was struck. The negro was killed, his body being completely riddled with bullets. The second negro made his escape.

ATLANTA CONSTITUTION
February 9, 1913

SECOND NEGRO LYNCHED
FOR CRIME OF ONE MAN

HOUSTON, Tex., Feb. 8—A mob of 1,000 persons conducted a mock trial in the courthouse yard here today, found David Rucker, negro, aged 30, guilty of murdering Mrs. J. C. Williams, and, in the presence of a sheriff and two deputies who were powerless to act, chained him to a steel pump in the middle of the yard, soaked his clothes with oil, piled wood about him and burned him alive.

Rucker was the second negro to die for the murder of Mrs. Williams who was clubbed to death in her home in the daytime Thursday. Friday a mob hanged a negro named Andrew Williams for the same crime. Williams' innocence has since been established.

ATLANTA CONSTITUTION
February 16, 1913

NEGRO PREACHER IS FOUND
SWINGING FROM A LIMB

SHREVEPORT, La.—The body of Charles Tyson, negro preacher, residing near Myrtis, was found hanging to the limb of a tree late Friday afternoon by deputy sheriffs who, on the request of the dead man's wife, had been searching for him. It is not known who did the lynching or why.

BIRMINGHAM NEWS
February 27, 1913

TWO LYNCHED IN TEXAS

MARSHALL, Tex., Feb. 25—Two negroes were lynched here last night. A negro named Anderson was hanged by one mob for reasons unknown. Robert Perry was shot to death by another mob which charged him with horse-stealing.

MONTGOMERY ADVERTISER
March 13, 1913

NEGRO MOTHER AND CHILD KILLED

HENDERSON, N. C., Mar. 12—Two negroes, a woman and a child, were killed and two negro men probably fatally wounded early today when unidentified persons after pouring kerosene on the home of Joe Perry, a negro living ten miles from this place, set it on fire, and poured a fusilade of bullets into the blazing structure as its occupants attempted to escape. The dead are Joe Perry's wife and her child and the wounded Joe Perry and his brother John. There are no clews. Sheriff Royster has gone to the scene.

MONTGOMERY ADVERTISER
June 6, 1913

POSTS BAIL, IS SLAUGHTERED

BEAUMONT, Tex., June 6—Richard Galloway, negro, accused with two others of attacking a party of white men last Saturday, was riddled with bullets today as he left the jail after electing to go free on bail. His two companions have decided to remain in prison pending a hearing.

ATLANTA CONSTITUTION
June 22, 1913

MOB IGNORES MINISTER'S PLEA

AMERICUS, Ga., June 21—Four negroes are wounded and one is dead tonight as a result of the shooting today of Chief of Police William C. Barrow. The dead negro,

William Redding, is purported to have fired at Chief Barrow as the Chief was attempting to arrest him for intoxication.

Redding was taken to jail after his altercation with Chief Barrow but was soon seized by a mob of 500 who strung him up to an overhead cable. Shooting at him then began from every direction and four other negroes, all innocent bystanders, were wounded, one of them apparently fatally. Miraculously, no whites were wounded.

Before the shooting began, Rev. Robert Bivins, pastor of the Furlaw Lawn Baptist Church, pleaded with the leaders to spare the life of the negro. His pleadings lasted during the twenty minutes required to string the body up to the cable, and then yells of the crowd and the shots from many pistols drowned out his voice.

EDITORIAL FROM THE MEMPHIS COMMERCIAL-APPEAL
August 5, 1913

LYNCHING BAD FOR BUSINESS

The killing of Negroes by white people in order to fatten an average ought to be stopped, and killing Negroes just because one is in a bad humor ought also to be stopped.

Two apparently inoffensive Negroes, good farm hands, real wealth producers, were assassinated near Germantown a few days ago. The Negroes had furnished no possible motive for the deed. So far as any one knows they were quiet and orderly, as country people of their class usually are. They worked and played and loafed, just like other country Negroes.

Now, the Negro is about the only dependable tiller of the soil in these parts. Competition for existence is not keen enough to force many white people into the harder work.

The Negro also is very useful as a distributor of money. About all he gets goes through his fingers.

Commercially, then, he is a very valuable asset. It is not good business to kill them.

When the Negro enters into the contest with the white man he is already at a disadvantage, and therefore the truly brave white man never seeks a quarrel with Negroes. He knows that the Negro is at a disadvantage, and he does not desire to take advantage of him. Furthermore, the white man of courage can most always control the Negro without being compelled to resort to violence.

MONTGOMERY ADVERTISER
August 9, 1913

SHERIFF STAVES OFF MOB

SPARTANBURG, S.C., Aug. 8—"Gentlemen, I hate to do it, but so help me God, I am going to kill the first man that enters that gate!"

So spoke Sheriff W. J. White of Spartanburg county today to a mob of his friends and fellow citizens who were trying to lynch a negro prisoner in his charge.

None of the mob advanced past the gate.

MONTGOMERY ADVERTISER
August 12, 1913

NEGRO HANGED TO TRESTLE

LAURENS, S. C., Aug. 12—Richard Puckett, a young negro charged with attempted criminal assault near here yesterday, was taken from the jail here at 12:30 o'clock this morning by a mob estimated to number 2,000 men, and hanged to a beam of a railway trestle near the Laurens depot. Several hundred bullets were then fired into his body, and the mob dispersed, leaving the body hanging to be examined by a coroner's jury today. Puckett made a denial of his guilt just before he was strung up by the mob.

Puckett was charged with having attacked a young woman who was driving in a buggy along a lonely road near here yesterday morning. It is said he dragged her from the buggy, but fled when she called to her two brothers who were following her in another buggy. Laurens officers arrested Puckett soon after they had begun the search, but the young woman who had been attacked failed to identify him. However, it is said, blood hounds were then used to fasten guilt on him.

_____

BIRMINGHAM NEWS
August 21, 1913

SHERIFF RESCUES NEGRO AFTER HOLDING BACK MOB

SPARTANBURG, S. C., Aug. 18—Three men, Frank Eppley, J. C. Owensby and John Turner were seriously wounded tonight when a mob stormed the county jail in an effort to lynch Will Fair, a negro prisoner, charged with assaulting a young white woman near here to-day. Sheriff White and a deputy, facing the mob alone, repeatedly drove them back with pistol shots when they advanced with battering rams.

Members of the mob finally returned the fire and in the darkness the three men were struck. They were not fatally wounded but were taken to a hospital for attention.

The young woman was assaulted in a lonely farm house this morning in the absence of her husband.

Several charges of dynamite were exploded late tonight by the mob in an effort to enter the jail here. After they had blown down a portion of the outer wall they were impressed by the show of strength inside the jail and retired, but threats were made to return later with nitro-glycerine which they proposed, it was said, to obtain from a railroad construction camp. Hundreds of pistol and rifle shots were fired when the dynamite was let off, but so far as can be learned no others were injured.

Gov. Blease was appealed to late to-night to call out the militia to protect Fair. He refused, but announced that he would order a special term of court to try the negro.

SALISBURY (NORTH CAROLINA) PIEDMONT ADVOCATE

September 27, 1913

SPARTANBURG JURY ACQUITS NEGRO NEARLY LYNCHED

SPARTANBURG, S. C., Sept. 20—Despite the positive statement of a respectable white matron of high intelligence that he had assaulted her, Will Fair, a Negro, was found not guilty this afternoon at a special term of General Sessions Court called for the trial of the case. The jury was out 20 hours.

The verdict caused no surprise and was quietly received. A few people not entirely familiar with the case were reported to be muttering this evening. Fair was told it might be inadvisable for him to remain in this vicinity. He thought so himself. A position was offered him in a railroad construction camp 300 miles from here. He left for there this evening.

The acquittal of Fair is a vindication of Sheriff W. J. White, who, at the risk of his life, saved the Negro from being lynched. He stood off a large mob who stormed the jail on the night of Fair's arrest and went so far as to blow open the outer gate with dynamite. Hundreds of pistol-shots were fired and three men were wounded. Policeman S. J. Alverson, who was alleged to have shot one of the men and who was impelled by the force of public opinion to resign in consequence, has been exonerated by the City Council and today was reinstated on the force.

People were saying here tonight that Fair's trial and acquittal were epoch-making in South Carolina and made the best argument that has ever been advanced against lynching.

The woman is believed to have accused Fair in good faith, but to have been laboring under a delusion due to her physical condition. The circumstances surrounding the case did not bear out the woman's statement, although Fair admitted that he passed her house about the time of the alleged assault.

The jury, it is authentically reported never considered

a verdict of guilty. On the ballot six stood for acquittal. The other six wanted to report a mistrial and shift the burden upon another jury. Thus they stood until about 10 minutes before they finally brought in the verdict. Then Judge George W. Gage bade them be men. They filed into their room and soon emerged with the verdict. Judge Gage had asked them: "Do you think I may not say anything to help you in arriving at a conclusion in this case?

The foreman, Joseph Lee of Landrum, president of a hosiery manufacturing company: replied "We are hopelessly disagreed."

"It is next to impossible for us in matters of this kind to put away all outside considerations. I speak from my own experience and out of my own heart and my own knowledge. I was raised on a plantation with Negroes and I think I know them as well as any man knows them. I know their weakness and I know our weakness. They are here by a strange providence, but they are here. How our final relationship with them is to be determined no man knows and no man need question himself. If we go to our duty day by day and do justice man by man, the end will come and the God who made us and who made them and who put us here together will bring us safely to some common end.

"I know that men are almost incapable of weighing a nice balance of truth where the contest is between one race and another race, especially where the one race is charged with the awful crime of assault. I know the awful peril our country women are subject to. I was raised in the country, and I know its duties and its beauties, its glories and its perils, its joys and its sorrows and burdens; but the question for you in this case is: Did this man assault this woman and under all the testimony is it true beyond a reasonable doubt? If it is, it is your duty to declare, it is your duty to say 'Guilty.' If it is not true as you see it, if it is not true beyond a reasonable doubt, then to write a verdict of 'Guilty, in answer to anybody's demand would be to crucify the law, to degrade our courts and to stultify you men. I know there is such a thing as public opinion that drives and whirls men like a sandstorm, but I tell you this: a wave of public opinion in time of excitement is sometimes the most

uncertain thing in the world. The only certain thing is the knowledge which points to the truth, and which never errs. If you follow it, you are in the sure path, and if you leave it you are in quagmires all the way."
Then the jury reported that they found Fair not guilty.

MONTGOMERY ADVERTISER
August 25, 1913

NEGRO HALF-WIT IS LYNCHED; THREATENED TO LYNCH WHITES

BIRMINGHAM, Ala., Aug. 25—Deputy Sheriff Dave Kennebrook today reported the lynching of Wilson Gardner, a young negro half-wit who was found Sunday hanging by a belt. Gardner has gone around to the homes of white miners near Kilgore carrying a rope and threatening to hang them. This disturbed the miners who beat the half wit to death before hoisting his corpse to a railroad trestle.

ALBANY (NEW YORK) KNICKERBOCKER PRESS
August 28, 1913

LYNCHED NEGRO CLEARED

GREENVILLE, Ga., Aug. 27—Virgil Swanson, the negro lynched near here Monday as the murderer of L.C. Marchman, a wealthy planter, was innocent, as citizens who tried to save the negro from the mob contended. Swanson's innocence was proved today when Walter Brewster, another negro, was arrested and confessed that he killed Marchman in a dispute about rent.

MONTGOMERY ADVERTISER
August 28, 1913

NEGRO SHOT AFTER STRIKING MERCHANT WHO DIRTIED HIM

JENNINGS, La., Aug. 27—James Comeaux, a negro, was lynched by a mob here early today. He was taken from his cell in the jail some time after midnight, shot to death and his body left lying at the jail door. Comeaux had been arrested for striking A. W. Joseph, an Italian merchant, who had swept dirt on the negroe's shoes while the latter was passing the Italian's store.

BIRMINGHAM NEWS
September 4, 1913

WHITE WOMEN SEEK CLEMENCY FOR NEGRO SLATED TO DIE

ATLANTA, Sept. 1—Attorney R. G. Dickerson, of Homerville, appeared before the Prison Commission to-day and made a strong appeal for commutation of the sentence of Lige Lane, a Clinch county negro, from death to life imprisonment. Lane was convicted of criminal assault upon a white woman. The lawyer declared there were grave doubts as to Lane's guilt, and that there was a strong probability of mistaken identification on the part of the woman. The most unusual feature of the plea for commutation was the filing of a petition in behalf of the negro signed by 95 per cent of the white women of Homerville.

BIRMINGHAM NEWS
September 23, 1913

IMPERTINENT QUESTION

LOUISVILLE, Ky., Sept. 21—Henry Crosby, a negro, yesterday entered the farm house of Mrs. J.C. Carroll of

Parkinsville and asked her whether her husband was home. The woman, frightened by this question, grabbed up her infant and ran to a near-by house. Officers searching for Crosby this morning found his body hanging from the limb of a tree.

MONTGOMERY ADVERTISER
October 23, 1913

INSULTING REMARK

MONROE, La., Oct. 22—Warren Eton, a negro, who made an insulting remark to a white woman Monday, was taken from the jail here early this morning by a mob and hanged to a nearby telegraph pole. Two masked men held up the jailer with pistols but other members of the mob made no attempt to conceal their identities.

LETTER TO THE EDITOR OF
THE MONTGOMERY ADVERTISER
November 6, 1913

LYNCHINGS DECLINE

Editor of the Advertiser:
At the end of six months of the present year there had been twenty-four cases of lynchings. At the end of ten months, (November 1st), there had been forty-five lynchings; a reduction of four as compared with the same period in 1912.

In ten months, as stated above, forty-five persons have been put to death by mob-law. A reduction of the number by four, though small, means something in the way of a higher civilization.

BOOKER T. WASHINGTON

SEATTLE TIMES
March 31, 1914

COLORED WOMAN IS HANGED

MUSKOGEE, Okla., Mar. 31—Marie Scott, a negro woman, was taken from the Wagoner County jail early today and hanged to a telephone pole.

A mob of at least a dozen armed men overpowered the jailer, a one-armed man, threw a rope over the screaming woman's head, dragged her out of her cell and strung her up a block from the jail.

Marie Scott was charged with driving a knife into the heart of Lemuel Peace, a youthful white man who, in company with other young white men, had gone to the negro quarter of Wagoner last Saturday night.

BOSTON GUARDIAN
April 30, 1914

NEGRO YOUTH MUTILATED FOR KISSING WHITE GIRL

MARSHALL, Tex., Apr. 29—Because he is alleged to have hugged and kissed a white girl, daughter of a farmer, Charles Fisher, a negro youth, was recently badly mutilated by a mob near here. According to Sheriff Sanders and County Health Officer Taylor, the mob sheared off the youth's ears, slit his lips and mutilated him in other ways below the belt.

NEW YORK AGE
April 30, 1914

WAS POWERLESS TO AID SISTER WHO WAS RAPED AND LYNCHED

CLOVIS, N. M., Apr. 27—The brother of the young colored girl who was lynched by a mob of white ruffians

90

near Wagner, Okla., a few weeks ago, passed through this town on his way to Mexico. He gave a pathetic account of the lynching to colored citizens here.

The young man's sister was but 17 years old and of respectable parents. Two half-drunken white men walked into their home during the absence of the mother and found the girl dressing, locked themselves into her room and criminally assaulted her. Her screams for help were heard by her brother, who, kicking down the door, went to her rescue. In defending his sister, he shot one of the brutes. The other escaped.

Later in the evening the local authorities, failing to find the brother, arrested the sister, who was taken from jail by a mob at 4 o'clock in the morning and lynched. From his hiding place the brother, who is 21 years old, could hear his sister's cries for help, but he was powerless to aid her.

MONTGOMERY ADVERTISER
May 8, 1914

SHOE THIEF SUSPECT LYNCHED

GROVETON, Ga., May 7—Charley Jones, a negro, was taken from two officers near here late last night by a number of white men and lynched. It is said that Jones was suspected of having shop lifted a pair of shoes.

ATLANTA CONSTITUTION
July 1, 1914

TWO ACCIDENTALLY KILLED IN SWAMP HUNT FOR NEGRO

SHAW, Miss., June 30—A member of the posse hunting for Jack Farmer, negro, was accidentally shot and killed by a fellow member of the posse early today. Fred Young mistook James Jolly, a fellow posseman, for Farmer as they were both pushing their way through a swamp here where it was believed Farmer was hiding.

This is the second life sacrificed in the hunt for Farmer, who is wanted for fatally shooting Earl Chase, a leading citizen of this county. The other death was that of Jennie Collins, a negro woman, who was alleged to have assisted Farmer in his flight.

ATLANTA CONSTITUTION
July 15, 1914

NEGRO HANGED AS MULE THIEF

LAKE CORMORANT, Miss., July 14—James Bailey, a negro, was hanged today by a mob of about twenty masked men. He had been accused of the theft of three mules.

GALVESTON (TEXAS) NEWS
October 15, 1914

MOB TAKES SPARED LIFE

ANGLETON, Tex., Oct. 14—Governor Colquitt today commuted the sentence of negro Jim Durfee, a convicted murderer, from death to life imprisonment. Local citizens, enraged at the action of the chief executive, formed in a mob, secured Durfee from the jailhouse and strung him up until he died of suffocation.

ST. PAUL PIONEER PRESS
November 26, 1914

NEGRO AND WIFE HANGED, SUSPECTED OF BARN-BURNING

BYHALIA, Miss., Nov. 25—Fred Sullivan, a negro, and his wife, accused of burning a barn on a plantation near Byhalia, were hanged today by a mob which forced a deputy sheriff and his posse to watch the lynching.

NEW YORK HERALD
December 6, 1914

WOULD-BE CHICKEN THIEF

SPARTANBURG, S. C., Dec. 5—For the crime of crawling under the house of a white citizen, with the intention of stealing chickens, Willie Green, a young Negro, was lynched Thursday night by a mob at Cowards, a rural settlement near here.

CLEVELAND GAZETTE
December 13, 1914

LA. NEGRO IS BURNED ALIVE SCREAMING "I DIDN'T DO IT"

SHREVEPORT, La., Dec. 12—Charred remains of Watkins Lewis, the third negro to die at the hands of mobs as the result of the murder of Charles Hicks, postmaster at Sylvester, La., last week, were found today near Sylvester bound to a tree with coils of wire. The burning of Lewis makes a total of eight lynchings in this parish in the last year, five negroes having been put to death in the last ten days. Tobe Lewis and Monroe Lewis were lynched last week for their alleged part in the Hicks murder.

Stories here tonight tell of a mob of 200 white men, formed in the outskirts of Sylvester last night. Lewis, cringing with fear, was taken from the jail here, placed in a motor car, and whirled to the mob. Not a word was spoken as the little cavalcade formed, and with the negro in the center marched to a giant tree near the Texas line. Lewis was bound to the trunk. Fallen trees and branches were heaped about him. Before the fire was lighted Lewis repeatedly was asked to confess his part in the crime, or to divulge the hiding place of a large sum of money said to have been stolen from the postmaster's store.

"I didn't do it," he screamed as the flames leaped about him.

When the fire enveloped him the mob dispersed. Today the town of Sylvester was quiet.

CHICAGO TRIBUNE
December 31, 1914

1914 LYNCHINGS SHOW RISE

The number of lynchings in 1914 shows a small increase over that of 1913, being 54, as compared with 48 in 1913 and 64 in 1912. The following table showing the annual number during the last thirty years may be of general interest:

Year		Year	
1865	184	1900	115
1886	138	1901	130
1887	122	1902	96
1888	142	1903	104
1889	176	1904	87
1890	127	1905	60
1891	193	1906	60
1892	205	1907	65
1893	200	1908	100
1894	170	1909	87
1895	171	1910	74
1896	181	1911	71
1897	106	1912	64
1898	127	1913	48
1899	107	1914	54

NEW YORK WORLD
February 18, 1915

ANOTHER FLORIDA LYNCHING

TAMPA, Fla., Feb. 17—John Richards, a negro, was lynched by a mob near Sparr, Fla., last night. He is said to have insulted a white woman.

CHICAGO DEFENDER
February 31, 1915

NEGRO SHOT DEAD FOR KISSING HIS WHITE GIRLFRIEND

CEDAR KEYS, Fla., Feb. 26—Young Reed, Negro, of Kissimee, was shot to death by a white mob at Wednesday noon after he had been seen kissing a white woman named Belle Mann with whom he had been keeping company for the past two years.

Reed was kissing Miss Mann good-bye when he was seen by a group of white men. The men seized him, beat him unmercifully and placed him in jail. Shortly thereafter a lynching party was formed and Reed was shot to death.

Local men of the Negro race have sworn to burn down the homes of white men living with colored women to avenge the death of Reed.

ATLANTA CONSTITUTION
April 18, 1915

CHARGED WITH STEALING MEAT

VALDOSTA, Ga., April 17—Caesar Sheffield, a negro prisoner in the town jail at Lake Park, was taken from the prison last night and shot to death by unknown parties. No trail has been found of the slayers.

Sheffield was arrested yesterday charged with stealing meat from the smokehouse of Elder B. Herring and put in jail to await trial. The prison was forced open by unknown parties and cries were heard from the negro about 9 o'clock last night. Moses Oppenheim, who went to investigate the cries, was driven back by shots fired in his direction, and was unable to identify the men who were making off with the prisoner. Sheffield's body was found this morning in a field near the railroad station at Lake Park.

KANSAS CITY (MISSOURI) JOURNAL
September 9, 1915

LYNCHED ON SECOND ATTEMPT

DRESDEN, Tenn., Sept. 8—Mallie Wilson, a negro charged with having entered a room occupied by a white woman, was hanged by a mob at Greenfield, Tenn., early Saturday, according to a dispatch from Greenfield.

The negro was taken from the jail earlier in the night and preparations made to lynch him. The husband of the woman, however, refused to act as executioner and Wilson was returned to jail. Later the mob reassembled, took the negro and hanged him.

CHICAGO DEFENDER
December 18, 1915

RAPE, LYNCH NEGRO MOTHER

COLUMBUS, Miss., Dec. 17—Thursday a week ago Cordella Stevenson was found early in the morning hanging to a limb of a tree, without any clothing, dead. She had been hung Wednesday night after a mob had visited her cabin, taken her from her husband and lynched her after they had maltreated her. The body was found about fifty yards north of the Mobile & Ohio R. R., and the thousands and thousands of passengers that came in and out of this city last Thursday morning were horrified at the sight. She was hung there from the night before by a bloodthirsty mob who had gone to her home, snatched her from slumber, and dragged her through the streets without any resistance. They carried her to a far-off spot, did their dirt and then strung her up.

Several months ago the barn of Gabe Frank, white, was burned. The son of Mrs. Stevenson was suspected of the burning. Although Mrs. Stevenson and her husband Arch are regarded as hard-working people, having worked for the same employer eleven years, their son is regarded as shiftless.

Mrs. Stevenson was brought to the police station and questioned on the possibility that her son might have set fire to Frank's barn. Mrs. Stevenson said her son had left home several months prior to the burning and she did not know his whereabouts. Convinced of her truthfulness, the police turned her loose and she went home.

Nothing more was thought of the case until Thursday morning. They had gone to bed early, as usual, and, after hearing a knock at the door, according to Arch Stevenson, the woman's husband, who ran all the way in town after the mob had taken his wife. Before he could answer the knock the mob had broken the door down and seized his wife, putting rifles to his head and threatening him if he moved. At the first opportunity he ran 'mid the hail of bullets. After telling his story he left for parts unknown. The mob took the woman about 10 o'clock at night. After that no one knows exactly what happened. The condition of the body showed plainly that she had been mistreated. Sheriff Bell telephoned to Justice of the Peace McKellar to hold an inquest. He was out of town, and didn't return till Thursday night. The body was left hanging in view of the morbid crowd that came to gaze at it till Friday morning, when it was cut down and the inquest held. The jury returned a verdict that she came to death at the hands of persons unknown.

It was the same old verdict that all southern juries return in the cases of this kind. The United States is sending missionaries to teach the heathen, Ford has gone to Europe with his peace party, ministers preach on the good to humanity, but here in the South the same dastardly crimes are committed and no one volunteers to raise his voice against such a crime committed against a member of the race. But retribution comes to all. Belgium robbed the black people of the Congo States of their ivory and rubber and sold for gold the labors of these well-meaning people. If their work was not up to what the Belgians thought it should be, an arm was cut off or some other cruelty imposed. Now Belgium is suffering. The day of reckoning has come. So will it be with this country. As they sow, so shall they reap. Today the business men are trying their hardest to get into South America, and the Latin countries are only going to allow them in under certain conditions. Race discrimination and lynchings will find no upholders there. The people there brand the Americans as lynchers, and it will be hard for the Americans to convince them otherwise.

97

PHILADELPHIA INQUIRER
January 3, 1916

BLACKS LYNCHED FOR REMARK
WHICH MAY HAVE BEEN "HELLO"

HARTWELL, Ga., Jan. 2—Two negroes were lynched
and a negro woman was badly beaten as the result of a
remark to a white girl in Anderson County, South Carolina, according to reports received here tonight.

The three negroes were riding in a buggy when they
passed the girl. One of the men made a remark to the
white girl, at which she took offense. She reported the
encounter to a group of white men who quickly caught up
with the blacks, lynched the men, beat the woman and
ordered her out of the state.

Reports concerning the nature of the allegedly insulting remark are conflicting. Officials of Georgia county say
that one of the negro men yelled out, "Hello, Sweet-
heart." The negro woman asserts that all they said was
"Hello."

ATLANTA CONSTITUTION
January 3, 1916

NEGRO CHURCH AND LODGES
BURNED AFTER 6 LYNCHINGS

BLAKELY, Ga., Jan. 2—While no more attempts have
been made on the lives of negroes since last week's outbreak, in which six negroes were killed, reports reached
here today that a negro church building, in the western
part of this (Early) county, was burned last night.
Some half dozen lodge buildings have been burned since
angry whites went out to avenge the death of Henry J.
Villipigue, an overseer residing in the western part of
the county, but until last night, negro churches, it was
said, had been spared. Villipigue was murdered by negroes for having whipped one of them, according to
statements by neighbors.

Mike and Ulysses Goolsby, negroes accused of complicity in Villipigue's death, generally are believed to have escaped from the county. John T. Beaseley, of Blakely, left here last night for Montgomery, Ala., on hearing reports that the negroes had gone there. A deputy sheriff was expected to follow him later.

Idlers in and around the courthouse square late today were given a surprise when a pistol dropped from the hand of a man who had been using it to illustrate the part he said he had taken in the hunt for negroes last week. One cartridge of the pistol exploded, the ball going through the fleshy part of the leg of the narrator. No one else was hurt.

NEW YORK HERALD
January 22, 1916

FIVE LYNCHED IN GEORGIA

SYLVESTER, Ga., Friday—The bullet-riddled bodies of five negroes found hanging from a tree near Starkville, Ga., to-day, increased the total of negroes lynched in that section to fourteen within the last five weeks. The victims of the latest lynching were accused by a mob of having knowledge of the killing of Sheriff Moreland of Lee County.

Four of the victims were of one family—Felix Lake and his three sons, Frank, Dewer and Major. The fifth victim was Rodius Seamore.

ATLANTA CONSTITUTION
February 23, 1916

ALL FIVE LYNCHED NEGROES WERE GUILTLESS, SAYS KEITH

TIFTON, Ga., Feb. 22—Jim Keith, sentenced to a life term in prison for complicity in the killing of Sheriff Moreland of Lee county, talked freely of the crime today as he was carried to Richmond county to begin serving his term. He declared that Rodius Seamore and old man

Lake and his three sons, who were lynched last month for Sheriff Moreland's death, were entirely guiltless. This fact is now generally believed.

While fleeing from the place where he shot Moreland, Keith said, he stopped at the home of the Lakes because it was the first negro house in reach. The old man was gone and did not get back until a few minutes before the posse came. Keith had no opportunity to tell him about the trouble, and old man Lake did not know that Keith was wanted by the officers, Keith said.

ATLANTA CONSTITUTION
February 7, 1917

KEITH ACQUITTED BY JURY

SYLVESTER, Ga., Feb. 6—Jim Keith, a negro, who, charged with the murder of Sheriff Moreland of Lee county, on December 18, 1915, was saved by Worth county officials from a mob which lynched five other negroes for the crime, was acquitted by a white jury in superior court here last night.

At his first trial here a year ago, Keith was convicted on the theory that he was in the conspiracy which resulted in the murder of the Lee county sheriff and was given a life term. Further evidence, however, has led to the general belief that another negro, who escaped, is the murderer.

Keith, in January of 1916, was removed from the Worth county jail and carried to a place of safety shortly before a mob, supposedly from Lee county, took five innocent negroes to Starkesville, in Lee county, and there lynched them.

EDITORIAL FROM THE NEW YORK TIMES
February 12, 1917

THE AFTERMATH

A Georgia sheriff was murdered something over a year ago. Naturally, there was intense excitement in Worth County where the crime was committed and of the six negroes who were arrested, five were promptly hanged by a mob. The sixth, Jim Keith, chanced to be rescued from the lynchers, much to their indignation. He was put on trial and convicted of complicity in the murder, but not of actual participation in it, and he was sentenced to imprisonment for life. Recently some new facts came to light and in the second trial that was accorded to Keith, because of their importance, not only was he cleared by the jury of having any hand at all in the killing, but it was also proved that the five negroes who were lynched were equally guiltless.

EDITORIAL IN THE CHICAGO DEFENDER
February 12, 1916

HOW MUCH LONGER?

In four weeks the intelligent and cultured citizens of the commonwealth of Georgia have lynched sixteen colored people, which is a record. Despite the emancipation proclamation and constitutional amendments, ostensibly conferring equal rights, the world knows how cheaply the life of a black man is held in those regions that are still stained by the memory of a legalized system of servitude.

But it would seem by this time that the people of the South would have made at least some small progress toward controlling and finally eliminating mob murder. Instead of diminishing, the number is increasing, and in at least four instances it later developed that the persons put to death were innocent of the offenses charged.

Whenever Georgia is able to execute legally the leaders of a lynching mob she will have made a step forward that will promise much for her future. The discouraging part is that as disgraceful and degrading as these occurrences are, the "best citizens" appear to have developed a pride in this hideous work. It is a species of provincialism and local conceit of a peculiarly ugly and grotesque kind that produces such a feeling, but it is plain that something of the kind exists among a large class there. As ghastly as are the horrors of the European war, man's inhumanity to man is not confined to our brethren across the sea. We have this same hideous story every year. Are we ever going to do anything about it?

BIRMINGHAM VOICE OF THE PEOPLE
April 1, 1916

BUMPS INTO GIRL; IS LYNCHED

CEDAR BLUFF, Miss., March 31—Jeff Brown was lynched by a mob here late Saturday afternoon. Brown was walking down the street near the car tracks and saw a moving freight going in the direction in which he wanted to go. He started on the run to board the moving train. On the sidewalk was the daughter of a white farmer. Brown accidentally brushed against her and she screamed. A gang quickly formed and ran after him, jerking him off the moving train. He was beaten into insensibility and then hung to a tree. The sheriff has made no attempt to find out who the members of the mob were. Picture cards of· the body are being sold on the streets at five cents apiece.

ATLANTA CONSTITUTION
April 4, 1916

LYNCHED FROM COURTHOUSE

IDABEL, Okla., April 3—After listening to the evidence at the preliminary hearing here today of Oscar Martin, a negro charged with having attacked a 13-year-old girl, a mob of five hundred men overpowered court attaches and hanged the negro from a second story balcony of the courthouse.

Evidently at a previously arranged signal the mob sprang up from among the spectators at the conclusion of the evidence and while court officers were held prisoners, dragged the negro to the balcony from which he was thrown after one end of a rope had been placed around his neck and the other made secure to a post.

The mob dispersed within a few minutes. To-night the town is quiet.

NEW YORK WORLD
May 16, 1916

15,000 WITNESS BURNING OF NEGRO IN PUBLIC SQUARE

WACO, Tex., May 15—Screaming for mercy until the flames silenced him, Jesse Washington, a negro of eighteen years, was burned to death by a mob in the public square here to-day. Many women and children were among the 15,000 who witnessed the lynching.

Just a week ago the lad assaulted and killed Mrs. Lucy Fryar, a white woman, in her home at Robinson, seven miles from here. There was no question of his guilt, and he got one of the quickest trials on record in this part of Texas. The proceeding ended this forenoon, when the jury brought in a verdict of guilty, carrying with it the death penalty.

"I'm sorry I done it," said the prisoner in a whisper, shaking with fear as he saw the crowd in the court room rising threateningly all around him with the pronouncement of the verdict.

"Get that nigger!" was the shout raised by some, and it was chorused by the mob. The leaders made a rush, sweeping officers and lawyers aside. The negro was seized and then was dragged from the court room.

The first suggestion was to hang him from the suspension bridge, and a chain was tied around his neck and he was dragged, yelling, in that direction.

"Burn him!" roared hundreds of voices all raised at once, and the idea pleased the mob. So the negro was dragged by the chain to the City Hall square. There the ringleaders stood him under a tree and threw the chain over a limb. Boxes and sticks of wood were piled around him and then he was hoisted over the pile.

His clothing was saturated with oil and a match was applied. At a signal the negro was hoisted further in the air, then was let fall into the flames.

It was all over one hour from the rendering of the jury's death verdict. When the fire had burned itself out the charred body was put in a sack and was dragged behind an automobile to Robinson, where it was hanged to a telephone pole for the colored populace to gaze upon.

NEW YORK WORLD
July 29, 1916

NEW YORK NEGROES STAGE
SILENT PARADE OF PROTEST

Leaders among the negroes of New York City decided that a silent parade would be the most dramatic and effective way to make felt the protest of their race against injustice and inhumanity growing out of lynch law.

And this silent parade was staged with real impressiveness and dignity and with an indefinable appeal to the heart in Fifth Avenue yesterday afternoon.

From the time that the 3,500 or 4,000 men, women and children marchers left Fifty-sixth Street shortly after 1 o'clock until they were completing their dispersal in Twenty-fourth Street about 3 no note of discord was struck.

Police Inspector Morris, who, with upward of one hundred policemen, was in charge of the arrangement down to Forty-second Street, expressed his warm admiration for those in the silent lines.

"They have done everything just right," he said to a reporter for The World. "They have been lovely."

And it might be mentioned that this was the first time that the reporter, who has observed many parades in the past few years in New York, ever heard a police official use the adjective "lovely" to describe those whom it is his task to keep in order.

Of the many printed signs prepared by the marchers, Inspector Morris doubted the good taste of only one. It showed a colored mother crouching protectively over two cowering children with the caption, "East St. Louis." And then it showed a photograph of President Wilson and his assertion that the world must be made safe for democracy.

"I asked them if they did not think it was in bad taste too," the Inspector said. "And they agreed that it was and put it aside. They made every effort to have this parade exactly what it was planned to be."

The only sound as the marchers passed down the avenue was the slow, —Tum, tum, tum—tum—tum. And except for little cries of sympathy and admiration from women when they saw a tiny, bright-eyed, kinky-haired baby peeping solemnly over the moist neck of its marching mother, the silence of the parade spread to and enveloped the watchers on the sidewalk too.

There must have been as many colored men and women and babies on the sidewalk as there were in the parade. Probably there were more. And they too showed the same restraint and sense of decorum that governed the marchers.

The parade was led by a drum corps of boys in khaki. Then there were fourteen lines of young girls. After them were six rows of boys, eighty-five rows of women, many of them mothers with babies in their arms, and fifty-five lines of men. The lines appeared to average twenty persons.

In the line of march were doctors, lawyers, ministers, school teachers and trained nurses. Many veterans of the Spanish-American War were there too. The Grand Marshal, Capt. Hubert Jackson, served in Cuba and the Philippines as Captain of Company L of the Sixth Massachusetts. Clifton G. A. French, a lawyer, was in the Twenty-third Kansas. He explained the purpose of the parade this way:

"We love our Government. And we want our Government to love us too."

The banners carried aloft bore the following inscriptions:

"Thou shalt not kill."

"Unto the least of these, my brethren."

"Mother, do lynchers go to heaven?"

"Suffer little children and forbid them not."

"Give me a chance to live."

"Mr. President, why not make America safe for democracy."

"The first blood for American independence was shed by a negro, Crispus Attucks."

"Put the spirit of Christ in the making and the execution of laws."

"Your hands are full of blood."

"We have 30,000 teachers."

105

"Race prejudice is the offspring of ignorance and the mother of lynching."

"Ten thousand of us fought in the Spanish-American War."

"Three thousand negroes fought for American independence under George Washington."

"No negro has ever betrayed his country or attempted to assassinate a President or any official of the Government."

"Patriotism and loyalty presuppose protection and liberty."

"America has lynched without trial 2,867 negroes in thirty-one years. Not a single murderer has suffered."

"Memphis and Waco, centres of American culture?"

"Twenty thousand black men fought for your liberty in the Civil War."

"The world owes no man a living, but every man an opportunity to earn a living."

"Thirty-four negroes have received Carnegie hero medals."

"Our music is the only American music."

"A square deal for every man."

And there was another one to the effect that if there is any fault to be found with color, either white people or God is responsible.

ATLANTA CONSTITUTION
August 20, 1916

5 HANGED ON ONE OAK TREE

GAINESVILLE, Fla., Aug. 19—Five negroes, three men and two women, were taken from the jail at Newberry, Fla., early today and hanged by a mob, and another negro was shot and killed by deputy sheriffs near Jonesville, Fla., as the result of the killing yesterday of Constable S. G. Wynne and the shooting of Dr. L. G. Harris by Boisey Long, a negro. The lynched negroes were accused of aiding Long to escape.

PHILADELPHIA ENQUIRER
August 27, 1916

LYNCHED DESPITE PROTESTS OF RAPE VICTIM'S PARENTS

SHREVEPORT, La., Aug. 26—A mob of 1000 yesterday took Jess Hammet, a negro, from the jail at Vivian, twenty miles north of here, and hanged him to a telegraph pole. He was identified by a white woman as the man who had attempted an assault upon her. The woman's parents pleaded with the mob to desist. Hammet, as a servant years ago, cared for the woman he is said to have attempted to outrage.

PROVIDENCE BULLETIN
August 31, 1916

SHERIFF NEARLY LYNCHED

LIMA, O., Aug. 31—Sheriff Sherman Ely of this county was slashed, kicked and nearly lynched by a mob of 3,000 last night when he refused to divulge the location of a negro prisoner wanted by the mob.

The mob descended upon the local jailhouse before dusk and demanded surrender of Charles Daniels, a negro, held for questioning in connection with 'the assault of Mrs. John Barber, a white woman. The Sheriff refused to surrender him.

The mob smashed its way into the jail, searched it cell by cell and realized that the prisoner had been spirited away and hidden elsewhere. The mob seized the Sheriff, stripped him of his clothes, kicked, beat and cut him, dragged him to the principal street corner of this town and tied a noose around his neck threatening to hang him to a trolley pole unless he told where he had hidden the negro.

With blood streaming from a dozen cuts and with two ribs fractured, the sheriff refused. The mob then dispersed.

MINNEAPOLIS TRIBUNE
September 3, 1916

LYNCH LEADERS DECLARE LYNCHING WAS "HUMANE"

You have heard about Southern chivalry all your life. Now a new phase of it has developed in the application of ethics to lynching.

If you were to be lynched by a mob, you would appreciate it greatly if you were "shown every courtesy" during the proceeding. To all persons who yearn to be the guest of honor at what used to be facetiously termed a necktie party, therefore, the gentlemanly and humane mob of Stuttgart, Ark., is recommended without reservation.

Down in Stuttgart last week a negro was lynched. He had been accused of attacking the daughter of a white planter near the town. The mob worked quietly and expeditiously, but necessarily without the limelight. After it was all over unauthorized versions of the affair were circulated and accepted by the public. It was to set the public right that the lynchers decided to proclaim just how genteel it really was. So the following "card" was sent to the Free Press, the town's newspaper, which published it on August 11:

"We, members of the committee that hanged the negro Wednesday morning, have, after listening to the false stories about the affair, concluded that it is due to the public that they may be made acquainted with the true facts.

"The criminal was taken from jail at De Witt, brought to the scene of execution, and hanged in as humane a manner as possible.

"Quite recently, in England, a man was hanged for high treason. He suffered the tortures of strangulation for nine minutes before he was pronounced dead by the attending physicians. We give you our word that the criminal we 'lynched' did not live nine seconds after his feet left the ground, as the bullet wounds on his body will prove.

"The only request made by the criminal was that he be hanged or shot, and not tortured or burned. That his request was granted was self-evident to everyone who saw the remains.

"For obvious reasons we must withhold our names and beg to sign ourselves:

"Yours for the proper and unfailing enforcement of the law,

"THE COMMITTEE."

ATLANTA CONSTITUTION
September 30, 1916

TWO SAVED FROM FIRST MOB ARE LYNCHED BY SECOND MOB

NOWATA, Okla., Sept. 29—Two negroes were saved from lynching today by the eloquent plea of a Methodist minister only to be lynched later on by a second mob.

John Foreman, negro, and another negro, unnamed, were arrested on the outskirts of town last night in connection with the shooting of Deputy Sheriff James Gibson. Foreman was wounded in the course of the arrest and was not immediately molested by the mob. The unwounded negro, however, was seized by the mob, which had grown to large proportions, and a parade through the principal streets began with the negro, at a rope's end, screaming for mercy.

When the mob reached the Methodist church a large tree offered the opportunity the rope around the negro's neck suggested. "Let's lynch the nigger on holy ground," shouted one man. The prisoner was swung clear and was being choked to death when Rev. Perry E. Pierce appeared, attracted from his study by the negro's screams. He rushed into the midst of the crowd and began his pleadings for the seemingly doomed man's life.

"Men, I beseech you in the name of God not to desecrate this holy ground," pleaded Mr. Pierce. "Do not stain the name of our city by going into this terrible affair."

With great earnestness he demanded that the law be allowed to take its course. Five minutes the pastor

109

spoke, until one of the mob leaders, turning to his fellows, said: "Men, Mr. Pierce is right. Take the nigger back to jail and let the law take its course." The suspended negro was cut down, unconscious but alive. The mob led him back to jail. Nowata was quiet following the episode, but quiet was only the lull before the storm. Shortly after the dinner hour Foreman and the other negro who had been rescued in the afternoon were taken from the jail by another mob, a larger one, and were strung up on the grounds of the courthouse.

ATLANTA CONSTITUTION
October 9, 1916

NEGRESS TAKEN FROM JAIL AND RIDDLED WITH BULLETS

ARLINGTON, Ga., Oct. 4—Mary Conley, the negro woman whose son, Sam Conley, killed E. M. Melvin, a prominent white planter, near here Monday, was taken from the guardhouse in Leary some time during the night and lynched. Her body, riddled with bullets, was found by the roadside by parties coming into Arlington during the early morning hours.

When Melvin reprimanded Sam Conley for the way the latter was neglecting his work the negro's mother showed resentment. It is claimed that Melvin then slapped and grappled with her, whereupon Sam Conley picked up an iron scale weight and struck the white man on the head in defense of his mother. Melvin died a short time later.

Conley escaped, but his mother was captured and put in jail here.

The mob had no difficulty in breaking into the guardhouse, which was unguarded, the officers not anticipating trouble. The lynching was very quiet.

MONTGOMERY ADVERTISER
October 10, 1916

NEGRO INSULTS WHITE WOMEN; IS SHOT AND STRUNG UP

DeWITT, Ark., Oct. 9—Frank Dodd, a negro, who was arrested yesterday charged with having insulted two young women, was taken from jail here early today, and hanged. His body was riddled with bullets and left hanging to a tree in a negro settlement on the outskirts of DeWitt.

NEW YORK EVENING GLOBE
October 16, 1916

2 LYNCHED; 1 HAD VOICED APPROVAL OF OTHER'S MISDEED

PADUCAH, Ky., Oct. 16—Two Negroes were lynched by a mob here to-day and their bodies burned. One was charged with attacking Mrs. George Rose, a white woman, at her home in the suburbs last Friday, while the other was accused of voicing approval of his action.

AN EDITORIAL FROM THE PITTSBURGH LEADER
January 23, 1917

THE COWARDICE OF LYNCHERS

The cowardliness of the mob intent on lynching has often been illustrated, but seldom in so striking a manner as in two recent instances reported from southern states.

In one of them Governor Stanley of Kentucky, alone and unarmed, held off the mob by a display of personal courage that does not have its parallel in the history of such outrages.

When the news reached him that a mob was being organized in Murray, Kentucky, to lynch a colored prisoner the governor immediately went to the jail, confronted the howling pack and cowed it with a few words that proved his magnificent courage, as well as his devotion to the duties he had been elected to perform.

The governor dared the mob to attack him before attacking the prisoner.

The mob melted away like snow beneath the sun.

And now comes another illustration from Columbia, S. C., where, according to the news reports, a 14-year-old girl, armed with a revolver which she did not know how to use, kept a mob of lynchers at bay.

The mob surrounded the jail and demanded the person of a colored man who had been arrested for assaulting a white man. The jailer's daughter was the only one left to protect the prisoner and she immediately took her stand in front of the jail and defied the mob to test her ability to riddle it with bullets.

The child was in control of the situation when her father arrived and took charge of it himself.

There is nothing so cowardly as a mob of lynchers.

NEW YORK GLOBE
July 25, 1917

2 HUNG FOR JOSTLING HORSE

MONTGOMERY, Ala., July 25—Will and Jesse Powell, negroes who were arrested here to-day on a charge of threatening the life of a white farmer and his negro helper, were to-night taken by a mob from deputies in Lowndes county and lynched to a nearby tree.

The trouble is said to have arisen when the negroes brushed against the farmer's horse.

PICTURE CAPTION IN THE CHICAGO DEFENDER
September 8, 1917

GRIM REMINDER

Above is the head of Ell Persons, Negro, who was burned to death in Memphis, Tenn. on May 18th. This head was

112

cut off the body and is seen here on the pavement of Beale Street, the principal business street of the Negro section. Both ears have been severed from the head by souvenir hunters, along with the lower lip and nose. Copies of this photograph are sold in Memphis for a quarter apiece.

CHICAGO DEFENDER
October 13, 1917

BOY UNSEXES NEGRO BEFORE MOB LYNCHES HIM

HOUSTON, Tex., Oct. 12—Eight hundred oil-field workers—whites, Mexicans, Germans and Italians—employed at Goose Creek, a suburb of this city, seized Bert Smith, a member of the Race, and brutally hung him to a tree and riddled his body with bullets and horribly mutilated it with sledge-hammers and butcher knives after cutting it down. Smith was accused of committing an outrage on his employer's wife.

Smith, who was employed as cook on the oil reservation, made complaint to the head of his camp concerning the indecent remarks that were recited to his sister and mother, who came to see him occasionally, and pointed out several men who had annoyed them A crowd of whites were standing nearby and heard Smith's complaint, and it is claimed that a heinous crime against Smith and his relatives was hatched by this bunch. A week later Smith's sister was on her way from Houston to the camp at Goose Creek, and was seen approaching by three whites who secluded themselves behind some shrubbery. When the girl passed they leaped out, gagged and bound her, and carried the body into the woods, and the three in turn committed outrages on her. After satisfying their beastly natures they stripped the girl of her blood-stained garments and hung them over her head on the limb of a tree. She was found late in the afternoon by several small boys who were out berry picking.

The day following one of the men came near Smith and said, "Hey, nigger, did you see that ugly black wench they picked up in the woods yistidy?" and also uttered

113

other horrible phrases concerning the outrage that would not look good in print. In the midst of these remarks Smith dealt this white a vicious blow that felled him. The argument was closely watched by a number of oil drillers who immediately attacked Smith and placed a rope around his neck, hammered his mouth in with a sledge and pierced his body with sharp instruments, and then forced a 10-year-old white lad who carried water around the camp to take a large butcher knife and unsex him. Smith, who was still alive, begged that all his feelings be taken from him. He was dragged down the main thoroughfare near the camp houses and viewed by citizens including women.

CHATTANOOGA TIMES
February 13, 1918

BLOOD-CURDLING LYNCHING WITNESSED BY 2,000 PERSONS

ESTILL SPRINGS, Tenn., Feb. 12—Jim McIlherron, the negro who shot and killed Pierce Rodgers and Jesse Tigert, two white men at Estill Springs last Friday and wounded Frank Tigert, was tortured with a red-hot crowbar and then burned to death here tonight at 7:40 by twelve masked men. A crowd of approximately 2,000 persons, among whom were women and children, witnessed the burning.

The negro was brought to Estill Springs on passenger train No. 5, arriving here at 6:30. A crowd of about 1,200 persons met the train and joined the captors. Shouts of "Burn him; burn him!" filled the air.

Twelve men, with faces masked, stepped forward from the crowd and took possession of the negro. Simultaneously, as if this was a signal, others scattered among the crowd apparently trying to keep strict order. McIlherron, who was badly wounded and unable to walk, was carried to the scene of the murder, where preparation for a funeral pyre was begun. The negro was swearing with every breath and attempting to put part of the blame upon the son of Lynch, the negro preacher who was inadvertantly killed yesterday by members of the posse.

114

He said that he was persuaded to kill the young men by the preacher's son.

Several prominent citizens of Estill Springs made speeches and implored that mob to take the negro out of town to burn him, in order that the women and children might not witness the gruesome affair. After deliberating some time the executioners agreed to their request. The captors proceeded to a spot about a quarter of a mile from the railroad station and prepared the death fire. The crowd followed and remained throughout the horrible proceedings. The negro was led to a hickory tree, to which they chained him. After securing him to the tree a fire was laid. A short distance away another fire was kindled, and into it was put an iron bar to heat.

When the bar became red hot a member of the mob jabbed it toward the negro's body. Crazed with fright, the black grabbed hold of it, and as it was pulled through his hands the atmosphere was filled with the odor of burning flesh. This was the first time the murderer gave evidence of his will being broken. Scream after scream rent the air. As the hot iron was applied to various parts of his body his yells and cries for mercy could be heard in the town.

After torturing the negro several minutes one of the masked men poured coal oil on his feet and applied a match to the pyre. As the flames rose, enveloping the black's body he begged that he be shot. Yells of derision greeted his request. The angry flames consumed his clothing and little blue blazes shot upward from his burning hair before he lost consciousness.

The negro was captured at 11 this morning after about a thousand shots had been exchanged. The posse which was pursuing McIlherron surrounded him in an old barn, five miles west of McMinnville this morning at 4. The pursuers waited until daylight before attempting his capture. Several times he attempted to get away, and each time was driven back by a fusillade of bullets. It is thought that he received his wounds in these attempts to escape. Many tricks to cause him to waste his ammunition was resorted to—hats were stuck out from behind trees, and each time the negro would catch sight of one he would open fire, sometimes losing two or three shots.

At 11 this morning his guns were silenced and the

posse rushed forward. About fifteen shots were exchanged at this time, but no member of the mob was hurt. McIlherron was found lying on the floor of the barn with one eye shot out, a bullet in his arm and his body sprinkled with BB shot.

He was then taken to McMinnville on a hand car and from there carried to Tullahoma, thence to Estill Springs.

CHATTANOOGA TIMES

February 14, 1918

GRUESOME DETAILS GIVEN ON ESTELL SPRINGS LYNCHING

ESTILL SPRINGS, Tenn., Feb. 13—The body of Jim McIlherron, the negro who was burned at the stake last night, was taken down today from the tree to which it had hung since the burning, by his relatives.

The lower part of his body was burnt to a char, from the waist up the body was cooked to the bone. The marks on the neck were the only ones that could be distinguished.

While it is said to be generally known who the executioners are, no names are being mentioned.

Having accomplished its purpose the community is now quiet and every one is going about his business.

The Times' special correspondent, who witnessed the burning Tuesday night of Jim McIlherron, negro, who shot and killed two white men and dangerously wounded another at Estill Springs last Friday, reported in person to The Times yesterday afternoon.

The reporter gave The Times the facts of the burning over the telephone a few minutes after it occurred. He stated that while he was telephoning the facts of the burning into this office, one of the members of the mob stood at his side with a gun warning him not to give out any names.

The following was taken from his notebook:

Five O'Clock—Word reaches here that boy's slayer is captured and is being brought to Estill Springs. All afternoon little groups of men, with firm jaws set and

116

determined looks upon their faces arrive on horseback, all are heavily armed. Reported that a wire has been sent to Gov. Rye asking for troops to prevent lynching.

Six-thirty—Approximately 1,500 people are crowded around the railroad station and along the side of the tracks. The train arrives and the posse alight with the negro, who is lying on a stretcher. A prominent citizen jumps to the station platform and asks the crowd to keep order; he then asks that the negro be taken out of town to be burnt.

The negro's captors carry their prisoner to the exact spot where the boys were murdered and orders are given for these desiring to look upon him to form single file and march by. They are asked not to do violence to the murderer or to spit in his face. The crowd does as bid and marched by; the negro, with one eye shot out, an arm hanging limp, the result of a bullet wound received in the battle with the posse and his clothing covered with blood, was a gruesome sight. He is glaring at the spectators and cursing with nearly every breath. A female relative of one of the slain boys come up to the negro, kicks him in the ribs and spits in his face. When an attempt is made to dissuade her she become hysterical and cries for a pistol, begging that she be allowed to end the life of the black. Among the spectators were women with babies in their arms and little children hardly able to toddle.

Seven-thirty—The negro is being chained to a hickory tree and the funeral pyre is being made ready; every one wants to give a hand, several little boys carry wood for the pyre.

Seven-forty—A red-hot crowbar is brought forward by a masked man, who jabs it at the negro's body. The negro grabs it with his bare hands and the odor of burning flesh fills the atmosphere. McIlherron groans and curses. The iron is then applied to each side of the negro's neck, searing the flesh. Screams that were heard for half a mile rent the air. The negro then implicated the son of Lynch, a negro preacher who was killed the day before by a mob.

Seven-fifty—Eleven more masked men appear on the scene and prepare the fire. Coal oil is poured upon the negro's legs and feet. One of the executioners strikes a match that starts the death fire. As the fire eats its way

117

upward the negro begs for mercy and asks that some one shoot him. He is jeered at. When the flames reach his hair the victim becomes unconscious.

The body hung upon the tree as a warning to other negroes all night and part of the following day.

CHICAGO DEFENDER
April 5, 1919

NEGRO VETERAN LYNCHED
FOR REFUSING TO DOFF UNIFORM

BLAKELY, Ga., Apr. 4—When Private William Little, a Negro soldier returning from the war, arrived at the railroad station here several weeks ago, he was encountered by a band of whites. The whites ordered him to doff his Army uniform and walk home in his underwear. Several other whites prevailed upon the hoodlums to leave Little alone and he was permitted to walk home unmolested.

Little continued to wear his uniform over the next few weeks, as he had no other clothing. Anonymous notes were sent him warning him not to wear his Army uniform "too long" and advising him to leave town if he wished to "sport around in khaki." Little ignored the notes.

Yesterday Private Little was found dead on the outskirts of this city, apparently beaten by a mob. He was wearing his Army uniform.

KNOXVILLE EAST TENNESSEE NEWS
May 1, 1919

ILLITERATE NEGRO LYNCHED
FOR WRITING IMPROPER NOTE

SHREVEPORT, La., Apr. 29—A Vicksburg, Shreveport and Pacific train was held up by an armed mob about five miles from Monroe, La., today, and George Holden, negro, accused of writing an insulting note to a white woman named Onlie Elliot, was taken from the train and shot to death. Holden was taken from a stretcher in the baggage car. He had been wounded in two previous attempts to lynch him.

Holden was being sent to Shreveport for safekeeping. He was shot in the leg Monday night by unidentified persons shortly after the woman received the insulting note. Later he was beaten into insensibility. When the local sheriff heard of this, he placed Holden aboard the V,S&P train for the purpose of taking him to Shreveport for safekeeping. Local citizens, hearing of this, raced ahead of the train in automobiles and reaching the next station pulled the helpless negro from the train, took him to a nearby tree and riddled his body with bullets.

The note sent to Mrs. Elliot was written in plain handwriting. Acquaintances of the Negro state that he had no education and could hardly write his name.

CHICAGO DEFENDER
May 10, 1919

WHITE MAN BLACKENS FACE IN ATTACK ON WHITE GIRL

DADE CITY, Fla., May 9—Luther Wilson (white) blackened his face and attacked a 16-year-old girl while she was on her way to school here last week. According to the girl, Wilson, with his face and hands blackened with a grease paint, waylaid her as she was passing through a strip of heavy timber. He tied her arms behind her back and in doing so rubbed some of the paint from his hands. She recognized him after a due course of time and pleaded with him to give up his purpose on the theory that she would not tell anybody. Wilson is a relative of hers by marriage. The girl later told a neighbor.

A mob gathered and made for Wilson. He was located at a creek washing the black substance from his face and hands. The girl stated that Wilson had told her if she said anything about it, he would swear his innocence and put the blame on a black man. Everyone would believe him, he said.

VICKSBURG (MISSISSIPPI) HERALD
May 15, 1919

NEGRO INTRUDER LYNCHED

Lloyd Clay, 24-year-old negro laborer, was roasted to death here shortly after 8:00 o'clock last night. He had been charged with entering the bedroom of Miss Lulu Belle Bishop, aged 19, and attempting to violate her.

At an early hour yesterday, Clay forced his way through a screened window and entered Miss Bishop's bedroom. The young lady shrieked for help and fought him. Her father, Charles Bishop, attempted to go to her assistance, but could not break the door, which had been locked from within. The negro became alarmed and escaped through a window.

Charles Gantt's bloodhounds were brought from Crystal Springs. The hounds made two runs. On the first, they lost the scent. On the second they ran within ten feet of Clay who was standing at the A&V Railroad Station, as though waiting for the train to Jackson. They bayed at him and he was taken to jail. The young lady was taken to the jail to identify him, but she was not certain as to his identity.

A mob of between 800 and 1,000 men and women soon descended on the jail. Using rails for battering rams, they snatched the prisoner from the sheriff.

The negro was taken to the corner of Clay and Farmer Streets, covered with oil, set aflame and hoisted to an elm tree. As the flaming body was pulled aloft, a fusillade of shots was fired into the negro's frame. A stray bullet struck Charles Lancaster back of the left ear, fracturing his skull. He is in the Vicksburg sanitarium in serious condition. A collection is being taken up for Lancaster's family.

NEW YORK AGE
June 14, 1919

NEGRO WAS LYNCHED TO SAVE WHITE WOMAN'S SECRET LOVER

JACKSON, Miss., June 3—A reader of THE AGE residing here has just completed an investigation of the recent lynching of a colored man by the name of Clay, at Vicksburg, and as often is the case, an innocent Negro met death at the hands of white men.

Anent the Vicksburg outrage the writer says: "I have been told by responsible colored men that it is generally accepted now that the party who went into the young white woman's room was a white man with whom she had been on intimate terms. The white man had visited the girl and was heard leaving the house when a member of the family called out and wanted to know who was up in the room. Then she screamed.

"The white man had employed a colored chauffeur to bring him to Jackson, the same chauffeur who had taken the couple for midnight drives on other occasions, and who had driven them earlier on the night of the outrage. The white man got away.

"The police went to the chauffeur's house upon his return to Vicksburg from Jackson and arrested him along with two other colored men, and they were taken to Jackson for 'safe-keeping.' When the chauffeur told all he knew in connection with the case the authorities turned all three loose and ordered them to leave the country.

"The girl failed completely to identify her assailant, and stated positively that Clay was not the man. Her father likewise pleaded with the mob not to lynch Clay, saying he wanted no innocent man killed and that if he found the right party he would need no mob to handle the case for him. But the bloodthirsty violators of the law wanted to murder somebody and put Clay to death."

DUBLIN (GEORGIA) HERALD
July 2, 1919

FATALLY WOUND WRONG NEGRO

A negro, Cleveland Butler, was shot and fatally wounded by four white men in Twiggs county yesterday, according to news reaching Dublin, when he was arrested by the men on suspicion that he was Hubert Cummings, the negro badly wanted in Laurens county. After the negro had died, parties from Dublin saw him, and stated positively that he was not Cummings.

According to the story told by members of the Laurens county parties who went to identify the negro, the four white men implicated were Messrs. Tharpe, Griffin, Myers, and another man they did not know. These men stated they heard of a strange negro working in the chalk mines just over the line in Twiggs county, and after seeing him, decided that he very much resembled Cummings. They decided to capture him, and laid their plans. Learning that he was asleep at a negro house near the mines, they went to the house Tuesday, and went into the room where the negro was sleeping. They stated they called to him twice, and when he did not answer, they decided he might be preparing to shoot at them through the coverings, and decided to shoot first, which they did. The load from a shotgun fired at close range tore away a portion of the negro's jaw and chin, teeth and tongue, making an ugly wound. Neither of the men was an officer of any kind, but they carried the negro to the sheriff of Twiggs county, who refused to take him, telling the men that the negro should go to the hospital at once, and if he proved to be Cummings, Macon was the place to carry him. They carried the negro to the jail in Macon, but here again the sheriff refused to take him but told the men to rush the man to the hospital at once. They carried him to the Macon hospital, where he died a few minutes after being taken in.

While this was going on Deputy Sheriff Lester Watson had been notified by Sheriff Griffin of the negro's capture, and he gathered a party who knew Cummings well, and went to Macon to identify the negro. The Dublin party saw the negro about ten minutes after he had died, and immediately stated that he was not Cummings. Although he favored Cummings, the dead negro was reported lighter in color, with an old scar on his face that Cummings did not have. The men from this county were positive that it was not Cummings.

Just what will be the outcome of the case against the white men who were responsible for the negro's death is not known here, but they are in a rather peculiar and somewhat uncomfortable position as a result of the affair.

NEW YORK TRIBUNE
July 5, 1919

LYNCHINGS ON DECLINE

MOBILE, Ala., July 4—Lynchings during the first six months of 1919 were fewer than during the same six months of 1918 but more numerous than in 1917, according to the record kept by Tuskegee Institute.

The total for the current year to date is twenty-eight, in comparison with thirty-five in 1918 and fourteen for the first half of 1917.

Of those lynched in 1919 one negro woman was included.

NEW YORK SUN
August 29, 1919

LYNCH NEGRO, BURN CHURCH

EASTMAN, Ga., Aug. 29—A mob of white residents attacked Eli Cooper, a leader among the negroes, as he was in a church at Ocmulgee, Ga., and shot him to death yesterday.

The mob then burned the church. Later other negro churches and a lodge were burned. The attack on Cooper grew out of the rumor that the negroes were planning to rise and exterminate the white residents of the section.

CHICAGO DEFENDER
September 6, 1919

CHURCH BURNINGS FOLLOW NEGRO AGITATOR'S LYNCHING

EASTMAN, Ga., Sept. 5—The charred body of Eli Cooper, an aged farmer who resided two miles from Caldwell was found in the ashes of Ocmulgee African church which was burned by a crowd of white men at an early hour on the morning of Aug. 28. Three other churches and several lodge halls were burned by the same band of outlaws during the day. The men who visited the community near Caldwell and dragged Cooper from his home are known to officials here. However, no arrests have been made and none are expected.

Cooper is alleged to have said that the "Negro has been run over for fifty years, but it must stop now, and pistols and shotguns are the only weaons to stop a mob." When the whites learned of this they formed a posse and made for Cooper's home. A crowd of twenty men battered the door of Cooper's home and pounced upon him with knives and axes. He was killed as his wife looked on. The body was tied to a buggy and dragged to the church. Torches were applied to the house of worship, and when the flames were licking high into the air Cooper's nude form was thrown into the blaze.

The church was discovered in flames about 1 o'clock in the morning. When neighboring negro farmers endeavored to extinguish the flames a crowd of about fifty white men held them at bay with revolvers. Cooper's body could be seen leaning against a tree, and the men were taking shots at it. It is estimated that over 500 shots pierced the dead man's body. A foot from the dead man's form was found a few yards from the church. Cooper, it is said, worked on the plantation of A. P. Petway, and sought to organize the farm laborers into a union for the purpose of demanding better wages. He has been unpopular with the whites ever since this became known and some warned him that unless he discontinued his efforts to organize the laborers he would be found

124

dead on the streets "some bright morning," as one communication to him stated.

It is near the scene of the burning that Berry Washington, aged 65, was lynched by a mob in May. Washington, bowed by the weight of his age, shot in defense of his daughter's honor, who was in the clutches of a white man. The girl's assailant entered Washington's home, drove the old man into the kitchen of the dwelling at the point of a revolver, and ordered the daughter, a maiden of 16, to accept his affections in the parlor of the home. Washington secured a revolver, crept around the outside of the house to the front window and fired on the intruder. The man fell mortally wounded. Washington summoned the sheriff and surrendered. It was shortly after the shooting that he was taken from the jail, carried to a lonely spot and strung to a tree. The lynching was kept a secret for three months, but came to light when a minister wrote a letter to organizations in New York and Chicago telling of the brutal crime.

A reward of $1,000 has been offered by Governor D'Orsey for the apprehension of the parties guilty of burning four churches and three lodge buildings near Cordell, Ga. The buildings were burned on different nights, and followed in the path of the lynching of James Grant, a returned soldier. The churches were worth approximately $5,000 each and the lodge hall slightly less. After the churches were fired hundreds of citizens left the vicinity and plantations were literally deserted. At a mass meeting held by white people in the courthouse yard appeals were sent out requesting our people to remain lest the crops go to ruin unharvested.

MONTGOMERY ADVERTISER
September 29, 1919

MAYOR OF OMAHA IS DEAD OF LYNCH MOB INJURIES

OMAHA, Sept. 29—Mayor Edward P. Smith, who tried vainly last night to prevent a mob from lynching a negro prisoner, died shortly after midnight from injuries inflicted by the mob which began to lynch him, too.

OMAHA BEE
October 5, 1919

JOE COE LYNCHING RECALLED

The lynching of Will Brown in Omaha Sunday night was the first that has occurred in this city since Saturday, October 10, 1891, when Joe Coe, alias George Smith, was hanged to a wire supporting the Harney street trolley wire in front of the Boyd theater, Seventeenth and Harney street, just one block from the scene of the hanging of Brown Sunday night.

Smith, alias Joe Coe, was charged with brutally assaulting a 5-year-old girl named Lizzie Yates, who was reported dead the afternoon before Coe was lynched. The alleged death of the little girl later proved to be without foundation.

The accused negro was taken from the city jail Friday afternoon and driven to the home of the girl's parents living at 1712 North Eighteenth street, for the purpose of identification. He was dressed in different clothes than he wore at the time of the attack, but Mrs. Yates was quite certain he was the negro who had been prowling around the house representing himself to be a garbage man.

She said she would not be willing to swear positively as to his identity. The little girl was still timid and very nervous from her experience, and could not be induced to look at the negro, so nothing could be obtained from her in the way of identifying her assailant.

At 8:30 a crowd collected around the city jail, but they were told that the accused negro had been taken to the county jail. By 9 there was a crowd of over 1,000 around the county jail yelling "bring out the nigger," numerous cries like this and almost at exactly the same time were heard at the courthouse Sunday night.

After a good deal of howling, some one yelled, "Let's break the door," and soon a line of men appeared carrying a long, heavy post. Sheriff John F. Boyd appeared and standing on the steps said: "Gentlemen and fellow citizens, as sheriff of Douglas county, I command you to disperse. I know what you want, but Smith is not here, he was taken away about supper time."

126

"A fake, a lie," the crowd howled. After a moment the sheriff was able to continue, and said that he must do his duty and protect the jail.

"If I had my way," said Boyd on closing, "I would furnish the rope to hang the wretch."

Governor James E. Boyd was sent for, and crowding his way to the steps, attempted to speak, but the howling stopped only for a moment, while the governor said:

"For the honor of Omaha, men, desist. Your actions are a disgrace to the city and will bring shame to every man in it. I implore you to cease and let the law take its course. Be men and disperse."

Councilman Moriarty grabbed hold of the bars over the window of the jailer's office and urged the mob on. Moriarty started things by thrusting his cane through the bars and breaking the windows. A couple dozen men took up the heavy post and using it as a ram, started to break through the steel bars. This could not be done, and attention was turned to the window casing. Every stroke of the timber was greeted with lusty cheers.

An old white-haired man, Uncle Jimmie Cannon, who was as much of a leader as any one, said he would go and started to climb into the window, but he was met by Jailer Lynch, who held a heavy revolver at the old man's head and told him to get out. Then a 20-foot plank was brought up and shoved into the room, clearing it of its occupants, who retreated into the hall.

Once inside, the crowd made short of the door opening from the office into the corridor. The door opening into the large cell on the lower floor was broken and the crowd made its way upstairs to the room where the negro spent the last hours of his life.

The door leading to his room was broken open and the crowd rushed in, surrounding the steel cage, in one corner of which crouched the miserable object of their search. A blanket was wrapped around him and he was endeavoring to conceal himself. The sight of the steel cage did not daunt the attacking party and demands for sledge hammers, crowbars, cold chisels, etc., shouted through the window met with quick response from those outside and soon the noise of resounding blows awakened the echoes outside.

Meanwhile a dozen policemen stood outside, but they

were utterly helpless and did not attempt to do anything. The crowd was constantly receiving accessions, until about 10,000 people were collected. The hill about the jail was literally black with people, and Harney street, from Eighteenth to Sixteenth, was filled with a howling surging mob.

At this time the fire department arrived on the scene, but every attempt of the men to connect a hose was stopped by members of the mob, the same as occurred last Sunday. The hose was cut into bits. Seeing all attempts to turn the hose on the crowd were useless, the firemen were withdrawn.

At 12:25 the leaders of the mob called to the crowd to give them room to get out of the window of the jail office. With a blood curdling yell, the crowd gave way for the leaders and the doomed man.

Several men sprang out of the window with the rope in their hands, and others shoved the half dead brute out the window. Then the most fearful work ever witnessed at the hands of a mob in Omaha, up to that time, was performed amid the piercing yells of thousands of desperate men.

The rope was grasped by nearly a hundred men, who ran down to Seventeenth and Harney streets. The accused negro was dragged by the neck all the way and was nearly dead before he had been dragged 100 feet. The mob rushed upon him, kicking and jumping upon him as he was jerked down over the rough pavement, his clothing being almost torn from his body and the skin and flesh bleeding in a shocking manner.

The leaders in the rope brigade made for a telegraph pole at the southwest corner of Seventeenth and Harney streets. One of the lynchers climbed up the pole, but found no projection to throw the rope across, and quickly descended to lead the way to a pole that stood diagonally across the street, directly north and across the street from the Boyd theater.

Within a short time the end of the rope was returned to the mob below, and in a second the body of the negro was dangling in the air. Beneath the dangling body stood the mob, looking up at the object of their fearful revenge, gleaming in the electric light, and their voices filling the air with the cries of a vengeance fully satisfied.

While the majority of the great crowd quietly left for home, fully 1,000 persons remained and completely blocked the streets and sidewalks near the dead man. Calls for speeches were sent up by the crowd. Julius S. Cooley was first spotted and compelled to make a talk. Cooley didn't say much of anything beyond claiming a great saving to the county by such action, and advocated the laws of Judge Lynch on account of celerity and economy.

Heafy & Heafy's undertaking wagon drove up as the speech ended and was greeted with cheers. Some cried: "Let him hang, d—n him, let him hang." Amid such remarks the body was lowered into the box, after having hung one hour, and with one final hurrah the wagon drove down Farnam street on a gallop.

Notwithstanding the terrific jam, no serious accidents occurred, though several persons were more or less injured, being knocked down and walked over.

Coe was a married man and had a wife and child, who resided in the alley between Eleventh and Twelfth streets in the rear of the Wells-Fargo Express company.

ATLANTA CONSTITUTION
October 4, 1919

SUMTER NEGRO FOUND DEAD AFTER SPREADING PROPAGANDA

AMERICUS, Ga., Oct. 3—The body of Ernest Glenwood, a negro, was found yesterday in Flint river near the line of Sumter and Dooly counties by Tom Shirer, a fisherman. The negro, who formerly lived in the vicinity of Lily, Dooly county, disappeared September 22, when he was taken in custody by three masked men.

Glenwood, it is charged, had been circulating incendiary propaganda among negroes in Dooly county, and when he was seized it was believed he would be whipped and made to leave the community. When the body was found yesterday a rope was about the neck and another stout cord about the right wrist. It is not known how Glenwood came to his death, but it is believed after he had been severely whipped and set free that he fell from the river bridge, 14 miles from Americus and only a short distance from where the body was found.

ATLANTA CONSTITUTION
May 9, 1920

TRAIN PORTER LYNCHED
AFTER INSULT TO WOMAN

ʾTAMPA, Fla., May 8—Riddled by forty or fifty bullets, the body of an unidentified negro porter was found beside the Lakeland-Bartow road, about 8 miles from the former city, shortly before midnight. The man was porter on Atlantic Coast Line train No. 82 northbound, and was taken from his train when it passed Lakeland about 10:30 p. m., when a young white woman enroute to Bartow stated that he had insulted her.

She proceeded to Bartow and sent Chief Deputy Sheriff Clyde Olive back for the negro. The deputy later stated he was alone with the handcuffed negro, driving to Bartow, when overtaken by three auto loads of armed men who demanded the black and ordered the officer to proceed on his way.

A card beside the negro's body bore the legend: "This is what you get for insulting a white woman."

NEW YORK NEGRO WORLD
May 29, 1920

WOMAN'S IMPATIENCE REVEALED
AS CAUSE OF PORTER'S DEATH

LAKELAND, Fla., May 10—The motive behind the lynching of Henry Scott, a Negro pullman porter who was killed by a mob near here two days ago, was revealed today in greater detail.

Scott was lynched because he had allegedly insulted a white woman, according to the woman's own story. Scott denied having insulted her. His story was that the woman had asked him to arrange her berth while he was

130

engaged in arranging another woman's berth. He asked her to wait until he was finished what he was doing. She became highly indignant.

The woman sent a telegram to the next station stating that Scott had insulted her. When the train stopped, Scott was removed by a deputy sheriff. From there the story followed the usual lynch pattern. A mob "overpowered" the sheriff and killed the Negro. The coroner's jury returned the usual verdict, "Death at the hands of parties unknown."

BROOKLYN TIMES
June 16, 1920

THREE ROUSTABOUTS LYNCHED AFTER MOCK TRIAL IN MINN.

DULUTH, Minn., June 16—Three circus roustabouts, all negroes, were lynched here last night by a rioting mob of 5,000 for the alleged crime of attacking a 17-year-old white girl.

Isaac McGhie, Elmer Jackson and Nate Green were hanged at intervals of eight minutes after a mock trial had been held by the mob. The three men, held on suspicion of the crime, had been removed from the jail by the mob.

McGhie was the first victim. A noose was placed around his neck at 11:30 last night. He declared his innocence and pleaded for mercy.

Two Catholic priests begged the crowd to let the law take its course.

Rev. Father E. J. Howard climbed fifteen feet up a telegraph pole and under the dim glare of an arc light prayed for the crowd to release the negroes. He was hooted by the crowd.

McGhie was jerked into the air three times. The rope broke on the first two attempts. He begged for mercy until an impassioned speech was cut short by his third ascent.

Jackson was the next victim, followed by Green. Both declared they were not guilty of the attack.

Officials here said it was the first manifestation of

mob spirit in Duluth in years. The storm last night broke slowly. Reports of the attack on the white girl were spread about town by afternoon newspapers. Groups collected in the streets.

"All of a sudden," Police Lieutenant E. H. Barber said, "the groups melted into one huge mass which came tearing down the street toward the jail.

"We refused to give up the prisoners, of course. Then they got timbers and began wrecking things. We couldn't stand them off.

"We called on the firemen. They came on the gallop, laying lines as they came. They poured water into the mob, using the highest possible pressure. The outskirts of the mob melted away, but the main body stood firm. Some of the men were caught in the face and strangled as the water caught them. Most of them just humped their backs and went on battering the doors. When they got inside, the men quickly determined that three of the black prisoners were guilty, hauled them out and hanged them.

"As soon as the three were dead the crowd dispersed and all was quiet. It happened so quickly it didn't look real."

ATLANTA JOURNAL
June 21, 1920

HUGE MOB TORTURES NEGRO TO AVENGE BRUTAL SLAYING

Within a few hours after he had been captured near Stilson in Bulloch county yesterday Philip Gathers, the negro who brutally murdered Miss Anza Jaudon near Rincon ten days ago, was lynched on the spot where the body of the young woman was found.

The murder of the beautiful young woman was avenged in a manner that ought to strike terror to those who might be tempted to commit a similar crime. After his body had been mutilated, while he was alive, the negro was saturated with gasolene and burned, and while he was burning his body was literally riddled with bullets and buckshot.

The mob numbered several thousand, and was composed of men and women from Effingham, Bulloch, Chatham and Screven counties. The crime was committed in Effingham about three miles from Rincon. And it was there that the black brute paid the supreme penalty for the crime.

The execution of the negro was witnessed by hundreds of persons, and many thousands who were in the crowd literally fought to get close enough to see the actual details. Almost every person who had a firearm, and it seemed that every one carried a gun or pistol, emptied the weapon into the man's prostrate body. He was not shot until he had been mutilated and saturated with gasolene and a match touched. The infuriated mob could hold itself in check no longer. One shot was fired from a revolver and it was the signal for a thousand shots which made mince meat of the body.

Four young women from the crowd pushed their way through the outer rim of the circle and emptied rifles into the negro. They stood by while other men cut off fingers, toes and other parts of the body and passed them around as souvenirs.

After all of the ammunition had been used more wood was piled on the remains and gasolene poured on the pile. Later the charred remains were tied to the limb of a tree and left dangling over the road. The lower part of the body hung so low there was hardly room for automobiles to clear it.

The first news of the capture was received in Savannah by the Morning News. It was telegraphed from Stilson by J. S. Kenan, the Morning News correspondent at Statesboro, who had been with the Bulloch posse almost constantly since Saturday morning when Gathers was first discovered in Bulloch.

The news spread rapidly. Chief Harley of the county police sent around the corner to the Grantham Motor Company and borrowed a new Apperson car, driven by George Waters. In this he and County Policeman O'Neal and a Morning News reporter, made a quick trip to the scene of the murder.

Mr. Kenan telegraphed that Gathers had been captured a mile and a half from Stilson and that he would be taken to the home of Miss Jaudon's mother, three miles from Rincon. This automobile went to Rincon and was directed via McCall's road to the Jaudon home. None of the captors had arrived so the party drove into the narrow road through the swamp to the scene of the murder. There they found the exact spot where the body of Miss Jaudon was found. Two other machines were already there.

Shortly afterward cars began arriving from every direction. Within an hour there were nearly 500 machines in the swamp and the crowd was rapidly swelling. An hour and ten minutes after the first car arrived on this lonely road where Miss Jaudon was murdered, the posse from Bulloch arrived with the negro.

His arrival was heralded with a shout, but there was really no disorder at that time. Older heads commanded the hot-bloods to be careful and not shoot.

Among those waiting were a brother and sister of the victim. The crowd was forced back and they were allowed to talk to Gathers.

The sister begged the negro to tell her what her sister's last words were, but he refused to admit that he committed the crime. The brother had said he hoped a confession would be obtained before the lynchers did their work, but he said afterwards that he was absolutely certain the right man had been punished.

A pile of wood had been placed on the spot where the body was discovered a week ago yesterday. As Gathers was being dragged, pushed and shoved along men reached over the shoulders of comrades and struck the negro on the head with the butts of their guns. Others slashed him with knives. One man stabbed him several times. While he was being chained to a small tree over the wood pile he was treated to further surgical punishment below the belt. Through it all he never murmured.

A match was applied after he had been chained around the chest and legs to the sapling. The wood was wet and soggy and burned so slowly the mob became impatient and somebody called for gasolene. Up to this time not a shot had been fired and the crowd was remarkably quiet under the circumstances.

Two quarts of gasolene was drawn from an automobile. It was poured over the negro. The blaze enveloped the body and caused the crowd to fall back. With a yell the

134

negro lunged forward and broke the chains that held him to the tree. The force with which he tore himself free carried him ten feet away. As he fell a shot was fired, and then it sounded like a hundred machine guns had cut loose.

There was a scrambling for cover, and it was remarkable that many were not shot, as men standing in a complete circle about the body were firing as fast as they could pull the trigger and reload. After all of the shooting was over it was discovered that H. J. Haterick of Oliver had been hit by a stray bullet. He was hit in the left leg about half way between the knee and ankle. Dr. Usher examined and bandaged the wound and said the bullet had glanced off the bone and come out without doing serious injury.

The original program of the searchers was to take the negro by the home so Mrs. Jaudon could see him, but this was not done as she was almost prostrated. The captors left Stilson about 9 o'clock and made the trip around by Oliver, and Springfield. No effort was made to interfere with them.

The lynching took place at 12:15 o'clock.

Just before the prisoner was delivered to the scene of the lynching it was reported that the Savannah Home Guard had been called out. This did not cause the crowd a great deal of concern as they expected to finish their task before the military could arrive. And they did.

The first of the Guard reached Montieth in time to meet the crowds returning from the lynching.

NEW YORK MAIL
July 8, 1920

LYNCHING IN CHURCHYARD

DURHAM, N.C.—Edward Roach, negro prisoner, age 24, held on a charge of attacking a 13-year-old white girl, was taken from the county jail at Roxboro by a mob of more than 200 masked men and hanged yesterday from the limb of a tree in a rural negro churchyard.

RALEIGH (NORTH CAROLINA)
INDEPENDENT
July 10, 1920

NEGRO LYNCHED AT ROXBORO

ROXBORO, July 7—As the result of attempted criminal assault upon Annie Lou Chambers, a 14 year old white girl, Ed. Roach, a 24 year old Negro from Reidsville, was lynched early this morning by a mob comprising approximately 200 men. An investigation held today failed to disclose the identity of any member of the mob.

Miss Chambers, who is the daughter of Mr. Edward Chambers of Chatham county is visiting her uncle, Mr. Garland Chambers, who lives several miles south of Roxboro. Yesterday afternoon she was found badly bruised and with Roach's finger prints on her throat and face.

Roach was next seen boarding a Norfolk and Western train at Helena, seven miles south of here, about six o'clock yesterday afternoon. Dr. George Gentry of Roxboro, who was near the station heard that the Negro was on the train and raced the locomotive to Roxboro, arriving in time to have Roach arrested at the station. A pistol was said to have been found in Roach's pocket.

Miss Chambers was brought to the jail and positively identified Roach as her assailant.

No move was made to seize Roach until two o'clock this morning, when a mob of about 200 men formed at the Person county jail where Roach had been held since his arrest. Sheriff N. S. Thompson was at the jail and pleaded with the crowd to disperse and permit the law to take its course. The response of the crowd was that it would give the sheriff three minutes to leave the jail. Fifty shots were fired to intimidate the sheriff. He left.

No further effort was made to thwart the mob and Roach was taken to the graveyard of a Negro Church three miles south of here on the national highway and hanged to a tree. After the lynching the corpse was riddled with bullets. The scene of the lynching is not far from the Chambers home.

There have been no indications of any race trouble as a result of the lynching. However, the entire road force

136

of which Roach was a member comprising about 75 men, has quit. The force was engaged in the construction of sand clay roads in the county. The Negroes declared they will not work any more in Person county.

THE RALEIGH INDEPENDENT
July 17, 1920

NEGRO LYNCHED AT ROXBORO WAS WRONG MAN, SAYS BOSS

DURHAM, July 12—Ed. Roach, the Negro who was lynched by a Person County mob last Wednesday morning was innocent of the crime for which he died, according to a signed statement made by Nello Taylor, widely known contractor and employer of the mob victim.

The infuriated mob, in the opinion of the contractor, made a ghastly mistake when they dragged Roach from the Person County jail, hanged him to the church-yard tree and riddled his body with bullets, while the brute who committed the crime was allowed to escape.

"When this Negro was lynched," Mr. Taylor says in his statement, "as innocent a man was murdered as could have been, had you or I been the victim of the mob."

Continuing, the contractor says: "Roach was working for me and was a quiet, hard-working inoffensive humble Negro. On Monday he came to me and stated that he was sick and wanted to go with me to Durham that night to see a doctor. Instead I arranged for him to go Tuesday night to Roxboro. He continued his work all day Tuesday until 5:30 (Bear in mind that the crime for which he was lynched occurred between 2 and 3 o'clock that afternoon), when he asked permission of his foreman to stop and go to Mt. Tersa station to catch the train for Roxboro. Permission was given him and he left for the station walking. At 5:45 he passed the State's bridge crew (white men) and two men who were out searching for the guilty Negro saw him and followed him up the road to the Mount Tersa station, where he sat down and waited for the train. These two men sat down on the railroad near him. When the train came he got on and paid the conductor his fare to Roxboro and got off the train there. He was not arrested until he got off the train. I am advised by the chief of police he asked what they had him for and told them he had not done anything, but he was not told until he got in jail what they had him for. He asked to be taken to my office to see my superintendent with whom he had arranged to carry him to the doctor, but permission was refused him."

Mr. Teer says the right Negro was probably one that worked at his camp only a few hours.

"A Negro man about Roach's size came to my camp on Sunday night, was employed on Monday and went to work Tuesday morning. About 8:15 a. m. he drove my team out to the side of the road and had been gone twenty-five minutes when my foreman missed him. My foreman took out one of the mules and went to look for him, saw him going up the road toward's Mt. Tersa Station, the Negro saw him and broke and ran over on the east side of the railroad, going towards Lynchburg. This was about 10:30 a. m. Tuesday morning and in approximately three-quarters of a mile of the scene of the crime. This man was dressed practically the same as Ed. Roach, with cap and overalls was about the same size, but a little darker in color."

In conclusion Mr. Teer says:

"I make this statement in the interest of truth and justice, yet with a full knowledge of the odium I am bringing down upon my own head in doing so, but with the hope that this fearful crime may so shock our people as to make its likes again an impossibility."

KANSAS CITY (MISSOURI) TIMES
July 7, 1920

FAIR GROUNDS FLAGPOLE SCENE OF DOUBLE LYNCHING

PARIS, Tex., July 6—Two negroes were burned at the stake by a mob here tonight at 8 o'clock. The pair, Irving Arthur, 19, and Herman Arthur, 28, brothers, were accused of the murder last Friday of their landlord and his sons, John and William Hodges. A dispute over money was said to have been the cause.

138

The negroes were taken to the fair grounds, lashed to the flagpole, doused with kerosene and burned alive. The flagpole had been the scene yesterday, Monday, of Fourth of July celebrations and oratory.

NEW YORK NEGRO WORLD
August 22, 1920

LETTER FROM TEXAS REVEALS LYNCHING'S IRONIC FACTS

NEW YORK, Aug. 18—On July 6, two colored boys, Irving and Herman Arthur, 19 and 28 years of age respectively, were lynched by a mob and their bodies burned, when they were accused of shooting their landlord following a dispute over settlement for a crop. Below we give verbatim a letter written to the National Association for the Advancement of Colored People by a reputable citizen of Paris, Texas, where the lynching occurred. His name is withheld for obvious reasons:

"I am writing you concerning a lynching which occurred here last month. Doubtless you have long since gotten the details, if not I will give you facts as I witnessed them. Herman and Irvin Arthur, Negroes, with their parents were tenants on Hodges Farm. They were working on halves, a system whereby the landlord furnishes his tenants and at harvest time takes half the crop and the amount with interest which he furnished his tenants during the year.

Against the usual custom here, Hodges wanted them to work all day every Saturday. This they did for a while, washing their clothes on Sunday. When they refused to work Saturdays, Hodges came to their house on the farm three days before the murder and took the family dinner off the cook stove, threw it into the yard, his son holding a gun on the Arthur family.

"He also threw the furniture and cook stove out of the house, made the boys pull off their overalls and shoes; the girls were forced to surrender their dresses and other clothing, which Hodges carried away with him, together with groceries, claiming they were in debt to him. After

139

this occurred, the family decided to move and secured a truck for the purpose.

"Hodges fired on them when they were attempting to load the vehicle with their personal effects. One of the Arthur boys ran to the house, got his shotgun and killed the white man and his son.

"The Arthur boys were soon arrested and pleaded self defense in the murder of the Hodges. They were brought to the jail in Paris. Hours before, signs were displayed throughout the city announcing the forthcoming lynching. One that I saw said, "Niggers caught. Black brutes who killed Hodges will be burned in the fair grounds. Be on hand."

"A mob of about 3,000 awaited the arrival of the prisoners. Preparations had been made to burn them at the fair grounds, and "Old Glory" was pulled from the flag pole and to this the men were chained, tortured, saturated with oil and burned to a crisp. Their charred, smoking bodies were then chained to an automobile and dragged for hours through the streets, particularly in sections inhabited by our Race. It was a regular parade of seventeen cars and a truck, all filled with armed men, crying aloud: "Here they are; two barbecued niggers. All you niggers come see them and take warning."

"The three Arthur girls, aged 20, 17 and 14 were in jail on the pretense of protection. They were severely beaten for screaming while the mob was taking their brothers from the jail. Later on in the night they were taken to the basement, stripped of all their clothing and there assaulted by 20 white men, after which they were given a bucket of molasses, a small sack of flour and some bacon and told to hit the road.

"Hundreds of Negroes have left Paris since this occurrence. Others who have real estate are planning to leave as soon as possible."

NEW YORK MAIL
October 29, 1920

LYNCHING MOTIVE DISPUTED

JOHNSON CITY, Tenn., Oct. 28—Cooksey Dallas, negro, was lynched by a mob here last night. Some local citizens say that he made improper advances to a white woman. Others say he refused to sell moonshine whiskey to white soldiers.

ATLANTA CONSTITUTION
November 24, 1920

NEGRO DRAGGED FROM TRIAL AND LYNCHED BY MISS. MOB

TYLERTOWN, Miss., Nov. 23—Harry Jacobs, negro, while being tried for his life for an assault on a white woman here today, was taken from the courtroom and lynched by a mob. Members of the mob, who had been barred from the courtroom during the progress of the trial, gained access to the courtroom by breaking down the doors.

After forcing an entrance to the courtroom despite efforts of court officials and others to prevent violence, the negro was seized, a rope placed about his neck and dragged two blocks through the main street of the town after which the rope was tied to the axle of an automobile, which dragged him to Magee's creek bridge, where the lifeless body was swung to the limb of a tree and riddled with bullets.

Cleveland Strange, of Jayess, Miss., was accidentally shot through the abdomen during the affray and tonight is said to be in a critical condition. Strange is said to have been hitting the negro over the head with a pistol, holding it by the barrel, when the pistol was discharged, the load taking effect in the stomach. He was taken to a hospital at McComb, Miss.

Harry Jacobs, the negro lynched today, was a brother of Ben Jacobs, who was lynched by a mob about two weeks ago for an attack on the husband of the woman attacked by Harry Jacobs on October 30. Since his arrest he has been in jail at Magnolia, Brookhaven and Jackson to prevent mob violence.

A special term of court was convened here this morning to try the case with Judge D. M. Miller presiding. A grand jury had been organized and the work of selecting a petit jury was being started when the mob stopped the proceedings by pounding on the doors for admission, with shouts of "Let us have him; we must have him."

Appeals were made by Judge Miller, other court officials and the husband of the woman assaulted to permit the court to proceed in an orderly manner.

With shouts of "Come on, let's get him," the mob broke down the doors to the courthouse, rushed up the stairs to the witness room, where Jacobs was being held, and dragged him to the street.

After the body had been hanged to the tree it was left there for several hours and great crowds of curious visited the scene throughout the day. Everything is quiet in town tonight, the mob having dispersed soon after the lynching.

NEW YORK TIMES
November 25, 1920

FUGITIVE'S BROTHER LYNCHED

DEWITT, Ga., Nov. 24—The body of Curley McKelvey, a negro, brother of Ophelius McKelvey, who yesterday shot and killed James E. Adams of Worth County, was found hanging from a tree here early today. The body had been riddled with bullets. The negro is believed to have been shot by one of the posses looking for his brother. Adams was killed in a quarrel with three McKelvey brothers over the use of a road across the Adams plantation.

KNOXVILLE EAST TENNESSEE NEWS
December 2, 1920

ATTEMPTED TO SHIFT BLAME
TO "LECHEROUS LOOKING BLACK"

RALEIGH, N.C., Nov. 30—Charles E. Davis, prominent Wake county farmer, committed suicide by hanging himself in the city jail today. Davis was arrested on suspicion of having murdered his wife after authorities began to doubt his story that she had been killed by "a lecherous looking black."

142

KNOXVILLE EAST TENNESSEE NEWS
December 2, 1920

SHE DENIES RAPIST WAS BLACK

MOULTRIE, Ga., Nov. 30—Miss Bessie Revere, daughter of one of the most prominent women at Quitman, Ga., gained consciousness just in time to prevent departure of a search party that had been formed to scour the country for "the big, black brute" who had been described in the press as her rapist. Miss Revere said the man who assaulted her was James Harvey, a prominent white man.

JACKSON (MISSISSIPPI) LEDGER
January 1, 1921

LYNCHINGS CONTINUE TO DROP

TUSKEGEE, Ala., Dec. 31—Lynchings were less numerous during 1920 than in 1919, records compiled at Tuskegee Institute show. Sixty-one persons were put to death by mobs this year as compared with 83 last year and 64 in 1918.

The lynchings by states were: Texas 10; Georgia 9; Mississippi, Alabama and Florida 7 each; Minnesota, North Carolina, Oklahoma and California 3 each; Arkansas, Kansas, Illinois, Kentucky, Missouri, Ohio, South Carolina, Virginia and West Virginia one each.

MEMPHIS PRESS
January 26, 1921

MOB TAKES LOWRY FROM TRAIN

SARDIS, Miss., Jan. 26—Henry Lowry, negro, accused slayer of a prominent planter and his daughter at Wilson, Ark., was removed from an Illinois Central train by a mob of determined men when the train stopped here this morning.

143

Lowry was being taken to Little Rock, Ark., by two Deputy Sheriffs to stand trial for his alleged crime. The Deputies were overpowered by unmasked men who announced they were going to return Lowry to the scene of his alleged crime and lynch him there at 6:00 p.m. this evening.

MEMPHIS NEWS-SCIMITAR
January 26, 1921

LOWRY ENROUTE TO LYNCHING

MILLINGTON, Tenn., Jan. 26—A party of seven in two automobiles, with Henry Lowry, negro murderer, stopped here at 12:30 o'clock this afternoon. The party is en route from Sardis, Miss., where they took the prisoner from officers, to Wilson, Ark., where Lowry is said to have murdered two members of the Craig family and where the party intends to lynch him.

The party stopped at Fowler's restaurant for lunch. The negro was taken into the restaurant and kept under observation while the party ate.

The negro said nothing, but showed the intense strain he was under. He realized he was on his way to death. A number of Millington citizens were attracted to the restaurant and conversed with him while the white men ate.

Nothing has occurred to mar the serenity of the party's journey. The party ate leisurely and after finishing went to E. A. Harrold's store, where a quantity of rope was purchased.

MEMPHIS PRESS
January 27, 1921

LOWRY ROASTED BY INCHES
BEFORE WIFE AND CHILDREN

NODENA, Ark., Jan. 27—"Cap, I want to be buried at Magnolia, Miss." These were the last words spoken by Henry Lowry, negro murderer, who was burned at the stake last night, three-quarters of a mile east of here.

More than 500 persons stood by and looked on while the negro was slowly burned to a crisp. A few women were scattered among the crowd of Arkansas planters who directed the gruesome work of avenging the deaths of O. T. Craig and his daughter, Mrs. C. O. Williamson. Among those in the crowd were Lowry's tearful wife and children.

The setting was a natural amphitheater between two bluffs, with the Mississippi River on one side and a huge lake, created by backwater, on the other. The negro was chained to a log. Members of the mob placed a small pile of dry leaves around his feet. Gasoline was then poured onto the leaves, and the carrying out of the death sentence was under way.

Inch by inch the negro was fairly cooked to death. Lowry retained consciousness for forty minutes. Not once did he whimper or beg for mercy.

As flesh began to drop away from his legs and they were reduced to bones, once or twice he attempted to pick up hot coals and swallow them in order to hasten death. Each time the coals were kicked from his grasp by members of the mob.

As the flames reached his abdomen, two men closed in on him and began to question him. The slayer answered their questions freely and the general impression was that he was telling the truth when he admitted his guilt in killing the man on whose farm he was a tenant and his daughter.

A big six-footer put the questions to the condemned man, while another wrote the answers down in a note book. It resembled a courtroom scene, with prosecuting attorney and court reporter. Other members of the mob crowded around, but not once did they attempt to interrogate the negro, leaving this to the pair who appeared to have been assigned this duty.

Words fail to describe the sufferings of the negro. Yet only once did he cry out. This was shortly before he lost consciousness as flames began to lick at his chest and face. He cried out some appeal to one of the many negro lodges of which he was a member.

Then gasoline was poured over his head and it was only a few minutes until he had been reduced to ashes.

After Lowry had been reduced to a charred mass,

members of the mob headed in the direction of Osceola. It was whispered that they were planning to raid the jails at Marion and Blytheville in order to secure possession of five more negroes, in order to raise the total number lynched to an even half dozen.

The mob, after riding back and forth across the country for several hours, finally began to disperse and go home. It was evident that the leaders were practically exhausted from their long trip with Lowry.

KNOXVILLE EAST TENNESSEE NEWS
February 3, 1921

LYNCHED AFTER REFUSING TO DANCE ON WHITE'S COMMAND

CAMILLIA, Ga., Feb. 1—Jim Roland, Negro, was lynched near here yesterday after shooting Jason I. Harvel, a white man, who had held a pistol on him and ordered him to dance.

Both men were well-to-do farmers. Each was standing with friends of his own race in front of a country store. Harvel pulled out a gun and ordered the colored man to dance for the amusement of himself and his white friends. Roland grabbed for the gun and it went off, killing Harvel.

Roland fled but was soon found by a posse which riddled him with bullets. Before doing so, the posse leader commanded Roland to dance. He refused.

NEW YORK TIMES
March 14, 1921

FIFTY KY. MEN HANG NEGRO JURY FAILED TO CONVICT

VERSAILLES, Ky., Mar. 13—Richard James, a negro, charged with the murder of Ben T. Rogers and Homer Nave, at Midway, this county, on October 8 last, was taken from the Woodford County jail by a mob early today and hanged from a tree two miles from this city.

The mob, composed of about fifty men, came to Versailles between 1 and 2 o'clock in the morning and wrested James from the jailer after overpowering him with a blackjack.

The trial of the negro for the murder of Rogers and Nave, who were guards at a Midway distillery, ended Saturday night, when the jury reported to Circuit Court Judge R. L. Stout that it was unable to reach a verdict.

NEW YORK POST
March 15, 1921

LYNCHED FOR REMARKS TO LADY

TAMPA, Fla., Mar. 15—William Bowles, a negro, was lynched near Eagle Lake, Polk County, soon after three deputy sheriffs had arrested him yesterday on a charge of making improper remarks to a young white woman.

MEMPHIS TIMES-SCIMITAR
March 18, 1921

MIDNIGHT TERRORISTS LYNCH NEGRO BRAKEMAN ON THE Y&MV

LAKE CORMORANT, Miss., Mar. 17—A series of warnings by masked white men to negro brakemen of the Yazoo and Mississippi Valley Railroad to quit their jobs was culminated by the lynching here last night of Howard Hurd, of Memphis. Hurd mysteriously disappeared from the freight train he was working when it was halted at Clayton, Miss., for a hot box. He was found riddled with bullets 500 yards north of the Lake Cormorant station at 5 o'clock this morning. The following note was found in his overalls:

"Take this as a warning to all nigger railroad men."

Hurd had been employed by the Yazoo and Mississippi for several years. For the past five weeks negro brakemen have been terrorized by gangs of white men who stop Y&MV trains between Memphis and Clarksdale, Miss., and molest them. Several negro trainmen have been severely beaten.

Walter Banks, of Memphis, speaking to railroad investigators there recently, told of being pulled off his freight train when it stopped at Lakeview. "Come with us, nigger," they ordered.

While Banks' train pulled out on its way south, the masked men, none of whom could be identified by the black, took him to a field and gave him a severe beating, warning him to leave railroad work for white men. Then, according to Banks, the men told him to run toward the lake. They fired several shots and forced him to jump into the lake.

Banks could swim, and he made his way across an arm of the lake. For several minutes the masked men kept firing at him continually. Banks reached the shore and made his way back to Memphis, a distance of 14 miles, on foot.

Robert Grant was another negro taken from his train and given a warning to quit work, according to railroad investigators. John Jackson and Charles Haron are other negro brakemen said to have been similarly treated.

The method of the midnight terrorists, it is said, is to ride freight trains out of Memphis, or to board them at points south of here. When the trains reach points where they want to take the negro brakemen off, the angle cock is opened, throwing on the air brakes the entire length of the train. The masked men seem to know the location of the negro brakemen, and take them quickly, and without commotion.

They are said never to be seen by the white members of the crews who will have nothing to say about the mysterious occurrences.

Superintendent V. V. Botner, of the Memphis division of the Y.&M.V. road, was out of the city Thursday. General Superintendent Egan was also away from the city. Their assistants would not comment on the case.

"The case is a very delicate one," said one under-official Thursday, "and we do not want any publicity given it."

This official, in the absence of the superintendents, denied emphatic reports that three negroes have met death on the road within the last few weeks.

"Hurd is the only negro killed," said the official.

Reports which have gone as far as Chicago offices of

148

the Illinois Central railroad, contend that two negroes have been slain mysteriously and buried by section hands on the right-of-way of the Y.&M.V.

Several negro railroad men are expected to leave the road, due to the murder of Hurd.

OMAHA HERALD
March 23, 1921

PLEADED IN VAIN FOR TRIAL

MONTICELLO, Ark., Mar. 22—Phil Slater, a negro, 50, who tonight confessed he attacked a white woman near Wilmar last week, was taken from the jail here tonight and lynched. In making his confession he said: "I did it, but please give me a trial."

RICHMOND PLANT
May 21, 1921

LYNCHING AT McGHEE, ARK.

LITTLE ROCK, Ark., May 21—A negro, whose name has not been learned was lynched at McGhee, Wednesday night for alleged participation in an attack on J. P. Sims and a young white woman while they were riding in an automobile along a lonely country road.

The lynching occurred after Sims, a blacksmith for the Missouri Pacific Railroad, identified the negro as one of three negroes who stopped him on the road. Instead of complying with the negroes' demand that he leave the young woman, Sims opened fire and the Negroes fled. His description of the negroes led to the arrest of one of them and the subsequent lynching.

ST. LOUIS ARGUS
May 27, 1921

BOY LYNCHED AT McGHEE
FOR NO SPECIAL CAUSE

McGHEE, Ark., May 26—While returning from Halley on Tuesday night, May 17 at about 8:30, at a point not far from the cemetery, Miss Arbella Bond and her escort, J. Simms, were attacked by a Negro who had stationed himself in the road and commanded them to stop their car. The command was unheeded and shots exchanged between Mr. Simms and the Negro but neither was hit.

The matter was reported to the authorities and the Negro captured and locked in the city jail. It is said he made a confession. Some time Wednesday night a mob formed quietly, in some manner got possession of the prisoner and this morning he was found hanging to a tree east of town, his body riddled with bullets.

The above clipping is the account of the lynching of the Negro boy here a few days ago. The white folks' paper published here doesn't seem to try to prevent any facts in so grave an affair; it nevertheless tells of the affair about like all such affairs are related from this section of the country. The facts in the case are these: The boy lynched was not an unknown Negro as reported, but to the contrary, was well known here. His name is Leroy Smith, age 14, his home is Lake Providence, La., where his mother, sisters, brothers and stepfather lives, and he was working at the time of the tragedy for the Good Roads Company. When questioned at the jail after his arrest he stated that he had been out frog hunting, in company with two other boys, and after leaving the other two boys, he saw a car coming which he thought was the car of the foreman at the camp, and that he tried to stop the car in order that he could get a ride to the camp. But was shot at by the man in the car.

ATLANTA CONSTITUTION
June 16, 1921

NEGRO WHO ELUDED LYNCHERS MAINTAINS HIS INNOCENCE

COLUMBUS, Ga., June 15—John Henry Williams, Negro, accused of the murder of an 11-year-old white girl whose body was found with the throat cut in a pond near Autreyville, was brought here early today and placed in the Muscogee county jail for safe keeping, it became known tonight.

The negro, in custody of Sheriff Beard, of Thomas county, was chased over several counties by a mob Monday night, and spent last night in jail at Cuthbert. Talking with newspaper men today, Williams maintained his innocence and said he was a mile and a half away when the crime was committed. He also denied knowledge of wet clothes and shoes which officers said they found in his house.

BALTIMORE AFRO-AMERICAN
June 24, 1921

NEGRO BURNED ALIVE SINGING "NEARER MY GOD TO THEE"

MOULTRIE, Ga., June 20—Unable to wait until July 8th, the date set by court for the hanging of John Henry Williams, a small crowd of white men took him from an armed force of twenty officers and burned him at the stake Saturday.

Williams had just been convicted by the court of first degree murder and sentenced to be hanged. He left the court room, with ten officers on either side.

When he appeared on the steps of the court house shouts came from the crowd, "Let's get him." The officers gave up the man without a struggle and the mob rushed him to the spot where it is said he killed a twelve year old white girl. Williams denied his guilt at the trial and even after he was tied to a tree trunk near the edge of a big pond. Members of the mob scattered to gather enough wood to pile around their victim and drew gasoline from their automobiles in order to make the fire hotter.

So quietly was the seizure affected and arrangements for the lynching made that only a few persons arrived at the pond on the outskirts of the town by the time everything was ready. For nearly an hour they tormented Williams, poked him in the ribs, cursed him, spit on him and called him vile names in the effort to draw a confession. Finally when several hundred persons reached the spot a match was applied. Flames flared up and found their way to Williams' body. Now and again he cried aloud and his body went through horrible contortions. For a time the winds carried the flames and smoke directly in his face so that he could not speak. Later the winds shifted and members of the mob, unaffected, recognized the hymn he sang as, "Nearer My God to Thee."

At the trial today the jury was out less than one minute when it returned the verdict of guilty.

WASHINGTON EAGLE
July 16, 1921

INDESCRIBABLE TORTURES WERE INFLICTED ON WILLIAMS

From Moultrie, Georgia, scene of the burning of the Negro Williams, The Eagle has obtained the following facts by an eyewitness. It is clearly shown that sworn officers of the law were leaders in mob violence and burning, acting with impunity.

Says The Eagle's correspondent:

"There are many things about the Williams burning more disgraceful than have been published. A sick woman and her child, who had nothing to do with the matter, were beaten into insensibility and left to die because of hoodlumism of the mob. Colored churches were burned, all colored farmer's fences were torn down and wealthy colored farmers chased from their homes.

"Williams was brought to Moultrie on Friday night by sheriffs from fifty counties. Saturday court was called. Not a single colored person was allowed nearer than a block of the courthouse. The trial took a half hour. Then Williams, surrounded by fifty sheriffs, armed with machine guns, started out of the courthouse door toward the jail.

"Immediately a cracker by the name of Ken Murphy, gave the Confederate yell: "Whoo—whoo—let's get the nigger." Simultaneously five hundred poor pecks rushed on the armed sheriffs, who made no resistance whatever. They tore the Negro's clothing off before he was placed in a waiting automobile. This was done in broad daylight. The Negro was unsexed and made to eat a portion of his anatomy which had been cut away. Another portion was sent by parcel post to Governor Dorsey, whom the people of this section hate bitterly.

"The Negro was taken to a grove, where each one of more than five hundred people, in Ku Klux ceremonial, had placed a pine knot around a stump, making a pyramid to the height of ten feet. The Negro was chained to the stump and asked if he had anything to say. Castrated and in indescribable torture, the Negro asked for a cigarette, lit it and blew the smoke in the face of his tormentors.

"The pyre was lit and a hundred men and women, old and young, grandmothers among them, joined hands and danced around while the Negro burned. A big dance was held in a barn nearby that evening in celebration of the burning, many people coming by automobile from nearby cities to the gala event."

NEW YORK SUN
August 16, 1921

2ND LYNCH MOB DESECRATES BODY OF 1ST MOB'S VICTIM

COOLIDGE, Tex., Aug. 16—Alexander Winn, a negro, was hanged by a mob here yesterday at Datura. He had been accused of assaulting a seven-year-old girl. Today his body was burned after another mob had stormed the funeral parlor where it had been taken.

BALTIMORE AFRO-AMERICAN
August 19, 1921

MOB RESPECTS WOMAN'S REQUEST TO MOVE LYNCHING FROM LAWN

WINSTON, N. C., Aug. 18—A mob estimated at from 1,500 to 2,000 hung Jerome Withfield, Negro, suspected of having assaulted the wife of a white farmer. When Withfield got word early that he was suspected of the crime, he made an attempt to escape. Blood hounds tracked him down, however.

He was brought to the assault victim's home in an automobile. The woman expressed doubt that he was her assailant. The mob deemed the track-down of the hounds as conclusive evidence, however, and Withfield was hanged. The request of the farmer's wife that Withfield not be hanged on her front lawn was heeded.

After hanging him a mile down the road, the Negro was riddled by a thousand bullets, hundreds of them lodging in his flesh and bone. Undertakers who cut down the body said that it weighed twice its normal weight.

ATLANTA CONSTITUTION
October 2, 1921

SHOT FOR ALLEGED INSULT

QUITMAN, Ga., Oct. 1—Ray Newsome, a negro, was taken from the H. A. Woods farm, near Pinetta, Fla., late today and shot to death as he was either turned loose or escaped from the car. He was accused of insulting a white girl.

BALTIMORE HERALD
October 19, 1921

LOTS DRAWN FOR SOUVENIRS
OF LYNCHED NEGRO'S ANATOMY

LEESBURG, Tex., Oct. 11—Wylie McNeely, a 19-year-old Negro, was burned alive here last night, accused by a mob of 500 of having assaulted an 18-year-old girl. As he was chained to an old buggy axle, which had been driven into the ground to serve as a stake, he was heard to proclaim his innocence. Just before he was fired up, leaders of the mob drew lots for the part of the Negro's anatomy which they regarded as the choicest souvenir.

HOUSTON POST
November 19, 1921

LYNCH, SHOOT, BURN NEGRO

HELENA, Ark., Nov. 18—Will Turner, negro, charged with an assault on a young white woman here Friday, was taken by a mob from a sheriff's posse, while being removed to Marianna for safe keeping, and after being shot to death by members of the mob his body was brought back here and burned in the city park.

Turner was arrested soon after making the attack on the young woman, and lodged in jail here. Feeling against him was so high that Sheriff Mays ordered Tex Graves and John Rabb, two deputies, to take the negro to Marianna for safe keeping. The deputies were held up a short distance from this city by a mob of 25 or 30 armed men, who demanded the negro. Turner, according to the officers, was taken into the woods nearby and his body riddled with bullets.

Another mob had armed in front of the jail here and threatened to storm the building unless the negro was turned over to them. The second mob refused to believe Sheriff Mays when he told them that Turner had already been killed by a mob outside the city. They were pacified only when the brother of the victim of the attack was allowed to make an examination of the jail.

The second mob waited for Turner's body to be brought back to the city by the first mob and, surrounding the ambulance in which it had been placed, dragged out the body and carried it to the city park, opposite the court house, where gasoline was poured over it and the body was destroyed.

ST. LOUIS ARGUS
November 25, 1921

LYNCH VICTIM'S FATHER CALLED TO CLEAR AWAY SON'S ASHES

HELENA, Ark., Nov. 18—After it had been hanged and cut down by one mob and before it had been burned in a city hall bonfire by a second mob, the body of William Turner, Negro, aged 19, was hauled through Helena to provide a moving target for white men armed with pistols who lined the principal streets of this town and took pot-shots at it. Turner had been hanged earlier for allegedly assaulting a white telephone operator.

Turner's corpse was roped to the rear of an automobile and driven up and down the main streets of Helena at various speeds as white men hooted, yelled and perfected their marksmanship by shooting at the almost disintegrated remains. No colored folks were allowed on the streets. When the celebrants had had their fill, the body was burned.

August Turner, father of the mob victim, was summoned to the park to remove his son's charred remains.

MEMPHIS COMMERCIAL APPEAL
November 26, 1921

NEGRO AMBUSHED, LYNCHED FOR WRITING WHITE GIRL

LITTLE ROCK, Ark., Nov. 25—According to information received by the Arkansas Gazette here tonight,

Robert Hicks, negro, about 25 years old, was lynched Wednesday beside the public highway four miles southeast of Lake Village because of a note he wrote to a young white woman.

According to the Gazette's information, an effort was made to suppress the news of the lynching, but following a coroner's inquest today the verdict was telephoned to Little Rock, that the negro came to his death at the hands of persons unknown.

According to stories of the affair obtained later, the negro came to the girl's home Wednesday evening and asked if she had received his note. A band of men was waiting, seized the negro, took him about four miles from town and riddled his body with bullets.

FORT WORTH TELEGRAM
December 12, 1921

NEARLY DEAD STRIKE-BREAKER SEIZED FROM HOSPITAL, HANGED

Fred Rouse, negro packing house worker who last Tuesday shot and wounded two striking pickets at Armour and Company's plant, was taken from his bed at the city-county hospital here last night at 11:00 o'clock and hanged by a mob of 30 unmasked men.

The negro had sustained a double skull fracture in rioting at Armour's plant Tuesday. He had just finished work and was walking down a line of pickets when halted by the strikers. Some words passed and the negro drew a gun, firing twice. Tom and Tracey Maklin, brothers fell to the ground, wounded.

The negro ran, but a mob quickly formed, took him away from police officers and beat him with iron bars ripped from a street-car window. The mob left him for dead, so badly was he beaten that his eyes were invisible under facial swelling, and he was covered with blood.

When he was brought to the hospital, it was expected that he would not live.

Miss Essie Slaton, night nurse, gave an account of the mob's seizure of Rouse from the hospital last night:

"Several young men, they looked like boys ranging

157

from 18 to 25 years of age, appeared at the hospital as I answered a call at the door. They stated they wanted no trouble but were after the negro who had shot the two white boys. I was so surprised I hesitated and finally called their attention to the fact that it was awful to come to the hospital like that and besides there are other patients in the hospital to be considered. I said to them 'Why don't you wait until he is well?'

"They would not listen to that and finally I said I would call the superintendent. They told me they had come after the negro and were going to have him, but that they were willing to do it quietly.

"It was obvious that I was helpless and I led them to the basement to the colored ward and showed the men where Fred Rouse was being treated. I said he is the one in the corner, but overlooked the fact that there were two in the corner, and the men went to the wrong corner. They nearly took the wrong patient. They began to feel the back and head of the other negro, who was awfully scared and he began to shout that he was not the one wanted.

"I had told them before that for just two of them to go in and not all of them, stating that the negro was weak and could not offer resistance. I then came on back upstairs.

"I called their attention to the fact that he had no clothes and they replied that he would not need any.

"Pretty soon they came, bringing out the negro, Rouse, almost in a run. The negro offered no resistance, but was groaning very much. They went out the door with him and said 'Goodnight' to me. As soon as they left I phoned the police station.

"I was so excited, I did not get a chance to recognize any of the men."

Twenty minutes later, Rouse's body was found dangling from a tree by Chief of Police Harry Hamilton. He was bloody and his nude body was riddled with bullets. A revolver, presumably the one he had used on the strikers, was found underneath the tree.

Rouse was hanged to the same tree where last December another negro, Tom Vickery, was hanged.

MEMPHIS COMMERCIAL APPEAL
January 14, 1922

INTER-RACIAL LOVE AFFAIR
ENDED BY LYNCHING OF MAN

FLORENCE, S.C., Jan. 13—One negro was killed and another wounded Sunday by a mob of white citizens in the Black River section of Williamsburg county.

The dead man is accused of having been intimate with a white woman. The wounded negro was driving a buggy into which the other man had leaped in an attempt to elude the mob.

Letters from the white woman were found in the pocket of the dead man after the lynching. One of them read as follows:

"Dearest Ed:

"I thought of you all during the show last night, and wanted you with me. It is too bad that we cannot be together always. My love for you is greater than you can imagine. Sometimes I become so disgusted with conditions in Florence that I want to leave and go some place where people are sensible, where I can at least walk the streets with you in the daytime without danger and fear.

"You often impress on me the fact that you are Colored and can't take any chances. I know that, darling, but love is greater than color in my case, and we must do the best we can until both of us are in position to leave Florence.

"I suppose you got the package I sent by mail to the barber shop for you. I have to be careful in buying things downtown because my little niece goes along with me and is so nosey. I had a beautiful shirt for you, but had to give it to my cousin because niece saw me purchase it.

"Be a good boy and don't forget tomorrow. Yours,
"DEVOTED."

After learning of the lynching the woman spent Sunday night in the swamps, crossing over the county line to Kingstree on Monday to seek the protection of the sheriff there.

CHICAGO TRIBUNE
January 18, 1922

MOB HANGS STRIKE-BREAKER

OKLAHOMA CITY, Okla., Jan. 17—The body of Jake Brooks, a colored man who was kidnaped from his home here by a mob Sunday night, was found this afternoon hanging from a tree six miles south of here. Brooks had been employed at a local packing plant since the calling of the strike of packing house workers.

MEMPHIS COMMERCIAL APPEAL
March 23, 1922

LYNCH NEGRO BROTHEL OWNER FOR HIRING WHITE GIRLS

GULFPORT, Miss., Mar. 22—The body of Alex Smith, an aged negro, was found suspended from a bridge near here today. Smith was the proprietor of a house of ill-fame. Recently his establishment was raided and two white girls discovered therein.

NEW YORK AMERICAN
May 19, 1922

TORTURE, BURN NEGRO OF 15

DAVISBORO, Ga., May 18—Charles Atkins, a negro, fifteen, one of four taken into custody to-day in connection with the killing of Mrs. Elizabeth Kitchens, twenty, a rural mail carrier, was burned at the stake to-night.

The lynching occurred at the scene of the murder and followed an alleged confession from the prisoner. He was tortured over a slow fire for fifteen minutes and then, shrieking with pain, was questioned concerning his accomplices.

Atkins was said to have confessed his own guilt but to have exonerated his brother.

160

Members of the mob of 200 then raised the body again, fastened it to a pine tree with trace chains and relighted the fire. More than 200 shots were fired into the charred body.

NEW YORK HERALD
May 28, 1922

DOUBT LYNCH VICTIM'S GUILT

WACO, Tex., May 27—Disorder which ruled Waco yesterday and culminated in the burning of the body of Jesse Thomas, negro, on the public square, has subsided, and persons here are wondering whether the guilty man was lynched for the killing of W. Harrell Bolton, 25, and the attack on his companion, Mrs. Maggie Hays, 26, four miles from here late Thursday.

Thomas was seized on the public square by a telegraph operator while hundreds of citizens in a dozen posses were scouting the countryside. The negro was hurried to the home of Mrs. Hays, where the woman arose from her bed and screamed: "That's him." Sam Harris, father of Mrs. Hays, seized a pistol and killed the negro.

Mrs. Hays said Thomas told her the negroes were ready to launch an organized campaign against white women in revenge for the lynching of negroes.

During the night Waco officers quelled disturbances. A hearse and a coffin arranged by a negro undertaker to care for Thomas's body were destroyed.

Waco is a strong Ku Klux Klan center and has been the scene of numerous riots.

Members of the family of the negro lynched yesterday were to-day submitting strong evidence to show that the latest mob victim was at home when Mrs. Hays was attacked. The lynching of Thomas was the tenth accomplished by mobs in this section in the last three weeks.

NEW YORK CALL
May 29, 1922

DESPITE LYNCHING, 5 MORE
ARE SEIZED FOR SAME CRIME

WACO, Tex., May 28—Jesse Thomas, Negro, who was burned at the stake by a mob here Friday, may not have been the man who murdered Harrel Belton and assaulted his girl companion, authorities feared yesterday, and five other Negroes will be held in jail until further investigation has been made.

Officers were trying to link the murder of Belton with two other unsolved crimes committed here recently.

BROOKLYN CITIZEN
May 6, 1922

TRIPLE LYNCHING FOLLOWS
THRILLING TEX. MAN-HUNT

KIRVIN, Tex., May 6—Three colored men were burned here at dawn for the murder of Eula Ausley, pretty 17-year-old school girl, whose body was found near here yesterday with thirty stab wounds. The three men were tied, one after another, to the seat of a cultivator, driven into the center of the city square and burned before a mob of 500.

"Shap" Curry, 26, Mose Jones, 44, and John Cornish, 19, were the victims. All three worked on the huge ranch of John King, the girl's grandfather. Curry was burned first. There was some delay in starting inasmuch as the men maintained their innocence to the last. Third degree methods failed to bring confessions.

The men were not shot but their bodies were mutilated prior to burning. Ears, toes and fingers were snipped off. Eyes were gouged out, no organ of the negroes was allowed to remain protruding.

After this preliminary mob vengeance, preachers from the two churches which flank the square came forward and prayed for the salvation of the blacks' souls.

162

As Curry was saturated with oil and set aflame, he chanted over and over again, "O Lord, I'm acomin." As the flames mounted about his body, his chant rose higher and higher until he could be heard throughout the downtown part of town. Curry lost consciousness in ten minutes and died.

Jones was then roped and dragged over the hot coals and more wood was thrown on. In six minutes, he, too, was dead. Cornish received the same treatment. Still more fuel was added and the three bodies were roasted in a bonfire that was kept going for six hours.

The lynchings followed one of the most thrilling man hunts in the history of these parts. Farmers and business men of three counties joined together to comb every inch of the territory. Creek bottoms were beaten all day and acres of grassland were flattened. Finally the three men were captured and brought to Fairfield where a mob gathered and took them from the sheriff after storming the jail.

_____

NEW YORK CALL
May 7, 1922

SHERIFF HOLDS 2 WHITES IN CRIME THAT 3 BURNED FOR

FAIRFIELD, Tex., May 6—Cliff and Arnie Powell, two white men, were detained today for further questioning in connection with the murder of Eula Ausley, for which three negroes were burned at Kirvin this morning. Sheriff H. M. Mayo declared that tracks leading from the scene of the murder led to the home of the brothers.

"The shoes of the Powells fit the tracks," was the terse comment of the sheriff.

One of the brothers was arrested yesterday and the other surrendered after the mob had taken the Negroes from the jail here. Said the sheriff, "The King and Powell families had some kind of a fight some time ago, in which one of the Powells was badly cut. This is just another clue we are following up."

Miss Ausley was granddaughter of John King, wealthiest rancher in these parts. Apart from their family feuding, the Kings and Powells have been involved in legal battles against one another, too.

NEW YORK WORLD
January 2, 1923

FINDS TRIPLE-LYNCH VICTIMS WERE PROBABLY INNOCENT

There were sixty-one lynchings in the United States in 1922, according to records made public today by the National Association for the Advancement of Colored People.

Of these, the most ironic was the burning to death of three negroes at Kirvin, Texas, on May 6th. Says the report:

"The triple lynching was so horrible an affair that the association sent an investigator to the scene. The men were burned at the same stake by a mob of 500 men for their alleged implication in the murder of a 17-year-old white girl. Our investigator, Mr. Dan Kelly, a native white Texan, found that the girl had probably been murdered in the course of a long standing feud between her family and another white family."

NEW YORK GLOBE
June 24, 1922

NEGRO ABOUT TO BE LYNCHED TELLS OTHERS TO BE GOOD

HOUSTON, Tex., June 24—Warren Lewis, eighteen-year-old Negro, was hanged at New Dacus, Montgomery County, after confessing to a mob of 300 persons that he had attacked a young white woman living near the city.

Before hanging, the Negro was allowed to make a speech to scores of Negroes who had collected. He advised them to "do the right thing." All is quiet to-night over the county.

164

MEMPHIS COMMERCIAL APPEAL
July 29, 1922

QUARREL OVER BLACK'S RIGHT TO CUP ENDS IN LYNCHING

TEXARKANA, Ark., July 28—A quarrel over a drinking cup between a white street paving foreman and a negro laborer at Hope, Ark., about 35 miles northeast of Texarkana, was followed this afternoon by the lynching of the negro near Guernsey, four miles southwest of Hope.

John West of Emporia, Kan., was the negro lynched. He had been employed on the paving job about 10 days. The foreman was Henry Worthington of Topeka, Kan., who has been on the job about two weeks.

Worthington and West came to blows over the negro's right to use the road crew's common drinking cup. Both men were arrested and fined in police court for disturbing the peace. Later West is reported to have been advised to leave town and he boarded a train at Hope at 1:45 o'clock en route to Texarkana.

A mob of about 100 white men preceded the train to Guernsey, where West was taken off. He was carried a short distance from the track and shot to death, eight or nine bullets entering the body.

This is the second lynching at Hope within the last 18 months, Brownie Tuggles having been hanged here on the night of March 15, 1921, for an alleged attack on a white woman.

MEMPHIS COMMERCIAL APPEAL
August 23, 1922

REFUSES TO MOVE; IS LYNCHED

JACKSON, Miss., Aug. 22—The body of Parks Banks, a negro, was found hanging to a tree a few miles from Yazoo City this morning. It was said the negro had been warned to leave the vicinity.

NEW YORK NEWS
December 15, 1922

CLEARS PAL BEFORE DYING

PERRY, Fla., Dec. 14—Two negroes were captured here for the murder of a white school teacher but only one was burned at the stake tonight.

Before he died, Charles Wright, age 21, confessed that he alone had committed the murder of Miss Ruby Hendry, exonerating Albert Young who was also captured by a party of whites.

Following the burning of Wright, Young was turned back to the authorities and all hands scrambled for souvenirs of the remains.

MONTGOMERY ADVERTISER
December 16, 1922

CLEARED NEGRO ALSO LYNCHED

PERRY, Fla., Dec. 15—The second of two negroes arrested Friday in connection with the murder of Miss Ruby Hendry, school teacher, the previous Saturday, was lynched last night when Arthur Young was taken from the officers as they were attempting to transfer him to another jail. Charlie Wright was burned at stake Friday night after a mob of several thousand men had taken him from the officers as they brought the two negroes into town.

WILMINGTON (DELAWARE) ADVOCATE
December 16, 1922

POSSE LYNCHES INNOCENT MAN WHEN THWARTED IN ITS HUNT

STREETMAN, Tex., Dec. 11—A posse was unable today to track down a negro who allegedly attacked the wife of the local Sheriff. The posse tracked down the uncle of a negro who is suspected of the crime and lynched him instead.

NEW YORK NEWS
December 16, 1922

TEX. MOB HOLDS LYNCHING BEE

STREETMAN, Tex., Dec. 14—This town is noted for lynching or, rather, for burning men at the stake, as three colored men have met their fate in that manner during the last three months. So it was a matter of course for the mob which shot and killed George Gay, a young man residing in Fairfield.

Gay, aged 25, was accused by the mob of having attacked a young woman, who told the police that some man had placed a sack over her head and stuffed her mouth with cotton. No criminal assault was alleged, as the girl said that the man became frightened and ran.

A mob of 1,500 then gathered, bent on injuring some colored man. Word reached Fairfield, and hundreds of men and women drove to Streetman in buggies. The girl failed to identify Gay when confronted by him. However, he was locked up in a small house under heavy guard pending arrival of bloodhounds from the State penitentiary at Huntsville.

But a mob does not wait for bloodhounds, hence the guards were overpowered and Gay was brought out into the highway and shot to death. The mob then set fire to the Streetman Hotel, the only one owned by colored people in the city. The mob seemed bent on doing more damage, but was dispersed by the police.

PITTSBURG AMERICAN
December 29, 1922

2 LYNCHED AS WARNING "TO ALL NIGGER LOAFERS"

PILOT POINT, Tex., Dec. 29—Two Negroes, detained yesterday in connection with the theft of two horses, were missing from the jail this morning. An unsigned note was posted on the door of the local newspaper reading:

"Both niggers got what they had coming. Let this be a warning to all nigger loafers. Niggers get a job or leave town."

Two Negroes disappeared from the jail here in a similar manner several months ago. Nothing has been heard of them since.

ST. LOUIS ARGUS
January 12, 1923

DISCOVER THAT LYNCH VICTIM WAS DARK-SKINNED WHITE

SHREVEPORT, La., Jan. 9—Leslie Legget was kidnapped last Wednesday night by a band of masked white men and riddled with bullets on the outskirts of town. Police Chief Basar said complaints had reached him earlier that Legget was in the habit of associating with white women.

Legget's employer, a white grocer named Charles Papa, in whose house Legget roomed, later said that Legget was not a Negro but a swarthy-complexioned Spaniard.

CHICAGO DEFENDER
February 17, 1923

WHITES IN GEORGIA DISPLAY PARTS OF NEGROES' BODIES

MILLEDGEVILLE, Ga., Feb. 16—Fingers and ears of two Negroes lynched near this city last week are on display in a large bottle filled with alcohol on the counter of the town's only drug store. An inscription beside the bottle reads:

"What's left of the niggers that shot a white man."

Lindsay B. Gilmore, a white grocer, was shot when he took after two Negroes, unidentified, who were caught stealing some cheese and cash from Gilmore's store. A number of witnesses have stated that in the chase Gilmore was shot by a local officer whose aim was faulty. The Negroes were lynched, nevertheless.

NEW YORK WORLD
April 20, 1923

UNIVERSITY STUDENTS HELP MOB LYNCH JANITOR

COLUMBIA, Mo., Apr. 29—A mob that included many University of Missouri students, both male and female, today lynched James T. Scott, a Negro janitor at the University who had been charged with an attempt to assault the fourteen-year-old daughter of the head of the German Department.

About 500 citizens broke into the jail, aided by an acetylene torch, and dragged Scott through the streets to the Missouri, Kansas and Texas Railroad bridge that spans a deep ravine just outside the university section.

Professor H. B. Almstedt, father of the intended assault victim, hearing of the lynching, went to the scene and appealed to the mob to let the law take its course. The students and townspeople laughed and booed him down, crying, "Hang him, too!" Finally, the professor went to his home and, Pilate-like, washed his hands of the whole matter.

A rope was tied around Scott's neck, the other end secured to the bridge railing. Scott, bareheaded and with his shirt torn, repeatedly denied his guilt.

"Before God, I swear I am innocent," he cried. "The girl who was attacked said the attacker had been having trouble with his wife. My wife never has had trouble with me. Go down and see her. I can prove my innocence."

The negroe's plea brought some hesitation to the mob but then a young man, about 20, stepped forward, lifted Scott to the bridge railing and dumped him over the side. His neck snapped audibly.

Scott's body swayed in mid-air for nearly a minute as the mob mutely watched it.

ST. LOUIS ARGUS
June 15, 1923

OUTSPOKEN NEGRO KILLED

PALM BEACH, Fla., June 13—The body of Henry Simmons, Negro, riddled with bullets, was found today hanging to a tree on Palm Beach Island. Simmons was a native of the Bahama Islands. He is said to have been an industrious and conscientious worker at a local ice cream plant but he also made enemies because he was outspoken on the treatment of American Negroes by Southern whites.

BALTIMORE AFRO-AMERICAN
July 6, 1923

NEGRO FATHER IS LYNCHED; AIDED SON TO ESCAPE MOB

BRONSON, Fla., Jan. 4—Samuel Carter, 46 years old, a respected resident of this place, was shot to death by a mob last night after he had admitted aiding his son to escape a lynch mob.

Young Carter was sought by a posse because he was thought to know the whereabouts of an escaped convict charged with assaulting a white woman. The two were seen together several hours before the assault.

The elder Carter faced the mob when the leaders knocked on his door, admitted that he had helped to get his son away by hiding him in the back part of his buggy. He led the mob to the point where he said his son jumped out and continued on foot. When bloodhounds were not able to pick up the scent, the members of the crowd vented their anger on the older Carter by riddling his body with bullets.

MASS EXODUS OF NEGROES

YAZOO CITY, Miss., Aug. 6—Ten thousand colored peosons, including men, women and children, are said to have left the vicinity of Yazoo City since Sunday following the burning at the stake of Willie Minnifield in a swamp near here.

The emigrants left in all sorts of conveyances, railroads, automobiles, ox carts, and some on foot. Few of them remained long enough to dispose of their possessions, some even leaving crops on the ground.

Minnifield, who was found fishing in the swamp, was accused of attacking a woman with an axe at a point 26 miles distant. There was no indication to prove that he was the criminal. When the posse discovered him, he was in company with another man. Both were seized and charged with the crime. Minnifield's companion escaped.

Angered because he had slipped from their clutches, the mob prepared to burn Minnifield. He was dragged to a cleared space in the swamp, and a stake was driven into the ground, to which he was tied. Brushwood was then piled around until only his head was visible. A match was set to the brush, and as the flames crackled around the man, the woods resounded with the shouts of the mob.

As the flames died down, leaving the victim's charred skeleton lying upon the embers the mob took up the chase for the man who had escaped.

MEMPHIS COMMERCIAL APPEAL
August 26, 1923

REPORTS ARE CONFLICTING ON LYNCHED NEGRO'S GUILT

JACKSONVILLE, Fla., Aug. 25—The handcuffed, bullet-riddled body of a negro, found on a road shortly after midnight, Saturday, was identified today as that of Len Hart, 34, a farm hand. He had been suspected of being the negro who, early Friday morning, peeped into the window of a girl at the Three-Mile Ranch.

Reports to the sheriff's office, however, were said to indicate that Hart was innocent. Bartow Jones, employer of Hart, told the sheriff he and his son-in-law had seen Hart at 5 o'clock Friday morning at his logging camp, ten miles from Three-Mile Ranch. According to the girl's story, the man appeared at her window at 4 o'clock. Jones said Hart could not have walked the ten miles in one hour.

The girl told two deputies that she could not remember what the intruder looked like. Investigation revealed that Hart had been taken from the logging camp about 9 o'clock Friday night by men who came in two automobiles and wore badges, posing as peace officers. The four negroes in camp were lined up and Hart was selected to go with the men in the cars. That was the last he was seen alive.

ST. LOUIS ARGUS
November 9, 1923

KLAN HANGS OKLA. NEGRO FOR "PASSING AS WHITE MAN"

EUFALA, Okla., Nov. 7—Dallas Sewell, Negro, was seized by a group of men wearing garb of the Ku Klux Klan and, after a Klan trial in the barn of a well known Klansman, was hanged this morning to a barn rafter.

Sewell was found guilty of "passing for white and associating with white women" and he was therefore put to death in accordance with the Klan "Kode."

CHICAGO TRIBUNE
October 10, 1924

DOUBT BLUDGEONED NEGRO WAS ACCOSTER OF GIRLS

It appeared yesterday that the wrong negro may have been killed by a mob here Wednesday night in the Jewish

"Ghetto" section on West 14th Street. Two girls who had been accosted by a colored man while standing on a sidewalk there yesterday viewed the body of William Bell, the mob victim, and said that they could not be sure Bell was the man who had approached them.

"The negro who accosted us did look very much like Bell—that is, he dressed similarly—but I can't be sure it was Bell," declared Miss Bertha Deutsch, 1357 Miller Street, one of the girls. Her companion, Miss Betty Greenblatt, 1071 Maxwell Street, was equally uncertain when questioned yesterday at police headquarters concerning the mob murder of Bell, who lived at 1057 Frank Street.

At 11 o'clock Wednesday night a negro is said to have approached the girls who were standing in front of the sacramental wine shop of George Shapiro, 1014 West 14th Street, in the midst of the "Ghetto." "Come with me to my car; I have lots of money," the negro is reported to have said to the girls. He took hold of Miss Deutsch's arm. The girls screamed and the negro fled.

A crowd, composed principally of foreigners, quickly formed and Bell, who was standing on the sidewalk with two friends near the spot where the girls had screamed, was quickly seized. A mob of 100 men and boys began to kick and beat him.

Someone appeared with a baseball bat and delivered a terrific blow to the colored man's head. He collapsed. An ambulance was summoned but Bell was dead by the time it arrived.

Meanwhile, Otto Epstein, night watchman at Shapiro's wine shop, ran to the police station. "There's a race riot," he excitedly told the desk sergeant. "A man's been killed."

Thomas Clark, one of Bell's negro companions, had followed Epstein to the station. "Yes, and you're the one who killed him," he said. Epstein strenuously denied this but agreed to remain at the station for questioning.

At the police investigation yesterday the two girls expressed regret over what had happened. "Who would have thought such a thing could happen in America," said Miss Deutsch, a recent immigrant.

Racial tension in the "Ghetto" has been running high

173

lately since a number of negro families moved into the district.

BROOKLYN EAGLE
December 20, 1925

LYNCHED JUST MINUTES AFTER JURY FREES HIM IN MURDER

CLARKSDALE, Miss., Dec. 19—Lindsay Coleman, negro, was lynched here tonight, a few minutes after a jury in Circuit Court had declared him not guilty of the murder of Grover C. Nicholas, plantation store manager.

ST. LOUIS ARGUS
June 8, 1926

NEGRO LYNCHED FOR "ATTACKING" CHILD HE ONLY STARTLED

OSCEOLA, Ark., June 2—Albert Blades, 22, a Negro visiting here from St. Louis, was hanged and his body was burned Wednesday morning for an alleged attack on a small white girl. Following the lynching, doctors who examined the child said that she had not been attacked.

There appears to be some question of whether the child wasn't merely frightened by the unexpected appearance of Blades in a picnic grounds where she and her classmates were playing. Blades pleaded his innocence to the last.

FROM AN EDITORIAL IN THE BRISTOL (ENGLAND) WESTERN PRESS
October 1, 1926

THE ENGLISH VIEW

The Negro question in the United States is undoubtedly at the root of much of the violence and intimidation that

174

is practised there. We in Europe can show nothing to match the dementia of a mob that still tears a Negro to pieces or burns him alive for his alleged crimes . . . It is an odd illustration of the difference between theory and practice of democracy in the United States.

NEW YORK SUN
October 8, 1926

BLOOD-THIRSTY MOB LYNCHES 3 MEMBERS OF ONE FAMILY

AIKEN, S. C., Oct. 8—A mob early today stormed the Aiken jail, seized three negroes, one of them a woman, and shot them to death in a pine thicket just beyond the city limits.

The negroes were on trial for the murder of Sheriff H. H. Howard, of Aiken County, who was shot to death at the home of the negroes a year ago last April. A verdict of acquittal had been handed down yesterday for one of the negroes.

The mob victims were Demon and Bertha Lowman, brother and sister, and their cousin Clarence. Demon had been cleared of the murder charge yesterday and a verdict of "not guilty" was ordered in his behalf by Judge S. T. Lanham. The acquittal of the other two Lowmans was expected shortly.

NEW YORK AMSTERDAM NEWS
June 1, 1927

LONE SURVIVOR OF ATROCITY RECOUNTS EVENTS OF LYNCHING

Samuel L. Lowman, whose wife, son, daughter and nephew were murdered by whites in Aiken, South Carolina, a year ago, last Thursday night told his story to a meeting of the National Negro Development Union at Manhattan Casion, 155th Street and Eighth Avenue.

Mr. Lowman, soft-spoken and stoop-shouldered, contrasted sharply to the brightly uniformed members of the Universal African Royal Guards who flanked him on the platform, the old man held his audience spellbound as he recited events which led up to one of the South's most horrible multiple lynchings.

His story went back to April 25th, 1925, when Sheriff H. H. Howard of Aiken appeared with three of his deputies at Lowman's cabin thirteen miles from Aiken. Neither Lowman nor any member of his family had ever been in any kind of trouble and none of them knew the sheriff nor did the sheriff know them. The Sheriff had come on a routine whiskey check.

As the Sheriff and his deputies approached the cabin, Lowman's wife, Annie, and his daughter, Bertha, were out back, working. Mrs. Lowman was making soap, Bertha was sweeping the yard. Bertha looked up, saw the four men, who were dressed in civilian clothes, and was terrified. Two weeks earlier, other white men had come to the cabin and whipped her brother Demon for no reason at all. Softly she spoke to her mother who agreed it would be best to go inside the house.

The white men saw the women begin to move. They drew their revolvers and started running toward them. Sheriff Howard and Bertha Lowman reached the back steps of the house at the same time. Bertha screamed. With his pistol butt, the sheriff struck Bertha in the mouth. Mrs. Lowman saw this, heard her daughter scream and picked up an axe. As she started to her daughter's assistance, one of the Sheriff's deputies emptied his gun into the old woman and she fell to the ground, lifeless.

Demon and Clarence Lowman, son and nephew of Mr. Lowman, were working a field nearby and heard Bertha's scream. Demon secured a revolver from a shed and Clarence a shot gun. Two of the deputies started firing at Demon and he returned the fire. What Clarence did is not clear. In a few seconds, the sheriff was dead and Bertha had been shot twice in the chest, just above her heart. Clarence and Demon were also wounded.

Mr. Lowman emphasized last night that at no time did anyone realize that the white men were sheriffs. They wore no badges and gave no sign of authority. Five members of the Lowman family were arrested and placed in the Aiken jail. Mr. Lowman had been away at a mill

176

having meal ground. He came home to find himself a widower and with four of his children and a nephew in jail.

Three days later, a fraction of a quart of liquor was found in a bottle in the Lowman back yard. For this, Mr. Lowman was sentenced to two years on a chain gang, charged with possession of illegal liquor. Mr. Lowman emphatically stated last night that the liquor had been planted in his back yard in order to frame him.

Bertha, Demon and Clarence, whose ages were then respectively 18, 22 and 15, were tried for the sheriff's murder and swiftly found guilty. The men were sentenced to death and Bertha was given life imprisonment.

The three appealed their conviction and the South Carolina Supreme Court found that their trial had been unfair and a new trial was ordered. It was during this second trial, after Demon had been acquitted and it appeared that Bertha and Clarence would be freed, too, since the sheriffs had failed to notify the Lowmans that they were officers of the law and the Lowmans had every right to assume they were intruders—that the three were removed from the Aiken jail and lynched by a mob.

The date was October 8th, 1926. On that day the three were removed from the Aiken jail, driven to a tourist camp a mile and a half from town, liberated and told to run. As they started off, shots rang out and they fell. The boys were dead. Bertha was wounded. She thrashed around on the ground begging piteously for life. A mobster was quoted as saying, "She's bleating like a goat." This caused much laughter among his comrades. More shots were pumped into the girl. At last one found a vital spot and, with a spasmodic quiver, Bertha died.

During this period, Mr. Lowman was serving out his two year sentence on a chain gang. On February 23rd of this year he was released. He came immediately to Philadelphia, the home of his other children. Except for his watch, the old man left all of his possessions—including a new Ford—down South.

Mr. Lowman said last night that the real killer of Sheriff Howard was one of his own deputies who wanted his boss's job. Mr. Lowman gave his name but libel law prevents our reprinting it here. It was this same man who later led the lynch mob that killed his children and nephew, Mr. Lowman said. They were the only ones who could prove he was the murderer of Sheriff Howard.

At the end of the evening, ushers passed around the hat and $35 was raised as a purse to aid the old man.

CHICAGO DEFENDER
March 12, 1927

DARROW FORCED TO FLEE
AFTER ANTI-LYNCH SPEECHES

MOBILE, Ala., Mar. 11—Clarence Darrow, internationally known criminal lawyer of Chicago, champion of oppressed people, and advocate of free speech in America, was given an example of southern chivalry early this week when he was forced to leave a hall where he had spoken here, under protection of a squad of riflemen and special police. He was menaced by a mob and, although ill and in Alabama for his health, was compelled to leave hastily for Chattanooga, Tenn. where he will rest a few days before returning home to Chicago. Mr. Darrow's only crime was condemning lynchings and other inhuman practices for which Alabama is notorious. He spoke to two audiences—one composed of white people at the Lyric theater and one to members of our Race at a school. In both speeches he stressed the importance of mutual respect and co-operation, through tolerance, and less mob activity on the part of whites, and independence and backbone on the part of our people.

Immediately following the address to whites he was rushed from the theater back to the home of his host at Fairhope, where he has been recuperating from a severe illness for several months, and was prevailed upon to board a train at noon Tuesday for the North. He was informed that if he remained in the state even the militia would be unable to make his stay safe. He was denounced from pulpit and by the press and described as a meddling trouble maker from Illinois.

It was during his Lyric theater speech that the first intimation of the temper of an Alabama mob expressed

178

itself. Speaking to what he believed was an audience of the "best people of the South," he had just declared that lynchings "are a disgrace not only to the South but to the North and the entire United States." Suddenly there was a cry, "Lynch him!" But he continued his talk, ignoring the interruption, until it became impossible for him to continue. Then, as he started from the theater, the mob spirit became apparent. Women, children and others recognized in Mobile's business, professional and social world were conspicuous in the mob that followed him through the street to his car. Police with drawn weapons surrounded him and Mrs. Darrow, holding the mob at bay. As they passed through the crowd handbills signed by the Ku Klux Klan and denouncing him as an advocate of "social equality" were showered upon them.

In commenting upon the affair before leaving Mobile, Mr. Darrow stated that he had told only the truth. He urged both races' to work for a better understanding through the spirit of fairness and justice for all. In his speech at the school he is reported to have said in part:

"I can't help you; you will have to help yourselves; but I advise an attitute of defiance toward the white man who calls himself your 'friend.' How has he manifested his friendship?

"By hanging and burning you, by making you do his work and use his back door, refusing to let you enter the best hotels and use the best coach in the train, and making you sit in the rear of the street car.

"The only front place the white man has ever given you is in the battle line. There you can stop the bullets; but when you return home you can't use the sidewalks. You have to use the road. What can the Colored man do to help himself?

"I see you pray, but I don't see why. Your God must be a 'white' man, considering the way He treats you. No doubt there will be a 'Jim Crow' law in your heaven when you get there.

"You can sing. I heard you sing 'Sweet Land of Liberty,' but I don't see how you can. I don't sing it because I know it's not true.

"But you can work and gain a place for yourself if you can do better work than the white man. You are being

179

recognized and you have some friends who are not afraid to sit at the table with you."

Clarence Darrow, who is about 65 years old, has long been known as a friend of our people. He takes the position that the white people of America are injured by the lynchings, peonage and segregation in the South as are the people discriminated against. He first aroused the enmity of the South in 1925, when he went to Dayton, Tenn., to defend John T. Scopes, a young schoolteacher, who was being tried for violating the Tennessee law against the teaching of evolution. In this case he opposed the late William Jennings Bryan, the idol of the South, who fought valiantly against evolution, but was never known to raise his voice against lynchings.

Darrow is also an opponent of capital punishment and has fought consistently against it. Our Race is the chief victim of this practice south of the Mason and Dixon line.

NEW YORK TIMES
June 14, 1927

WHITE ATTEMPTS IN VAIN TO RESCUE VICTIMS

LOUISVILLE, Miss., June 13—Two negro brothers, Jim and Mark Fox, accused of having slain their sawmill superintendent after an argument over work hours, were seized by a mob early this morning, paraded through the streets of Louisville and then saturated with gasoline and burned to death at a telephone pole a short distance from town.

The terrified screams of the negroes touched one member of the mob who attempted to extinguish the blaze a moment after it had started, but the would-be rescuer was seized by others and dragged away.

NEW YORK WORLD
November 12, 1927

COURTHOUSE IS LYNCH GALLOWS

COLUMBIA, Tenn., Nov. 12—A courthouse balcony became a gallows when Henry Choate, 18-year-old negro accused of attacking a white girl, was hanged by a mob here yesterday. One end of a rope was fixed around Choate's neck and the other end secured to a balustrade. Choate was then thrown over the side. The courthouse was festooned with red, white and blue bunting for yesterday's Armistice Day celebration.

NEW YORK TIMES
January 12, 1930

FORESEES END OF LYNCHING

ATLANTA, Ga., Jan. 11—Lynching will be a lost crime by 1940—something for scientists to study and the rest of us to remember with unbelief—and it will be wiped out by radio, good roads and the newspapers, according to Will W. Alexander, director of the Commission on Inter-Racial Cooperation.

"In 1919, when the commission was born, eighty-three persons were lynched," said Mr. Alexander. "This year the records show but ten and those in only five States. The figures are startling when one finds 1,726 lynched between 1885 and 1894, our earliest records. All told 4,377 persons have been lynched since 1885, a good sized town.

"Ten years from now we will be wondering how it ever happened."

COLUMBUS (GEORGIA) ENQUIRER-SUN
May 10, 1930

UNABLE TO BLAST INTO JAIL, MOB BURNS IT TO KILL NEGRO

SHERMAN, Tex., May 9—A mob today burned the $60,000 Grayson county court house, cremating George

Hughes, negro, after unsuccessfully attempting to seize him from officers.

Hughes, who had pleaded guilty to assaulting a white woman, died in a vault in the court house in which he had been placed for safety by Texas rangers and local officers; when the mob stormed the building during the trial, crying for his life.

Driven back three times by officers who hurled tear gas bombs and fought with fists and clubs, but did not shoot into the crowd, the mob finally set fire to the court house. An earlier attempt to dynamite the structure had failed.

Three youthful leaders of the mob were seriously wounded in a clash with the guardsmen. Two of them were shot and one may die. Jed Brown, 18, was shot in the chest and physicians held little hope for his recovery.

Several of the guardsmen were struck by stones, bottles and missles hurled by the mob in its attempt to storm the county jail.

Meanwhile, another crowd battled a detachment of guardsmen on the Square when they attempted to drive the crowd from the grounds of the wrecked court house.

The negro quarter of the city was deserted and appeals were sent to neighboring towns to rush police officers here to assist Sherman authorities.

The flame of an acetylene torch was directed against the vault by the mob which did not believe Hughes had burned to death. Previously, two attempts to blast open the vault failed. Seven sticks of dynamite were placed under the vault door and exploded but failed to open the door. A can of blasting powder was set off and this explosion also failed to shake the structure.

Hughes, who had pleaded guilty to charges of assaulting a white woman, had been placed in the vault for safety by Texas rangers and local officers, when the mob stormed the court house, crying for his life.

After the guardsmen had repulsed the mob at the jail, machine guns were set up at strategic points around the building.

Sheriff Vaughan said the Negro was given his choice of running for his life, after the courthouse fire began, or being shut in the vault, and that he chose the vault.

When last seen alive by the officers he was sitting on a chair in the vault, his head bowed upon his folded arms.

COLUMBUS (GEORGIA) ENQUIRER-SUN
May 11, 1930

LYNCH FEVER RUNNING HIGH

SHERMAN, Tex., May 10—Culminating an orgy of mob-madness, a mob early today set fire to a negro drug store and nearby erected a funeral pyre for George Hughes, 41-year-old negro attacker of a white woman who was suffocated or otherwise killed in a fire which destroyed the Sherman court house yesterday.

The body was recovered at 11:45 o'clock last night from the vault in the court house. It was dragged through the narrow opening made by an acetylene torch and dynamite blasts, and a chain wrapped around it.

When the men who went into the vault shoved the body through the hole and dumped it to the ground two stories below, women screamed and clapped their hands and a great cheer went up from the mob.

The chain was fastened to the rear of an automobile and it was started through the streets toward the jail, dragging the body, as the maddened mob cheered wildly.

The state rangers and guardsmen remained at the jail, not attempting interference as the dynamiting was in progress at the court house ruins.

NEW YORK SUN
May 10, 1930

TEXAS MOB RUNS AMUCK;
BURNS BLOCKS OF NEGRO HOMES

SHERMAN, Tex., May 10—As an aftermath to the burning of the Sherman courthouse here yesterday, in which George Hughes, alleged Negro rapist, was killed, three blocks of Negro dwellings were burned by a raging mob here early this morning.

The mob, after seizing Hughes' body from the ruins of the courthouse, chained it to the rear of an automobile and started for the Negro section. Through the streets the mob dragged the body and the journey ended at a large Negro store which housed a drug store, beauty shop, undertaker, tailor and other enterprises. A tree was near by.

The body was strung up to the tree and boxes piled beneath. A fire was lighted. Then the drug store was set on fire.

After virtually destroying the drug store, the mob surged down a three block section of the Negro district, a stampede of humanity run amuck. Clubs, bricks, bottles and fists were wielded against windows and doors. Virtually every store was entered and its interior looted and wrecked.

Near 2 A.M. most of the mob dispersed, and harassed officials believed that most of their grief was over. Just then, a fresh fire broke out and the overtaxed fire department went clanging again into the Negro district. About seven hundred white persons, in knots of twenty to fifty each, were on the streets at that hour.

Every Negro had disappeared from the Negro Section, even from districts which were not burning. The frightened men, women and children were reported to be huddling in brush thickets on the outskirts of Sherman.

Later this morning hundreds of curious persons invaded Sherman. Highways were covered by solid strings of automobiles bringing visitors to this city which, because of its numerous colleges, churches and fine public buildings, is known as "The Athens of Texas."

CHICAGO DEFENDER
May 17, 1930

ADDED FACTS ON LYNCHING

SHERMAN, Tex., May 16—Millions of Americans have read about the recent conflagration which took place here in connection with the lynching of George Hughes. Nowhere in the white press has mention been made of these two important facts:

First, Hughes had not confessed to the rape he was charged with. As a matter of fact, a jury had just been sworn in and witnesses were beginning to testify when mob violence interrupted the trial. Hughes claimed he was innocent.

Second, the lynching and burnings took place on the anniversary of the birthday of the abolitionist John Brown.

ATLANTA CONSTITUTION
June 1, 1930

MOB OVERCOMES NAT'L. GUARD TO LYNCH ACCUSED RAPIST

CHICKASHA, Okla., May 31—Henry Argo, a 19-year-old negro accused of attacking a white woman, was shot in the head and stabbed twice near the heart today by a lynch mob which attacked him in his jail cell. Believed by the mob to be dead, he was removed in a blanket and taken to the University of Oklahoma Hospital in Oklahoma City, fifty miles away, where he died one hour later.

A fight between law enforcement officers and the mob that preceded the mob's entry into the jail resembled a pitched battle between two armies at war. Remarkably, no one was fatally wounded but the negro.

A mob of 1,000 men and boys massed in front of the jail early last night and made a number of unsuccessful attempts to seize Argo. Leader of the attacks was W. G. Skinner, husband of the women who is alleged to have been attacked by Argo. Argo was picked up on a highway two miles from the Sinner home soon after the attack and held on suspicion. Argo denied his guilt.

The mob's first advance on the jail was repulsed by deputy sheriffs shooting over their heads. Emboldened, the mob returned with battering rams and sledge hammers and began to break down the steel door of the jail.

Just then 30 National Guardsmen, ordered out by Adjutant General Charles F. Barrett, arrived in a truck. The Guardsmen fired blanks from a machine gun, aim-

185

ing over the heads of the mobmen who were momentarily driven back from the jail door.

The mobmen retaliated with a rain of bricks, pavement blocks and bottles that broke every window in the jail and sent the Guardsmen fleeing for cover inside the jail. The mobsters then set fire to a Guard truck, cut all power and telephone lines to the jail and snipped the hose of a fire brigade that had arrived to help disperse the crowd.

With the Guardsmen as virtual prisoners within the jail, trapped on the second floor, the mob stacked a pile of mattresses in a downstairs room, soaked them with gasoline and sent a dense smoke aloft.

The Guardsmen came down coughing. They came to terms with the mobsters, virtually surrendering. The mob permitted the Guardsmen to leave the building and to take with them all prisoners but Argo. The fire on the ground floor was then extinguished.

Rioters seeking clubs and brickbats raced through the building, tearing out water pipes and flooding the interior of the jail which added to the confusion. A number of mobsters advanced to the door of Argo's cell. Finding the door locked, they began to break open a wall.

Argo fought desperately, hurling everything within reach. At one point he wrenched an iron bar from one of the attackers and drove the rest back with it, flailing it wildly, injuring a number of the men.

It was during this confusion that a sniper, unnoticed, climbed up a vine outside the jail, aimed a pistol at Argo's head and shot him near the brain. Shortly thereafter, W. G. Skinner, husband of Argo's alleged victim, managed to enter the cell and stabbed Argo twice above the heart. With Argo a heap on the floor, the mob dispersed.

Argo was then taken to Oklahoma City, where he died.

Skinner, a tenant farmer in overalls who lives in a mud hut, was an important man in town today. He was much in demand at sidewalk gatherings and was asked time and again to tell and re-tell his part in the lynching. This afternoon he collapsed on the jail house lawn and was taken to a hospital suffering from over-exhaustion.

EDITORIAL FROM
THE NEW YORK TELEGRAM
July 12, 1930

A SOUTHERN STATESMAN

The question whether lynching is justifiable is figuring in the United States Senatorial campaign in South Carolina, unbelievable as it may seem.

Senator Coleman L. Blease, up for re-election, discussed the subject in a campaign address.

"Whenever the Constitution comes between me and the virtue of white women in South Carolina, I say to hell with the Constitution," Blease is quoted as having said recently at the scene of a recent lynching where he was seeking the local vote.

When he was Governor, he added pridefully, he did not call out the militia to protect Negroes against mobs, and asked that when a suspect was caught he not be notified until the next morning.

It would be difficult to equal such a statement for sheer barbarity and demagogism.

It is a deliberate invitation to the people of South Carolina by an acknowledged leader, who boasts that he has held more political offices than any other man in the history of the State, to supersede normal legal processes with lynch law and mob violence.

And there has been plenty of that in the South in recent weeks.

We cannot believe that such savagery reflects the views of the people of South Carolina.

Obviously men like Blease have no place in the Senate or in any other public office. It will be interesting to observe whether the decent people of South Carolina are willing to bear the stigma of having him again represent them.

ATLANTA CONSTITUTION
September 10, 1930

MOB DISBANDS AFTER TALK BY GLIB POLICE CAPTAIN

A nervy police captain with courage, a sense of humor and a gift of gab used all three Tuesday night to disperse an angry mob of several hundred men who gathered suddenly about the negro clinic of Grady hospital where Robert Glaze, negro held in connection with the fatal shooting Monday night of John B. McWhorter, street car operator, lay seriously wounded.

As the result of the smoothness with which Captain Grover C. Fain, under instructions of Chief of Police James L. Beavers, handled what was for a time a menacing situation, the crowd disbanded in an orderly manner and the suspect was quietly removed to Fulton county jail, where his alleged confederate in the robbery attempt, Willie Lee Cox, also wounded, likewise is being held.

Earlier in the night, according to police, Chief Beavers had instructed Captain Fain to keep an extra watch of reserves on duty, both at headquarters and at the hospital. Both watches were assigned by the night captain, the one at the hospital having instructions to notify headquarters in the event any untoward developments occurred.

Shortly after 8 o'clock Captain Fain received a telephone call from the hospital detachment. As a result he immediately telephoned Chief Beavers at the latter's home, ordered the reserves at the station and all available call officers to go to the vicinity of the hospital.

There it was discovered that a large crowd thronged the sidewalk near the negro clinic. It was a nondescript mob, composed largely of men in civilian clothes, police said. A buzz of excitement throbbed through its ranks as the police cars drew up. Chief Beavers was among the first of the officers to reach the scene.

One man, apparently a leader of the men, saw Captain Fain and stepped forward to meet him. It was then that

188

the captain employed his nerve, humor and diplomacy. Without displaying any official resentment or anger he began to talk to the unidentified leader and those who surged around him. He reminded them that they were supposed to be law-abiding citizens. He spoke sympathetically of the death of McWhorter, and called the attention of the leaders to the work of the officers on his watch who had captured the suspected slayers.

When the front ranks of the mob showed signs of restlessness and began once more to move forward, Captain Fain met nerve with nerve. Indicating an imaginary line across the sidewalk he adopted a law often used by old-time skippers of four-masted schooners.

"Now you men," he said, "are law-abiding citizens up to now. But you are just about to become lawbreakers, and the first man that steps across that line violates the law. I represent the law here, and whoever violates that law is going to have to answer to me and my men."

The tall leader and those nearest Captain Fain eyed him silently for a minute or so, saying nothing. Then the tall man turned and said:

"The captain is right, boys. Let's go back."

The crowd began to walk back toward Piedmont avenue. A certain element in it, however, still hummed with dissatisfaction, and the victory the captain had won was perilously near an open break when another unidentified man broke from the ranks and came up to the captain. In a rage he threw his hat to the ground in front of Captain Fain's feet. He surveyed Captain Fain with cold eyes, then challenged:

"Spit in that hat!"

But the police official's sense of humor came to the fore here. His eyes twinkling in the street light, Captain Fain placed his hands on his hips.

"Listen, fella," he scoffed. "You've got more sense than that, haven't you? Why, son, if I were to spit in your eyes I'd drown you! Now isn't that a fine way for a grown man to act—throw his best hat on the ground! And invite a captain of police to spit in it! You oughta be ashamed of yourself!"

The crowd began to laugh and the unidentified challenger, having been exposed to the ridicule of his own ranks, lost his point. Within five minutes the entire throng had dispersed.

ATLANTA CONSTITUTION
September 11, 1930

POSSIBLY ONE, MAYBE OTHER LYNCH VICTIMS WERE INNOCENT

DARIEN, Ga., Sept. 10—Of two negroes lynched here last Monday and Tuesday in connection with the killing of one policeman and the wounding of another, at least one positively was the wrong man, according to a statement issued here yesterday by Mayor R. A. Young. "We are convinced that the negro who was shot by a posse and taken to Savannah where he died was not one of the two suspected of intent to rob The Bank of Darien," said the Mayor's statement.

Two negroes loitering near the Bank of Darien were suspected of intent to rob the bank by Officer Ora Anderson here on Sunday night. Anderson hid in a shadow near the bank intending to observe the two negroes. One of the negroes caught sight of him crouching in the shadows and is said to have opened fire. Anderson was slightly wounded.

A posse quickly formed and a systematic search of swamps and outlying territory was quickly begun. George Grant, a negro, was located in the swamps. Before he was seized, he shot Officer Bob Freeman, fatally.

Grant was brought to the jail here in Darien where a mob shot him to death. Before dying, he was questioned about the man who was thought to have been his companion in front of the bank. Grant is quoted as having said that his name was Bryan.

An alarm went out and four negroes named Bryan were rounded up. Among them was Willie Bryan, 24, who was located at a house on "The Ridge," a place about four miles from Darien. As he and the search party were leaving his house, Bryan is said to have attempted to flee.

He was shot twice in the chest and soon died.

The location of bullet-holes in his chest was explained

190

by the posse as having resulted from Bryan turning around to fire at the posse as he fled.

Concluding his statement, Mayor Young said:

"Officer Anderson has given us the evidence that eliminates Willie Bryan as a suspect. On the basis of Officer Anderson's assurance, I am wiring the police heads of Savannah, Brunswick, and Jacksonville to keep a sharp lookout for Fred Bryan, the negro we really want.

"Officer Anderson, after seeing Willie Bryan, has reported to me that he is not the man who was Grant's companion. The negro shot weighed about 162 pounds and was dark. The negro, Fred Bryan, whom we want, weighs over 200 pounds and is ginger-cake in color.

"The most lamentable part of this whole affair is the death of Police Officer Bob Freeman, of Brunswick. Our sincere sympathy goes out to his family."

MONTGOMERY ADVERTISER
September 24, 1930

HUNTING NEGRO IN SWAMP

THOMASVILLE, Ga., Sept. 24—A crowd of several hundred men was reported searching a swamp near here tonight for an unidentified negro who today attempted to attack a 9-year-old white girl on her way home from school. Officers reported that highways in the vicinity of the swamp were choked with automobiles.

NEW YORK NEGRO WORLD
October 4, 1930

PRISON WARDEN DOUBTS GUILT OF NEGRO LYNCHED IN GA.

THOMASVILLE, Ga., Sept. 25—A mob of seventy-five men today wrested Willie Kirkland, a young Negro convict, from the hands of the sheriff, hanged him to a tree in the suburb of Magnolia Gardens and after riddling his body with bullets toted it through the town behind a truck and deposited it on the courthouse lawn.

Kirkland, who was twenty and a trusty at the country stockade, a prison camp, where he was serving out a term for stealing a horse, was said to have been twice identified by a nine-year-old school girl as the man who had attempted to attack her. But the warden of the camp expressed doubt as to Kirkland's guilt, saying the Negro did not leave the stockade yesterday, the day of the attack.

Prominent citizens of the town tried to reason with the mob and prevent the slaying. But as the sheriff brought Kirkland out of the stockade to take him to another jail for safekeeping, the father of the girl raised a shotgun to kill the Negro. Some one knocked the gun down, but the parent's action seemed almost a signal for the mob to attack.

The sheriff was disarmed and Kirkland placed on a motor truck and driven to Magnolia Gardens, not far from the winter home of Harry Payne Whitney and the former residences of the late Mark Hanna and John D. Archibald. There the Negro was hanged to an oak tree and shots were fired into his body.

When the mob was sure Kirkland was dead the body was cut down and towed back to the courthouse. This was the mob's demonstration of contempt for the law which would not have prescribed death for Kirkland under any circumstances since the assault was not accomplished. Witnesses told the sheriff they were unable to identify any members of the mob.

The attack on the girl was frustrated when her screams brought her mother to her aid. A posse was formed quickly and bloodhounds trailed the child's assailant to the stockade. Kirkland was arrested and the girl identified him. The next morning she again picked him out from four other Negroes as the man who had tried to attack her.

It was then that a restless crowd formed around the county jail, and word that Kirkland had been transferred to the stockade led it to the camp just as the sheriff was removing the Negro.

The sheriff, the only witness at the inquest, told the coroner's jury he was unable to identify any of the mob. The jury decided that Kirkland came to his death at the hands of unknown parties.

EDITORIAL FROM THE LITERARY DIGEST
January 31, 1931

MISSOURI'S IS THE SHAME

Almost all Maryville—3,000 strong, it is reported—turned out for the feast of blood.

A strong wind was blowing, and the little schoolhouse, with the Negro bound on the ridge-pole, and plentifully soaked with gasoline, made a spectacular blaze.

In ten minutes it was over—schoolhouse and Negro were reduced to ashes.

It was the first lynching of 1931, and Missouri's is the shame. The Negro had been on his way to the courthouse for a preliminary trial when he was seized by the mob, according to a dispatch from the St. Louis *Star*. Ample preparations for the funeral pyre had been made. All the furniture had been removed from the schoolhouse, and the Negro, showing remarkable coolness, was made to climb a ladder to the roof. Then a hole was cut in the roof, and through this the Negro was bound to the ridge-pole with a ten-foot chain, his head hanging down one side of the roof and his feet the other. One of the mob poured gasoline over the prostrate man. Gasoline was then sprinkled inside the building, and all was ready for the match. After the fire, the crowd, which had been looking on in silence, walked slowly away.

Thus was avenged the honor of a nineteen-year-old schoolteacher who, several weeks before, had been confessedly mistreated and done to death by the Negro on whom the mob wreaked its vengeance.

NEW YORK SUN
November 9, 1931

DOUBT OF GUILT FOUND IN MOST OF 1930'S LYNCHINGS

ATLANTIA, Ga., Nov. 9—Conclusions that two of the twenty-one persons lynched in 1930 "certainly" were innocent, and eleven others "possibly" so, were advanced today by the Southern commission on the study of lynching along with a criticism of hasty trials and "legal lynchings."

The commission listed as findings of a year's survey that:

1. There is real doubt of guilt of at least half the victims of mob violence.

2. Fewer than one fourth of the persons lynched since 1890 have been accused of assaults upon white women.

3. Claims that lynchings are necessary because courts do not convict Negroes for their crimes are fallacious.

4. Mob leaders can be identified without difficulty, although Grand Jury indictments seldom are brought.

5. Lynching is most frequent per tens of thousands of Negro population in sparsely settled areas.

6. There is direct relationship between lack of education, low economic status and lynching danger.

The report was made public here today by the commission's chairman, George Milton, president and editor of the Chattanooga News.

Regarding offenses that resulted in lynchings, the commission said: "One man was lynched solely because he had offended political opponents and another to prevent his appearance as a witness in a serious court case against white men."

In some cases, the commission said, it found reason to suspect victims had been deliberately "framed" for purposes of concealment or revenge.

Georgia led in contributing to the 3,603 recorded lynchings since 1889 with 465. Mississippi had 464, Texas 364 and Louisiana 349.

The commission concluded that lynching, while decreasing during the last three decades, was becoming more exclusively a Southern phenomenon with 97 per cent. of the country's lynchings occurring in the South in recent years.

NEW YORK SUN
June 14, 1932

SHERIFF AND NEGRO KILLED, 6 DEPUTIES WOUNDED BY MOB

WINNSBORO, S. C., June 14—Six deputies were wounded and Sheriff Hood was killed today when they fought a desperate battle in front of the court house to keep a mob from lynching a negro prisoner. Despite the posse's fight, the negro was wrested from them and the infuriated crowd shot him to death.

HACKENSACK (NEW JERSEY)
EVENING RECORD
February 20, 1933

LYNCH NEGRO FOR KILLING MAN WHO DEFENDED WIFE

RINGGOLD, La., Feb. 20—A Negro who kidnaped a banker and his wife in an attempted robbery and killed the man for defending the woman against attack, was lynched by citizens at the scene of the slaying yesterday.

Officers said the Negro, identified as Nelson Nash, 24, of Leesville, La., early yesterday morning entered the home of J. P. Bachelor, 50, of the Ringgold Bank, and forced Bachelor and his wife to take him to the bank and open the doors.

When Bachelor told the Negro he could not open the vault, the bandit forced the couple, still in their night-clothes, to accompany him down the railroad tracks about a mile north of the town, where he allegedly attempted to attack the woman.

Bachelor grappled with the Negro as his wife ran to a nearby cabin to summon aid. The husband was severely beaten about the head, and died of his injuries.

As news of the crime spread several hundred citizens organized posses and captured Nash 15 miles away and brought him back to Ringgold where officers said he confessed the slaying.

The crowd spirited the Negro away to the scene of the slaying, hanged him from a tree, and riddled his body with bullets.

INDIANAPOLIS RECORDER
March 4, 1933

LYNCHED FOR KILLING BANKER, NEGRO WAS THE WRONG MAN

RINGGOLD, La., Mar. 1—Nelson Nash, young Negro who was brutally lynched here February 19, was the wrong man. The perpetrator of the crime for which Nash was an unwilling victim may well have been a white man. This was revealed today after careful investigation of the circumstances surrounding the lynching had been made by a correspondent of this paper.

Just before the lynching, at a sheriff's questioning, the wife of the man for whose murder Nash was lynched positively refused to identify the lynched man as the one who murdered her husband, J. P. Batchelor, white local banker.

Batchelor and his wife were forced to leave their home by his murderer and accompany him to the Ringgold Bank. Batchelor was killed by the man when he refused to open the safe at his command.

The man wore no mask and Mrs. Batchelor had full view of his face and profile. Though she would not say whether her husband's assailant was white or colored, she did refuse to specify Nash as the guilty party.

First press reports failed to specify Batchelor's murderer as a Negro. They also originally placed the number of the lynch mob at 500 of this town of 1500 population.

A more careful check-up based on corroborating testimony of eye-witnesses places the number at 40 and it is said they were not mobsters from the poor section but wealthy businessmen and friends of Batchelor.

Nash was arrested shortly after the murder of Batchelor and taken before Mrs. Batchelor for identification.

Even after Mrs. Batchelor failed to connect Nash with the crime, the posse remained determined to avenge the crime with their own hands.

Protesting and proclaiming his innocence, Nash was taken to the woods outside of town. He asked the mob to spare him a few minutes to pray. The mob told him to open his mouth and stick out his tongue. He did so. The tongue was grasped with a pair of auto pliers and severed by a razor.

An attempt to burn Nash was made but it was found that the grass and wood was too wet to accommodate such a slow death. Instead, he was strung up from a tree. He protested his innocence until a volley of bullets killed him.

Nash, age 24, was known to be a peaceful young man and had never before been in trouble with the law.

NEW YORK HERALD-TRIBUNE
March 27, 1933

DOCTOR RESCUES NEGRO LAD

LOWELL, N. C., Mar. 26—A physician here today saved a Negro from a lynch mob by hiding him in his cellar. A twenty-year-old youth stealthily approached the home of Dr. James W. Reid and told him that a mob was searching for him, having accused him of attempting to assault Miss Kathleen Jenkins, a 16-year-old white girl.

The Doctor hid the youth in his basement as the mob combed the neighborhood around his house. After they left, the Doctor drove the Negro to Charlotte for safe-keeping in the Mecklenberg County jail.

ATLANTA CONSTITUTION
July 6, 1933

NEGRO AND WHITE SCUFFLE; NEGRO IS JAILED, LYNCHED

CLINTON, S. C., July 5—A negro truck driver who had come to blows with a white truck driver was found dead today.

Norris Bendy, Laurens county negro, had argued yes-terday with Marvin Tollis, white, after each had driven a truckload of Fourth of July picknickers to Lake Murray. When the men came to blows, the negro was arrested.

Sometime this morning the negro was spirited away from the Clinton Jail. Later, his body, showing signs of shooting, beating and strangulation, was found seven miles from here by Deputy Sheriff Thad Moore. It was hanging from a tree on the lawn of the Old Sardis Church.

KNOXVILLE JOURNAL
July 23, 1933

MYSTERIOUS LYNCHING IN MISS.

COLUMBUS, Miss., July 22—Mystery shrouds the lynching of a negro which took place at the little town of Caledonia, 15 miles north of here.

First reports merely stated that a negro had been lynched last Friday after he allegedly "insulted a white woman." Subsequent efforts by newsmen to secure details of the lynching met with outright denials that a lynching had taken place.

Later it was admitted, however, that an unnamed negro had been hanged. It was said that the negro went to a farm house and made an improper proposal to a white girl.

The white girl sent him away with the understanding that he was to meet her later in a nearby cotton field. When he appeared at the designated time, he was met by a band of white men who were waiting for him.

The band seized him, hanged him, riddled him with bullets and quietly dispersed.

S. C. LYNCHERS SLAY NEGRO; ONE TELLS OF POLICE HELP

NINETY SIX, S. C., Oct. 9—A coroner's jury ordered four men held late today on a charge of murdering Bennie Thompson, youthful Negro who was taken from the jail here last night and beaten to death.

The action was taken by the jury after Burley Leppard had read a statement admitting that he and three white men had taken the youth from his cell and whipped him with "automobile top tubes." The men implicated by Leppard were J. F. Morris, "Lesty" Mayes and "Toody" Webb. Leppard, a textile worker, and Mayes were in jail tonight, but officers were still searching for the other two.

"We and the others had some trouble with the Negro at a cafe last night and he drew a pistol on us." Leppard's statement said. "The Negro was arrested and put in jail. Later the four of us went to the jail and asked the jailer to turn the Negro over to us. He refused, telling us we would have to see the chief.

"Chief of Police Rush came in a few minutes later, and we made the same request of him. He told us to wait until dark and come back and we would find the jail unlocked.

"We went back to the jail a short time later and we found the door open and the lock hanging in the cell door, pushed together as if it had been locked.

"We took the Negro out and drove him down the road in my car. All of us beat him with automobile top tubes and left him beside the road still alive."

Leppard said this was at 7:30 o'clock last night.

Just after 8 o'clock this morning, the Negro's body, bearing many welts, was found in plain view of the highway by a small Negro boy.

Solicitor H. S. Blackwell, who attended the inquest, said he would ask that Chief of Police Rush be indicted as an accessory to the killing.

Chief Rush made a statement tonight denying the textile workers' charge that he had aided them in taking the Negro from his cell: "I have been an officer a long time and I will never be guilty of such a dirty trick as that," he said.

NEW YORK TIMES
October 19, 1933

MARYLAND WITNESSES WILDEST LYNCHING ORGY IN HISTORY

PRINCESS ANNE, Md., Oct. 18—In the wildest lynching orgy the state has ever witnessed, a frenzied mob of 3,000 men, women and children, sneering at guns and teargas, overpowered 50 state troopers, tore from a prison cell a Negro prisoner accused of attacking an aged white woman, and lynched him in front of the home of a judge who had tried to placate the mob.

Then the mob cut down the body, dragged it through the main thoroughfares for more than half a mile and tossed it on a burning pyre.

Fifty State policemen and deputies battled vainly with the crowd in front of the jail, tossing tear bombs in an effort to disperse it.

Five policemen were beaten to the ground and the others were swept aside by the fury of townsmen and farmers, who used a heavy wooden battering ram to smash three doors and reach the cell of the terrified prisoner, George Armwood, 24 years old.

Armwood was dragged by the neck through the streets to the home of Judge Robert F. Duer, who, earlier in the day, had called the Somerset County grand jury in special session next Monday to hear testimony against the Negro.

While the prisoner pleaded desperately for his life and members of the mob shouted "Lynch him!" a rope was placed about his neck. The other end was swung over the limb of a tree directly in front of the judge's dwelling.

To accompanying shouts of "let him swing," the struggling Negro was hoisted into the air. Five minutes later he was cut down, dead.

200

Then members of the mob, shouting, seized the loose end of the rope and dragged the body half a mile on Main Street to a blazing pile in the centre of the thoroughfare. The dead man was lifted high by half a dozen men and flung to the flames.

Hundreds of persons, packed so thickly about the fire that police could not fight their way through, watched the body burn.

Armwood, who was arrested on Monday night, confessed to police that he had waylaid Mrs. Mary Denston, 82, on a lonely road near Monokin, eight miles from this place, and had attacked her.

He was smuggled into the county prison this morning, but word soon spread that he was here. Men by the hundred began to gather about noon. They marched about the jail, shouting and demanding that the prisoner be surrendered to them.

A guard of thirty-five men augmented by deputy sheriffs, surrounded the prison. In the afternoon an emergency call for State police was sent to Governor Ritchie at Baltimore. A score of troopers reported in the late afternoon, armed with riot sticks and tear bombs.

In addition, the Governor directed that the American Legion be asked to guard the prisoner. E. C. Young, local post commander, spurned the appeal.

"I have no authority, as commander of this Legion, to call out its members as a military unit or for police duty," he said.

"I am willing as a legionnaire to protect the townspeople and their property. However, I have no desire personally as a citizen, as a legionnaire or as a commander of a Legion post to engage in police duty for the protection of a Negro charged with such an atrocious crime. The laws of our organization forbid such use."

Hoping to allay mob feeling, Judge Duer had recalled the grand jury to hear evidence against Armwood and announced that the Somerset court would convene in special session a week from tomorrow to try Armwood.

The crowd became more and more unruly as the afternoon and evening wore on, however, and about 9 o'clock the attack on the jail began.

The march to the scene of the lynching of Armwood was wild in the extreme. The mob members seemed crazed, continually leaping on the Negro, even after he fell to the ground and was unable to rise.

One boy, apparently about 18 years old, slashed the Negro's ear almost off with a knife.

Under the oak tree, despite the presence of women and children, all the victim's clothes were torn from his body and he hung there for some minutes nude.

After they had burned the body, the mob members disbanded.

Rumors are current that the mob will re-form later to lynch John Richardson, a white man, with whom Armwood was riding at the time he was picked up.

Richardson is in jail for safe-keeping.

NEW YORK TIMES
October 20, 1933

NEARLY LYNCHED BY ACCIDENT

BALTIMORE, Oct. 19—A Negro demonstrator was nearly hanged by accident here today as a large number of Communists and members of the International Labor Defense assembled in City Hall Plaza to protest the lynching of George Armwood.

The demonstrator, his neck in a noose under an imitation gallows, was standing in a truck which was labeled "Protest Lynching of George Armwood."

Police were escorting the truck to the meeting place when it hit a bump in the pavement. The Negro lost his balance and for a moment gave a realistic exhibition of a hanging. He was quickly restored to his feet.

NEW YORK HERALD-TRIBUNE
October 25, 1933

21 LYNCHING WITNESSES
SIGHTED ONLY "STRANGERS"

PRINCESS ANNE, Md., Oct. 24—Each of the twenty-one witnesses who testified at the coroner's inquest into the death of George Armwood, Negro lynched here last

Wednesday night, today testified they did not recognize a single member of the lynching mob. "I could not recognize any of them; they were strangers," stated Sheriff Luther Daughterty. Such, in substance, was the testimony of other officers and eyewitnesses. All insisted that the lynchers did not live in this vicinity.

BIRMINGHAM (ALABAMA) NEWS
November 29, 1933

LYNCH VICTIM'S CORPSE MAY HAVE BEEN DUG UP

PRINCESS ANNE, Md., Nov. 28—George Armwood, the Negro who was mauled and mutilated before he was lynched here last month and whose body was then burned and further desecrated, appears to have had his grave "tampered with" last Tuesday night, according to a statement by Steve Hopkins, superintendent of the Somerset County Almshouse on whose grounds Armwood is buried.

Hopkins said yesterday that the turf over Armwood's grave appeared to be churned up and covered with fresh dirt, indicating that whatever fragments of his corpse remained in his coffin may have been dug up.

NEW YORK WORLD-TELEGRAM
November 4, 1933

"A FEAR OF COMMUNISM" CITED AS LYNCHING CAUSE

CHATTANOOGA, Nov. 4—In a report issued today, the Southern Commission on the Study of Lynching, gave as one cause of lynching "a consuming fear of Communism." A recent triple lynching of Negroes near Tuscaloosa, Alabama, was directly traceable to this cause, the Commission said.

NEW YORK HERALD-TRIBUNE
November 29, 1933

REPORTER DESCRIBES ESCAPE
FROM MARYLAND LYNCH MOB

WASHINGTON, Nov. 28—The escape of newspaper correspondents and photographers from a Maryland mob today was described as follows by a reporter for "The Washington Daily News," one of the endangered writers:

—I now know what it feels like to have a mob get after you. I have just returned from Salisbury, Md., after a gang of about 500 angry men stormed the Wicomico Hotel there, demanding that the manager turn over to them seven newspaper men and photographers, who had stayed behind to send news stories to their papers.

After the infuriated mob members finally forced armed soldiers to leave Salisbury in a hail of curses and brickbats, they turned on us. I was just finishing my story over the telephone when the hotel manager stuck his scared face into the booth.

"Get out quick!" he said, "the mob's coming after you fellows." I dashed out of the booth and went into the manager's office. About that time a group of men rushed up to the desk.

"We want those newspaper men," one of the mob demanded.

"They are not here—they've gone," the manager stammered.

I backed into a small clothes closet.

"We don't believe it," said the mob leader, "and we're coming back."

I held my breath. It seemed like about five minutes. Finally the manager tugged at my coat. "Get upstairs to 318 in a hurry," he said. I ran for all I was worth.

Inside the room I found a group of reporters and photographers.

Outside, three floors below, you could hear the mob yelling for us. "We want those newspaper guys," they shouted.

About that time a bellboy knocked at the door.

"Boys," he said, "you all had better get in another room. I think them folks done seen you in here."

Some of us went across the hall. The others went farther down the hall. Then we waited. Outside we could hear them chopping something. Fred Cole peeped out.

"They're chopping up and burning my car," he said. About ten minutes later another bellboy came back.

"Come up to the seventh floor," he said. He looked scared.

On the seventh floor we were met by the manager.

"Now listen," he continued. "This thing's getting pretty bad, but we're telling them that you have all gone. We've checked you out and all that, but the mob is still suspicious."

"What do you think they would do to us if they caught us?" a photographer asked.

The manager smiled. "Give you a good beating," he answered. "I don't think it would be any worse than that."

I decided to make a break for the airport. Freddie Cole pushed two photographic plates under my coat. I handed some one my press card.

With the manager I walked downstairs. There were a lot of people milling about, of course. I imagined every one of them was a mobber. I waited for ten minutes. Then the manager eased up and said, "There's a taxi driver outside. He won't pick you up here. It's too dangerous. You walk down the street and hop on his cab at the corner."

I made my way to the taxi, and safely to the airport.

NEW YORK WORLD-TELEGRAM
November 29, 1933

CROWD CHEERED AND LAUGHED AT NEGRO'S HORRIBLE DEATH

ST. JOSEPH, Nov. 29—They didn't hang Lloyd Warner. They burned him alive. Here's how it all happened, from start to finish.

The mob started to gather about 5 P. M., but they were

good-natured then. The sheriff was kidding them and nothing would have happened had not three river workers taken charge of things. They didn't say much, except "get me that" or "do this" as they went about breaking into the jail. It was very business like.

Of course, excitement mounted and permeated the mob of at least 10,000. There were lots of women along and many sightseers who didn't take part. There was at least a thousand from out of town.

About 9 o'clock the mob tried to enter the jail through the Court House next door. Through a passageway they got to the second floor of the jail, but were unable to go further. So they went back to batter their way in.

On the third floor were Sheriff Otto Theisen, his deputies, two newspaper men and national guardsmen. They were armed with tear gas and pistols, but not a shot was fired except by the mob.

The mob fired plenty, but the bullets only scarred the jail walls.

Guardsmen en route with three tanks were stopped. The mob yanked the soldiers out of the tanks and mauled them.

After a section of oilfield casing or water main pipe failed to batter in the outside door, two five-ton trucks were backed up. Log chains were attached and the doors pulled from the walls.

The second door inside was battered down and but one remained when the sheriff went out the back door, came around to the front and said to the mob:—

"You are plenty of Irishmen and I am but one Dutchman. You are too many for me, boys. I'll turn him over to you."

The mob cheered and shouted.

The sheriff said he feared they would lynch all prisoners. He went for Warner, who was chattering in fear. Warner hung to his cell bars for life, until his fingers bled. He was pulled loose and taken downstairs. But the sheriff didn't show the prisoner yet.

"You fellows clear out," the sheriff said calmly. "Send four men in and I will let them have him."

This was done.

The Negro, clinging to every object he could reach, tried to hold himself back. Warner was dragged a block

206

toward the centre of town to a small tree across from the Hotel Robidoux (the city's leading hotel).

They tied an inch and a half rope around his neck. But for a hanging the job was bungled.

It was tied so that it only threw his head back instead of forward so as to break his neck. He hung and struggled as the crowd yelled. Laughter rang out on all sides. Men and women leaned calmly against buildings, witnessing the horrible sight.

Warner wanted to talk but they wouldn't let him.

Then some one ran across the street, got seven gallons of gasoline from a filling station. Warner had on pants, shoes and socks which they drenched and set afire.

Warner was still alive.

He was burned alive.

He didn't cry out.

The fire went out. More gas was thrown on him and lighted again. Then the rope burned in two.

As the body slumped, wood was piled around and the fire was lighted a third time.

The crowd cheered and laughed and made jokes.

NEW YORK HERALD-TRIBUNE
December 3, 1933

MOB VIOLENCE DISAPPEARING FROM AMERICAN WAY OF LIFE

Although the three recent lynchings in dissimilar communities have widely aroused public opinion throughout the country, the fact remains that lynching, as a typical American way of dispensing with the process of law, has always been with us. Since the Civil War lynchings have markedly declined, but outbreaks of mob violence continue to be frequent.

From 1889, when records of lynching began to be kept, to 1932, 3,745 persons have been killed by mob violence. This excludes several race riots in various Middle Western and Southern cities.

In 1889, 176 persons were lynched, while in 1932 eight met death at the hands of the mob. To date this year seventeen persons have been lynched, according to unofficial records, bringing the total since 1889 to 3,762.

Statements similar to that of Governor James Rolph of California promising protection to the San Jose lynchers have been made by other State Executives. Governors and officials have run for election on promises to relax anti-lynching laws. In many cases courts have refused to proceed against leaders of lynching mobs, although it would have been relatively simple for the state to make a case against them. When indictments have been returned, in a comparatively small number of cases, sentences have been usually light. Out of twenty-one lynchings in 1930 only forty-nine persons from the thousands in the mobs and on the sidelines have been indicted. Only four have been sentenced.

Cole Blease, when Governor of South Carolina in 1911, said: "Whenever the Constitution comes between me and the virtue of white women of South Carolina I say 'to hell with the Constitution!'"

Governor Dan Moody of Texas once said to National Guardsmen: "Hold the Negro, if possible, but don't shoot anybody." During the first six months of 1919, after President Wilson's plea to end lynchings, six men were burned. The National Association for the Advancement of Colored People demanded an investigation from the various Governors. Four, Theodore G. Bilbo of Mississippi, W. P. Hobby of Texas, Hugh M. Dorsey of Georgia and Charles Brough of Arkansas, refused to answer. One, Sidney J. Catts of Florida, took the association to task and said: "There is no use bringing lynchers to trial; the citizenship will not stand for it. . . . If any man, white or black, should dishonor one of my family, he would meet my fist square from the shoulder, and every white man in the South, who is a red-blooded American, feels the same."

The scenes of lynching are usually rural places below the general economic and social average or regressive towns. Many surveys have been conducted to determine this fact.

"It is a rural Southern county," writes J. H. Chadbourn in "Lynching and the Law," "characterized in general by social and economic decadence. For example, it is below the state average in per capita tax valuation, bank deposits, income from farm and factory, income tax returns and ownership of automobiles."

In such a belated frontier, the shiftless elements of the population, the propertyless younger group, without real jobs and without real responsibility, serve as good raw material for a lynching mob. The average age of the mob, according to Dr. Arthur Raper, of the Commission on Interracial Co-operation, in "The Tragedy of Lynching," is from eighteen to twenty-five. Frequently older men lead the group or make suggestions.

The cruelty of mobs has long furnished the students of crowd psychology with their best laboratory material. "Let him die slowly," is a cry that most observers of a lynching have heard from many throats. Anything to prolong the agony is resorted to.

In addition to its cruelty, the typical lynch mob has a complete disregard for property. Since the majority of the mobs are men without possessions and of a low sense of responsibility, they suffer no sense of personal loss in destruction. In the lynching of a Negro, accused of assaulting a white woman, at Sherman, Tex., in 1930, the mob destroyed the Grayson County Courthouse and then fired the entire Negro business section of the town, valued at between $50,000 and $100,000. It refused to let firemen play their hoses on the burning building, and to enforce its order, the rioters cut up the hoses into little pieces.

According to Dr. Raper, the mob, out of a mistaken desire to convince the world at large of its right to lynch a man, often holds a mock trial or forces a confession out of the victim by a mock third degree. In the lynching of two Negroes at Scooba, Miss., in 1930, the third degree was applied by the nooses which had already been slipped over the heads of the men. When they refused to answer questions, they were snapped off the ground, then lowered so they could answer. One man expired by strangulation, never confessing the robbery of which he was accused, while his partner, to end the agony, blurted out a statement before being swung aloft for the last time.

This tendency of the mob to believe rumors has also been good material for the psychologists. The craving of modern persons for violence, and the fierceness of usually peaceful people when aroused, partly explains their extreme willingness to believe anything which would contribute toward giving them a thrill and a sense of power. The lynching party and the man-hunt, the baying of the dogs in the dead of night, and the entire scene lit by the flaring of pine-knots or fuel-oil torches, affords a good road to emotional escape from drab lives most lynchers usually lead.

One of the most bruited untruths about lynching is the common statement of the lynching-apologists: "We've got to lynch a nigger now and then to protect our women." The records show, however, that 1,406 lynchings since 1889 were for homicide, while only 623 were for rape. At least eighty Negro women have been lynched.

"These assumptions have been kept alive," Dr. Raper says, "by certain types of politicians who keep themselves in office by appeals to racial fear and antagonism."

It is interesting to note here that in no country during peacetime, except the United States, does lynching and mob violence form such an important part in the roster of crimes. Revolutions, whether Fascist or Communist, have their own particular forms of mob violence and choose their victims in their own peculiar way. The American lynch mob batters down the jail door, attacks the sheriff, pours on gasoline and uses the rope.

Another common excuse for lynching is that "the law is too slow." As far back as 1893, according to Dr. Chadbourn, the Georgia Bar Association said that a growing distrust in the promptness and efficiency of the law caused many lynchings. Also the fear that sentence would not be severe enough was responsible for many more. Added to these feelings on the part of lynching mobs was the assurance that no action would be taken against the lynchers by the state.

Regarding the attitudes of sheriffs and peace officers, Dr. Raper quotes a common remark as explanation: "Do you think I'm going to risk my life protecting a nigger?" In most cases sheriffs and deputies act in connivance with the mob. In a Mississippi lynching several years ago the sheriff promised the mob to turn the prisoner over to it at 4 o'clock promptly.

Other times they are in sympathy with the lynching, and simply look the other way. Occasionally sheriffs put up a fight, take the word of their election promises seriously and try to protect the prisoners. But this subject usually depends upon the caliber and personality of the man. Politics, too, plays a part: the lynch mob is usually the sovereign electorate, and the sheriff cannot afford to antagonize it. The use of the National Guard, while usually effective, has a bad after effect. Bad blood is created, and the town or community usually goes into open rebellion against the state. Salisbury, Md., is a case in point, where the mob battled the troopers with a vengeance, and were dispersed only at the point of fixed bayonets and with tear gas.

NEW YORK WORLD-TELEGRAM
December 8, 1933

HEART AND GENITALS CARVED FROM LYNCHED NEGRO'S CORPSE

KOUNTZE, Tex., Dec. 8—David Gregory, a Negro ex-convict accused of attacking and slaying a white woman, was shot to death when he was said to have resisted arrest by a posse and his body later mutilated and burned by a mob which dragged it to a pyre in the Negro section of Kountze early today.

Officers and incensed citizens had been searching for the Negro since Mrs. Nellie Williams Brockman, 30, wife of a farmer, was found dead on a highway near here last Saturday.

Last night a posse trailed the Negro to his hiding place in the belfry of a Negro church at Voth, a town between Kountze and Beaumont. There he was shot and wounded when officers said he drew a pistol and resisted arrest.

The wounded Negro, unconscious, was taken to a hospital at Beaumont, but when officers received information a mob was forming at Kountze and starting toward Beaumont, they took the Negro away in an automobile, trying to protect him.

Without regaining consciousness or being able to make any statement as to his guilt or innocence, the Negro died as the car bearing him sped toward Vidor, six miles east of Beaumont.

211

The body was taken to Silsbee, another small town in the vicinity by Sheriff Miles Jordan of Hardin County.

On learning of these developments, the mob, slowly increasing in size, trailed the sheriff to Silsbee, took the body from him, tied it behind an automobile with chains, and dragged it for thirty-five minutes through the Negro section of Kountze to terrorize the negro population.

Members of the mob of approximately 300, cut out the Negro's heart and sexual organs before casting it to the flames.

NEW YORK TIMES
December 16, 1933

CLEARED BY JURY, THEN LYNCHED

COLUMBIA, Tenn., Dec. 15—Cord Cheeck, 20, a Negro, was found hanging from the limb of a cedar tree near here tonight. He was lynched following refusal of a Grand Jury to indict him for molesting an eleven-year-old white girl.

NEW YORK WORLD-TELEGRAM
December 26, 1933

SURVIVOR OF LA. LYNCHING
TELLS OF HIS ORDEAL

A story of being hanged by a Louisiana mob and of surviving the ordeal was told here yesterday by Norman Thibodeaux, 19-year-old Negro of New Orleans.

Another Negro lynched by the same mob was less fortunate. He did not survive. A white man afterwards confessed the murder of the white girl which inspired the lynchings.

"Ah tol' 'em Ah was innocent," Norman said. "They beat me worser yet. Ah couldn't breathe, and my eyes was poppin' out . . ."

Norman arrived here yesterday on funds furnished by the International Labor Defense and will tell his story

Thursday night at a mass meeting against lynching in Temple Baptist Church, 269 Lenox Ave.

A soft-voiced, readily smiling Negro, Norman was reared in New Orleans by his grandmother and went through the ninth grade at public school. Smoking cigarets incessantly, he told of the necktie party today in the I. L. D. offices.

"Ah went up to Labadieville to visit my other grandmother," he said. "It was on the 11th of October. When Ah got there I hear about this white girl, she been found dead in the canefield.

"They arrested this boy Freddy Moore and Wednesday night some mens take him and say they goin' hang him. They torture him and he say a Negro boy named Norman Jackson help him kill the white girl. Ain't no Norman Jackson, but my name is Norman an' they come for me.

"Seven mens come at three in the morning an' they say, 'Git up, nigger, an' put on your clothes.'

"The Sheriff, Ferdinand Richards, was leadin' the mob an' when Ah doan put on mah clothes fast enough the Sheriff he beats me with his gun."

Norman lowered his head, pointed to still obvious bruises and discolorations, and continued:—

"Ah'll tell you jus' how they did. They wouldn't let me put on only my pants and shirt and they was beating me an' cursing.

"They said they'd show me my pal hanging an' they said, 'Nigger, you went after a white woman,' an' I said I didn't know nothin' about it.

"They took me down to the bridge in a car an' sixty or seventy mens yanked me out an' they was beating me with guns an' they fists.

"They say if Ah tell 'em I did it they let me go, but I just say Ah is innocent an' Ah didn't plead nor nothin'. They said Ah helped Freddy Moore kill this woman, an' Freddy was hanging there, tortured. He was dead.

"One of these mens says 'let's hang this nigger an' be done with it,' an' another mans says, 'No, we hung one nigger, let's burn this one.'

"They decides to hang me an' one white boy gets a brand new rope. Ah was bleeding bad.

"They makes a loop in the rope, an' puts it aroan mah

213

neck an' throws one end to a fellow standing on the bridge right next to where Freddy Moore was hanging.

"They starts to pull me up an' Ah says to the last Ah is innocent but that don't do no good.

"They pulls me up in the air, and Ah couldn't breathe an' mah eyes was popping. Ah felt bad.

"Then this bridge tender—he name Cadeux—he say 'cut that nigger down, he just got here.' An' he son climb up on the bridge an' cut the rope an' Ah fell down almost unconscious.

"How it feel? How would you feel? Ah didn't want to stay up there no mo'.

"Well, the Sheriff, he grab me an' put me in a car with two other mens an they drive ten miles down a back road to Valencennes in the dark an' they stop longside a cane field an' Sheriff, he say, 'git out, nigger.'

"Ah gits out an' Ah walks 'bout twenty feet an' Ah hears the Sheriff holler, 'run, nigger.'

"Ah starts a running an' they starts shooting at me. Ah hears them bullets singing close to mah head as Ah runs.

"Ah stumbled an' fell in the cane an' I hears Sheriff say, 'come on, boys, we got that nigger,' an' they drive off.

"Ah lays there bleeding for a long time. Its dark, an' ah gets frightened. Ah gets sorta nervous with what's happened to me an' Ah gets afraid.

"Finally, Ah crawls across the cane an' gets to a colored lady's house an' she lets me hide till her son goes to work an' then she put me out. She says 'Git out. Ah doan want the sheriff comin here.'

"Ah goes to mah uncle's house an' hides in the corncrib all day an' he say 'yuh beter git away from here,' an' Ah tell him Ah just gotta see grandmother because she think they done killed me.

"Come night Ah went to the house of a gal Ah knows an' she get my grandmother. My grandmother, she ben crying all day because they tell her they'll find mah body in the cane in a day or so."

Norman's grandmother gave him clothes, money. That night he walked twenty miles to another town and caught a train for New Orleans.

In New Orleans he was arrested as a suspect in the

murder at the request of "the high sheriff" when he went to a hospital to have his wounds dressed.

He was not released until two weeks later, when the stepfather of the murdered girl—Ella La Rose—confessed he had killed her.

NEW YORK TIMES
December 27, 1933

TERMS LYNCH SURVIVOR "LIAR"

NEW ORLEANS, Dec. 26—Sheriff L. H. Himel of Assumption Parish tonight characterized as a "malicious lie" a statement attributed to Norman Thibodeaux, Negro, who was whipped and nearly hanged by a mob which a short time earlier had hanged Freddy Moore, Negro murder suspect. He warned Thibodeaux never to "put foot in this here Parish again."

Thibodeaux has been quoted in a number of northern newspapers as saying that the stepfather of Annie Mae Larose, who was found murdered in a cane field near Labadieville on Oct. 11, had confessed to the slaying of the girl but that the sheriff had not arrested him.

BIRMINGHAM (ALABAMA) POST
June 9, 1934

MOB VIOLENCE DEALT TO PAIR

CLARKSDALE, Miss., June 9—Two bodies hanging from a rickety wooden trestle three miles east of Lambert, Miss., this morning gave mute witness to Mississippi justice.

The bodies were those of Joe Love and Isaac Thomas, negroes, lynched at sundown, yesterday. The bodies were left hanging all night on orders of Greek Rice, district attorney. An inquest was held at the spot this morning. A verdict of "death at the hands of persons unknown" was returned.

Torn from the custody of Mississippi officers near

Hushpuckena at 6 o'clock last night, the negroes were dead an hour later. More than 150 men were in the mob that stopped the officers. They brandished guns, and disarmed the officers.

One of the negroes' ears was chopped from his head, before he died. They are said to have confessed an attempted assault on a Mississippi planter's wife.

DUBOIS (PENNSYLVANIA) EXPRESS
June 9, 1934

EYEWITNESS TELLS OF LYNCHING

CLARKSDALE, Miss., June 9—Despite the reluctance of witnesses to openly discuss the lynching of two Mississippi negroes that took place here yesterday, the local newspaper was able to secure the following eye-witness account of the affair from a man who, nevertheless, refuses to give his name for fear of retaliation by townsmen:

I saw them hang two negroes last night.

The negroes screamed and prayed, but they died.

Just before they died they called on the Lord to help them.

"It won't do you no good to pray niggers, where you're goin," someone in the crowd shouted to them.

Some of the men wanted to cut them up. "We better not waste too much time," someone else said, " 'cause the sheriff will be along any time."

It was getting pretty dark when we got to a bridge over a small creek near Lambert. "Here is a good spot to get rid of them niggers," a fellow in the car with them said.

We all stopped. There must have been close to 200 men from around the neighborhood. The negroes were thrown out of the car. Ropes were tied around their necks.

They screamed louder.

"Cut out that crying you black So and So's," someone shouted.

One of the negroes was hit in the ear. He fell down.

"Oh Lordy, save me," he shouted. Someone kicked him. He got up swaying from side to side as if drunk.

The crowd dragged the negroes to the edge of the bridge.

"Push them off," a voice cried.

They were pushed.

Swinging down you could hear their necks crack. It made me right sick for a minute.

The bodies started swaying around, spinning back and forth.

Around and around they spun, sort of like two black tops on a string.

"Shall we cut them down now?" someone asked.

"Hell, no," another man said. "Leave them up there for crow-bait."

For a while no one said anything. Everybody just stood still and watched them swing. Finally we started movin' away. I went home. I couldn't eat no supper.

I still saw them bodies swinging.

GALVESTON (TEXAS) TRIBUNE
June 21, 1934

WHITE GIRL IS JAILED, NEGRO FRIEND IS LYNCHED

NEWTON, Tex., June 21—A negro charged with associating with a white girl here was lynched last night by a mob of 200 armed men who over-powered two deputy sheriffs who were taking him to another city for safe keeping.

The nude body of the negro, John Criggs, was found at 2 a. m. today in front of a box factory. He had been hanged and shot.

The deputies were halted on the highway 27 miles south of here. The officers were disarmed and a noose was thrown around the negro's neck as he sat in the officers' car.

The negro was jerked from the car. The officers were told to "get going." They drove away immediately.

Deputy Sheriffs D. W. Smith and W. E. Davison were ordered by Sheriff T. S. Hughes to spirit the negro from the old Newton county jail last night when a howling mob of men and women gathered outside.

"We told the negro the jail was about to be stormed and that we were helpless," Smith said. "We asked him if he wanted to attempt to slip away and go to Orange with us.

"He accepted gladly."

The negro, crying frantically, was given a coat and hastened out the rear door of the jail to an awaiting automobile.

Smith said that about 27 miles from Newton the road was blocked by a mob of men standing eight men deep.

They were all armed with shotguns, rifles and pistols, Smith said.

As soon as the auto was stopped, Smith said other men came from the side of the road and the car was surrounded.

"I tried to plead with the men not to take the negro," Smith said, "but they jerked me from the car and took my gun. Davison got the same treatment.

"After they took the negro from the car they told us to get moving. There was nothing else we could do."

Griggs had been in jail for over a week on a charge of associating with a white woman. The woman had also been arrested and is still in jail on a charge of vagrancy. Her name is given as Joan Rivers, age 19.

Further details concerning the couple are vague. Some sources give Griggs' age as 38, others as 20. Some say they both worked in a local box factory, others say they attended the same Texas college.

FROM AN EDITORIAL IN THE
CHICAGO DEFENDER
June 29, 1934

COMMENTARY

In the state of Texas, a white woman may associate more freely with a dog than with a Negro.

NEW ORLEANS TRIBUNE
July 10, 1934

SUSPECT HANGED FROM OAK ON BASTROP PUBLIC SQUARE

BASTROP, La., July 9—A mob of 3,000 stormed the Morehouse parish jail tonight, dragged out Andrew McCloud, 26, Negro, suspected of attempting to assault a white girl, and hanged him to an oak tree in the public square.

The mob tore down a telephone pole intending to use it as a battering ram to gain entry to the jail. Three other Negroes imprisoned with McCloud were so badly frightened that one of them shouted out, "White folks; batter down the side of the building and we'll throw him out to you." This the mob proceeded to do.

Just then District Attorney Hawthoren arrived and made a speech. "I sympathize with your attitude, but I'm afraid you'll get into trouble," he said. "If you sympathize with us," one of the leaders shouted, "why don't you take off that straw hat and take a hold of this telephone pole?"

McCloud had been arrested Sunday, some hours after a white girl reported an attempted attack Saturday night. She and her escort were returning to Bastrop from a dance. Her escort had been drinking and he ran his car into a ditch. He was too intoxicated to go for help and the girl started out for a gasoline station on foot.

A Negro stepped out of the night, she said, and started to drag her into the woods. Before he could get her off the road, a car approached, frightening him away.

McCloud was later picked up at his home, twenty-five miles away.

After he was removed from jail by the mob, McCloud was taken to a tall oak on the village green. He was placed on top of a car, and a noose tied around his neck. The car was driven off. He fell with such force that the rope snapped. An unidentified man ran up with a knife and slit McCloud's throat from ear to ear. Nearly dead, he was strung up again. This time the rope held.

The lynching site was located across the street from a picture show where a horror film was playing. A number of women emerging from the theater saw the Negro hanging from the tree and fainted.

NEW YORK DAILY NEWS
July 11, 1934

BASTROP OFFICIALS YAWN OVER YESTERDAY'S LYNCHING

BASTROP, La., July 10—Parish authorities showed little interest today in the capture and punishment of a mob which lynched a colored man in the public square here last night. Sheriff J. F. Carpenter said he recognized none of his fellow townsmen in the mob. District Attorney F. W. Hawthoren, who had told the crowd he sympathized with its attitude, was non-committal.

ATLANTA CONSTITUTION
July 11, 1934

LYNCHED FOR "INDECENT" NOTE

BOLTON, Miss., July 16—Accused of writing an "indecent and insulting" letter to a young Hinds County white girl, James Sanders, 25-year-old negro, was riddled with bullets late today by a mob of armed citizens.

WASHINGTON TRIBUNE
September 1, 1934

ORIGIN OF WORD "LYNCH"

On Route 29, two miles north of Alta Vista, Virginia, stands an historical marker of the Virginia Highway Commission which tells the following story:

"One hundred yards west of here stands a walnut tree under which Colonel Charles Lynch held an informal court in 1870 for the trial of tories and criminals who were later whipped. This form of summary justice was first used by his brother, John Lynch, founder of Lynchburg. From this crude form of justice evolved the term 'Lynch Law.' It is claimed that John Lynch first used such methods of summary punishment to rid the neighborhood of escaped slaves."

MACON (GEORGIA) TELEGRAPH
October 26, 1934

BIG PREPARATION MADE FOR LYNCHING TONIGHT

GREENWOOD, Fla., Oct. 26—Local citizens have been preparing all day for the lynching of a negro scheduled to take place here tonight. This morning a mob seized Claude Neal, 23, from a jail in Brewton, Ala., where he had been held in connection with the murder of a white girl which took place here several days ago.

At noon a "Committee of Six" representing the mob announced a timetable for the lynching which was given in newspapers and over the radio as follows:

At sundown the negro will be taken to the farm two miles from here where Miss Lola Cannidy, the murder victim, lived. There he will be mutilated by the girl's father.

Then he will be brought to a pig-pen in the middle of a cotton field nearby, where the girl's body was found, and killed.

Finally his body will be brought to Marianna, the county seat, nine miles from here, and hung in the court house square for all to see.

The negro is presently being held at an undisclosed location in a swamp along the Chattahoochee River, not far from the Cannidy farm.

"All white folks are invited to the party," said the announcement issued by the mob's Committee of Six.

As a result, thousands of citizens have been congregating all afternoon at the Cannidy farm. Bonfires have been started, piles of sharp sticks have been prepared, knives have been sharpened and one woman has displayed a curry-comb with which she promises to torture the negro.

The crowd is said to have been addressed by a member of the Florida State Legislature who, in a humorous vein, promised that no one would be disappointed if the crowd maintained decorum.

Some misgivings are said to have been expressed by the Committee over the fact that the crowd is heavily armed and highly intoxicated. It is feared that shots aimed at the negro may go astray and injure innocent bystanders, who include some women with babes in arms.

During the early afternoon a party of men broke off from the crowd at the Cannidy farm and paid a visit to the cabin where Neal's family lives and burned it to the ground.

Early announcement of the lynching has had its repercussions outside the community. At Tallahassee, the Florida Council of the Association of Southern Women for the Prevention of Lynching has issued a strong appeal to law enforcement officials to do all within their power to prevent the mob from carrying out its plan. In Washington the Attorney General of the United States said that he was powerless to invoke the federal kidnapping law to rescue Neal because no ransom was involved.

In New York, Walter White, Secretary of the National Association for the Advancement of Colored People, sent a telegram to Florida's Governor David Sholtz urging him to "take immediate steps" to protect Neal. J. P. Newell, the Governor's Executive Secretary at Tallahassee, has replied that the Governor is "out of the capital" and can not be reached.

BIRMINGHAM (ALABAMA) POST
October 27, 1934

LYNCHING CARRIED OFF ALMOST AS ADVERTISED

MARIANNA, Fla., Oct. 27—The body of Claude Neal, 23, negro, confessed attacker and slayer of a white girl, swung from a tree on the courthouse lawn here today, victim of an enraged mob's vengeance.

A crowd of 100 men, women and children silently gazed

at the body, nude except for a sack reaching from waist to knee. The negro had been shot at least 50 times, burned with red hot irons and dragged through the streets behind an automobile.

An eye-witness to the lynching, which took place yesterday, said that Neal had been forced to mutilate himself before he died. The eye-witness gave the following account of the event which took place in a swamp beside the Chattahoochee River:

"Due to the large number of people who wanted to lynch the nigger, it was decided to do away with him first and then bring him to the Cannidy house dead. First they cut off his penis. He was made to eat it. Then they cut off his testicles and made him eat them and say he liked it.

"Then they sliced his sides and stomach with knives and every now and then somebody would cut off a finger or toe. Red hot irons were used on the nigger to burn him from top to bottom. From time to time during the torture a rope would be tied around Neal's neck and he was pulled up over a limb and held there until he almost choked to death, when he would be let down and the torture begun all over again. After several hours of this punishment, they decided just to kill him."

"Neal's body was tied to a rope on the rear of an automobile and dragged over the highway to the Cannidy home. Here a mob estimated to number somewhere between 3,000 and 7,000 people from eleven southern states was excitedly waiting his arrival. When the car which was dragging Neal's body came in front of the Cannidy home, a man who was riding the rear bumper cut the rope.

"A woman came out of the Cannidy house and drove a butcher knife into his heart. Then the crowd came by and some kicked him and some drove their cars over him."

What remained of the body was brought by the mob to Marianna where it is now hanging from a tree on the northeast corner of the courthouse square.

Photographers say they will soon have pictures of the body for sale at fifty cents each. Fingers and toes from Neal's body are freely exhibited on street-corners here.

Neal is said to have confessed to attacking and killing

the white girl when he was first brought to jail for safe-keeping.

NEW YORK POST
October 27, 1934

FATHER FEELS DEPRIVED OF CHANCE TO KILL NEGRO

GREENWOOD, Fla., Oct. 27—A bent, little old man to-day stood on the porch of his simple farm home and said a mob "done me wrong" because it killed the Negro accused of attacking and killing his twenty-three-year-old daughter after assuring the old man that he would "have the first shot."

George Cannidy, his red beard belying but his stooped frame attesting his sixty-odd years, wept openly at every mention of "my girl" as he told how Miss Lola Cannidy, his daughter, left her farm home last week to be killed at a pigpen, half a mile away in a cotton patch.

Claude Neal, young Negro, who officers said confessed to the killing, was shot many times, his body mutilated with knives and taken to Marianna, the county seat, where it was strung up by the neck from a tree limb in the Courthouse Square.

"They done me wrong about the killing," said the aged father as he wept. "They promised me they would bring him up to my house before they killed him and let me have the first shot. That's what I wanted."

EDITORIAL IN THE CHICAGO DEFENDER
December 29, 1934

STRANGER THAN FICTION

The State of Maryland, as late as 1856, enacted a law that provided that a Negro convicted of murder should have his right arm cut off, his head severed, his body divided into four parts and that the head and quarters should then be set up in the most public place near where the crime was committed!

NEW YORK TIMES
January 13, 1935

MOB SUPERCEDES COURT RULING; KILLS NEGRO WHO WON APPEAL

FRANKLINTON, La., Jan. 11—A mob superseded the Supreme Court of Louisiana here today, entering the Washington parish jail and shooting to death a Negro whose conviction for murder was reversed Monday by the Louisiana Supreme Court on grounds that his trial was unfair.

ATLANTA CONSTITUTION
March 13, 1935

LYNCHED WITH HYMN ON LIPS

SLAYDEN, Miss., Mar. 12—Ab Young, a negro, was hanged to an oak tree in a schoolyard three miles east of here this afternoon by a mob of about 50 white men.

The negro had been sought in connection with the shooting to death Saturday night of Hardy Mackie, 45, a state highway worker.

He was placed atop a small coach automobile, with a rope around his neck. The other end of the rope was suspended to a tree. The car was driven out from under him and he was left dangling at the end of the rope.

He met death with a hymn upon his lips.

BALTIMORE AFRO-AMERICAN
March 16, 1935

LYNCHING TERMED A TYPE OF DIXIE SEX PERVERSION

NEW YORK, Mar. 15—An inherent hatred, born of the white man's chagrin at finding male ex-slaves finally in position to partially protect the women of their race against the habitual ravishment to which masters and overseers had subjected them, forms the basis for the sex perversion responsible for Southern lynchings.

A well known psychologist says: "Much that is commonly stigmatized as cruelty is a perversion of the sex instinct. This perversion, technically known as sadism, occurs chiefly in males. Here the causing of pain or the sight of blood, is a direct satisfaction of sexual impulse." It is well to note that it is the white males of the South that display such ferocious hatred and inflict such brutal tortures. While five thousand men have been lynched, less than a dozen women have suffered a similar fate.

Whenever it is announced or claimed by any white person that a man has committed, or attempted to commit rape, or has become impertinent in any way to any white person, that announcement angers the sadist.

It causes a superfluous amount of hormones to flow out of the adrenal gland into the blood and through the pituitary gland to the brain cortex, and immediately the mind of the sadist becomes inflamed and frenzied.

The conscious and the sub-conscious complexes engage in a terrific conflict, during which time the sadist becomes a raving maniac and reason is dethroned.

The writer once saw a southern white man boastfully display a withered and dried-up right hand of a fourteen-year-old boy whom he had helped to lynch, and this gruesome souvenir was carried around in his pants pocket.

In the case of Claude Neal, a mob of Florida sadists tortured him for twenty-four hours, just as cats torture mice before killing them, castrating their victim, dismembering his genitals and stuffing them into his mouth to compel him to eat his own flesh.

There is no further need of a psychic research or a psychoanalysis to prove that Southern lynchings are caused by sex-urge sublimation.

BALTIMORE AFRO-AMERICAN
April 27, 1935

VISITED BY MOB AND SHOT; JURY RULES IT "SUICIDE"

HATTIESBURG, Miss., Apr. 24—On the night of March 25th, R. J. Tyrone, prosperous Negro farmer of Lawrence County, was found shot to pieces in the woods beside his house. He had been visited earlier by a mob of white men in connection with financial difficulties he was having with William Newton, a neighboring white farmer. Today a coroner's jury handed down a verdict that Tyrone had died as a result of "Suicide."

MACON (GEORGIA) TELEGRAPH
September 19, 1935

LYNCH MOB DECIDES CASE

OSFORD, Miss., Sept. 18—Ellwood Higginbotham, Negro on trial here for the murder of a white man, was taken from the Lafayette county jail last night and lynched by a mob. He was seized while a jury was out deliberating his case.

NEW YORK HERALD-TRIBUNE
February 9, 1936

GETS 2 YEARS ON CHARGE HE LYNCHED NEGRO FOR

ST. JOSEPH, Mo., Feb. 8—Carl "Cowboy" Fisher, 25, attired in levis and carrying a ten-gallon hat, was today sentenced by the Circuit Court to two years in prison for attempted rape. Three years ago Fisher led a mob in the lynching of Lloyd Warner, Negro, whom Fisher had accused of the same crime.

LYNCHED JUST BEFORE TRIAL

ROYSTON, Ga., Apr. 28—Lint Shaw, burly negro farmer once saved from lynching through the pleadings of an aged judge was shot to death by a mob of forty men eight hours before he was to have gone to trial on a charge of attempted criminal assault today.

His body was found at dawn, tied to a pine tree in a creek bottom near Colbert, Ga., his home.

Pierced by shotgun, pistol and rifle bullets, he died at the scene where two white girls reported he attempted to attack them after their motor car broke down April 10.

The mob, climaxing a series of demonstrations against the 45-year-old negro which once required the intervention of national guardsmen, broke into Royston's one-story jail about midnight, cornered Night Chief of Police W. A. Dickerson and smashed a lock on the prisoner's cell.

"I couldn't see exactly what happened," Dickerson said. "They just told me they wanted the negro. He didn't say a word when they dragged him out."

Plowlines, cotton ropes used for guiding work animals in the fields, were cut up to tie the negro to the tree.

The jail here was the third in which he had been held since he was identified by the girls as the man who pursued them with a knife and threw one into a gulley. The assailant was frightened away by their screams.

First he was taken to jail at Danielsville, Ga.

A mob of 100 men formed there and battered some bricks from the jail in an attempt to reach him.

Superior Judge Berry T. Moseley, 74, left a sickbed to warn the throng against a lynching, and deterred the leaders until a national guard unit, rushed to that city from tornado emergency duty at Gainesville, Ga., took the negro in custody.

"Stop violating the law by breaking into jail," warned the judge.

At Judge Moseley's suggestion, Sheriff T. L. Henley

deputized several members of the crowd to help keep order.

From Danielsville Shaw was taken to Atlanta, to save him from further mob outbreaks. He was returned to Danielsville last night to await trial before Judge Moseley, but a threatening crowd caused Sheriff Henley to move him to this city.

Inflamed citizens learned of the transfer and followed. Several hours after the lynching Shaw still was bound to the tree as throngs assembled on the nearby highway.

Terrified members of the negro's family refused to claim the body.

NEW YORK POST
June 18, 1936

FRUSTRATED LYNCH MOB BURNS DOWN WHITE'S CAFE

EL CAMPO, Tex., June 18—A mob of about 300 persons, balked by State Rangers in an attempt to lynch five Negro men and four Negro women who are being held here in connection with a slaying, gave vent to its frustration today by burning down a cafe in which the slaying took place. The cafe owner, a white man, had nothing to do with the slaying.

NEW YORK TIMES
April 14, 1937

MISS. LYNCHERS TORTURE, BURN 2 NEGROES ON TRIAL

WINONA, Miss., April 13—Two Negroes were tortured and lynched by a mob of more than 100 white men near Duck Hill this afternoon within two hours after they had pleaded innocent in Montgomery County Circuit Court to a charge of murdering a white man.

A third Negro, suspected by the mob of complicity in the slaying of George Windham, a country storekeeper, was severely whipped and run out of the county after narrowly escaping the fate of the other two Negroes.

Roosevelt Townes, who had confessed, Sheriff E. E. Wright said, that he shot Windham, was tied to a tree near his victim's store and tortured slowly to death with flames from a blow-torch.

A Negro identified only as "Bootjack" McDaniels, indicted with Townes in the Windham slaying, was shot by members of the mob and his body burned.

Townes and McDaniels were taken from Sheriff Wright and two deputies early this afternoon as they were being led from the court house to be returned to the jail to await trial Thursday.

The Negroes were handcuffed and placed in a waiting school bus. Members of the mob piled into the bus and others into automobiles. The caravan sped northward toward Duck Hill as the Negroes screamed for mercy. The bus stopped near the small country store where Windham was fatally shot through a window one night last December. The Negroes were tied to a tree and tortured.

Townes' eyes were gouged out with an ice pick and a blow torch was applied to parts of his body before he died.

McDaniels was flogged by members of the mob who took turns with a chain and a horsewhip. Still alive, he was riddled with buckshot.

Everett Dorroh, Negro farmer, happened to be passing the scene and was attracted by the crowd. Before he had fathomed what was going on or had had a chance to leave, he was named by someone in the mob as an accomplice in the white man's murder.

Dorroh was flogged and told to run. Buckshot was fired at him and some entered his leg but he somehow managed to escape with his life.

"This terrible thing will be immediately investigated by the grand jury," said Circuit Judge John F. Allen of Kosciusko, who was presiding at the regular criminal term of Circuit Court here when the Negroes were arraigned.

Judge Allen said he would hold a conference with the District Attorney and plans for investigating the double lynchings would be made immediately.

JACKSON, Miss., Apr. 13—"We are justly proud of the fact that Mississippi has not had a lynching in fifteen months," Governor Hugh White boasted in an address before the Farm Chemurgic Conference here this afternoon.

A minute later he was called from the conference to learn from his secretary that two Negroes had just been lynched at Duck Hill.

NEW YORK POST
May 25, 1937

GIRLS IN TEENS TAKE PART IN RAID ON FUNERAL HOME

BAINBRIDGE, Ga., May 25—Because police had killed Willie Reid, twenty-four, Negro, alleged murderer and rapist, a mob couldn't lynch him. But it broke into a mortuary, hauled his body off to the ball park and there burned it. Women and some girls in their teens were among its members.

The informal incineration occurred last night and until dawn today the embers of the pine boards that had been the ball park fence glowed against the night sky. The incinerators acted openly, even invited photographers to make pictures of the blazing pyre in which the dead body could be discerned with difficulty. They looked upon it as an object lesson.

The chain of events began last Friday when Mrs. Ruby Hurst, thirty, and Rita Mae Richards, sixteen, disappeared. Mrs. Hurst's body was found Saturday on the outskirts of town. She had been killed apparently by a hatchet and ice pick. Sunday it became known that Miss Richards had been seen with her Friday and a renewed search yielded Miss Richard's body, mutilated with the same type of wounds, 400 yards from where Mrs. Hurst's body was found. Miss Richards had been subjected to criminal assault; Mrs. Hurst had not been.

Soon afterward authorities went to Dothan, Ala., and there, in the attic of a Negro home, found Reid. According to Deputy Sheriffs H. C. Pollard and R. A. Stephens, Reid confessed.

The deputies knew that news of the capture preceded them and in order to stave off the possibility of mob violence they started with their prisoner toward a mob proof jail at Albayn, Ga. Before they reached Albany Reid was killed.

"Near the Georgia line," Stephens said, "the Negro suddenly leaped from the car. We opened fire instantly. He must have been struck by ten or twelve bullets. He was dead when we got him."

Stephens and Pollard brought the body to a mortuary. Soon afterward a car loaded with white men appeared, then another and another and another. The leaders went in, carried out the body and dumped it into a car and the motorcade drove on.

With every horn blowing continuously, the progression moved through town. Onlookers saw that some cars were driven by women, that women were their only passengers. Others seemed to carry family groups, a father, a mother and girls in their teens. More and more cars were joining and by the time it reached the ball park, it was estimated to number seventy-five cars.

Men climbed out, the boards of the ball field fence were pulled off and piled up. The women assisted. Then the body was thrown on and in an instant a great fire was roaring, illuminating the intense emotion-choked faces of the incinerators.

NEW YORK TIMES
June 5, 1937

"WRONG MAN WAS LYNCHED," ALABAMA JURY WAS TOLD

MONTGOMERY, Ala., June 4—A jury hearing the impeachment trial of Sheriff J. L. Corbitt, charged with failing to protect a Negro from a mob, was told today the mob "lynched the wrong Negro."

Wesley Johnson, Negro, accused of attacking a white woman, was taken from the Henry County jail on Feb. 1, hanged to a tree and shot.

Attorney General A. A. Carmichael told the court "we will be able to prove, beyond all reasonable doubt, that the popular indignation was so great that the Sheriff was forced to arrest the wrong Negro."

Later Mr. Carmichael called the woman whom Johnson was accused by warrant of assaulting to show that the alleged incident occurred "at 11:15 A. M."

Then John H. Oates, Henry County road supervisor and former employer of Johnson, testified he saw the Negro on the day of the alleged assault "about noon—a little before noon."

NEW YORK TIMES
November 22, 1938

ALLEGED ATTACK ON WOMAN, 74, LEADS TO LYNCHING OF YOUTH

WIGGINS, Miss., Nov.. 21—Wilder McGowan, 24-year-old Negro, was lynched today by a mob of about 200 white men who had trailed him several hours with bloodhounds after a 74-year-old white woman allegedly was criminally attacked and robbed.

Sheriff S. C. Hinton said the mob seized the Negro while he and his deputies were six miles away.

The elderly woman, according to Sheriff Hinton, was alone in her home last night when a Negro broke in the door and attacked her.

"The woman," the Sheriff said, "furnished a description but could not name the Negro who raped and robbed her. I don't believe the woman, in spite of her years, is in a serious condition. She is the mother of a Wiggins physician and is a member of a socially prominent family."

The Sheriff said he did not know where or how the youth had been found by the mob, which grew from eight men in the early morning hours to about 200 at daylight,. when the Negro was hanged from a tree beside a highway.

One man said the mob found the Negro preparing to leave for Gulfport, dragged him away and strung him up.

PHILADELPHIA TRIBUNE
December 15, 1938

NAACP SAYS RAPE CHARGE WAS MERELY A PRETEXT

NEW YORK, Dec. 13—An investigation by the N. A. A. C. P. proved, last week that Wilder McGowan, who was lynched in Wiggins, Miss. on November 21, was innocent of any crime.

The lynching of McGowan, the NAACP reported, was the culmination of the "pent-up-anger of whites against an innocent Negro who had refused on numerous occasions in the past to accommodate himself to the attempt of white ruffians to frighten colored citizens.

McGowan was lynched after members of a mob accused him of attacking an elderly white woman on Sunday, November 20. The woman said according to reports, that she was attacked by a "light-colored Negro with slick hair."

McGowan is a man of dark complexion and, the NAACP report said, was not in the vicinity when the alleged attack occurred.

NEW YORK TIMES
May 10, 1940

SOUTH GOES WHOLE YEAR WITHOUT SINGLE LYNCHING

ATLANTA, May 9—The modern South ended its first year without a lynching last midnight, and today a foe of mob rule credited this new record to effective education, plus swift work of police radio patrols.

Mrs. Jessie Daniel Ames, executive secretary of the Association of Southern Women for the Prevention of Lynching, said midnight marked the close of the first twelve-month lynchless period since tabulations were started in 1882.

In contrast to this is the peak mark of 231 mob killings recorded in 1892.

Mrs. Ames said swift action made possible by police radio alarm systems, particularly as used by highly mobile State trooper units, was an efficient and relatively new technique in combating mobs.

She declared the twelve months just past, and the previous year's record of only three lynchings, represented the fruits of long years of campaigning to bring about "lynch-consciousness." Formerly, she said, lynchings were "hushed up" and therefore soon forgotten.

"Now, however, we get the facts and see that they are publicized," she added. "When we hear a lynch-mob has assembled, we make a direct appeal to law enforcement officials, so that a lynching cannot take place without the authorities knowing of it."

The association, representing about 41,000 Southern women and now in its tenth year, Mrs. Ames said, campaigned especially against public opinion that has "accepted too easily the claim of lynchers that they acted solely in the defense of women."

Of the previous year's three lynchings, she asserted, none involved a crime against women.

NEW YORK POST
May 13, 1941

FLORIDA KILLERS DRAG NEGRO FROM AMBULANCE

QUINCY, Fla., May 13—The body of A. C. Williams, 22, Negro charged with assaulting a 12-year-old white girl, was found on a bridge five miles north of here today, several hours after he had been abducted from authorities for the second time. He had been shot to death.

Williams was taken from the Gadsden County jail last night by four white men. Later he was found in the home of another Negro with several bullet wounds in his body, and suffering from a beating about the head. His assailants apparently thought he had been killed.

Sheriff Luten had Williams placed in an ambulance for

transportation to a Tallahassee, Fla., hospital, after a physician said he had a good chance to recover.

The ambulance left without guards after the sheriff said he did not "anticipate any more trouble," and on the way was stopped by "a group of persons" who took Williams from the vehicle.

Will Webb, Negro driver of the ambulance, said the vehicle was halted by "four or five men," and the wounded man was pulled out and taken away.

"One of them said they wanted the man I had in the ambulance and they didn't want any trouble," he said. I told them they wouldn't get any trouble out of me, because I didn't even have a pocket knife.

He said he did not recognize any of the men.

NEW YORK AMSTERDAM NEWS
August 26, 1944

MISS. MINISTER LYNCHED

NEW ORLEANS, Aug. 20—A lynch-killing of a 66-year-old minister last March 26 in Amite county, Miss., because he hired a lawyer to safeguard his title to a 220-acre debt-free farm, has just been revealed in an affidavit sworn to by Eldridge Simmons, son of the murdered man.

Rev. Isaac Simmons was going peacefully about the business of running his farm and had no trouble until it began to be suspected that there was oil on his land. Whites then tried to "muscle in" and take his property away. When they found he had consulted a lawyer, they got together a small mob and killed him in the presence of his son, who was later driven from the county.

Eldridge Simmons sent his affidavit to the NAACP in New York which in turn has asked Governor Thomas L. Bailey of Mississippi to investigate. The NAACP also has asked Attorney General Francis Biddle to examine into the possibility that Federal conspiracy statues have been violated.

The dramatic story of the lynching is told in the following paragraphs from the affidavit:

"Between 11 a. m. and 12 o'clock noon, March 26, 1944—which was on a Sunday—a group of white men including Noble Thompson, two of his brothers, Harper Eliot, Rabbit Hastings, and a man I did not know, came to my house which is located about a mile from my father's house, both being on property owned by us.

"The men asked me if I knew how the property line ran. I told them I thought I did. They told me to come and show them.

"I went down the road with them for some distance then we came to a car. The car was a late model Studebaker, I believe, with the gear shift on the steering wheel. It was grayish in color.

"I got in the back seat of the car and they drove about a quarter of a mile from my father's house. The man I didn't know did the driving. They kept telling me that my father and I were 'smart niggers' for going to see a lawyer.

"Three of them remained in the car with me; three walked up to my father's house.

"Some time later, I saw the three men returning with my father. They were Noble Thompson, Harper Eliot, and another man.

"Noble Thompson and the other man were walking on either side of my 66-year-old father, Isaac Simmons, while Eliot walked behind him kicking and punching him.

"When they reached the car, they made my father get in the front seat. They all got in the car.

"My father begged them and prayed with them not to hurt him or me as they drove down the road. Two of them kept beating me as I sat in the back seat.

"Some distance down the road they stopped the car near a side road where there were lots of thickets. 'Let's take them down here,' one of the white men said.

"They told my father to get out of the car. He got out and started to run from the road. One of the men leveled the shotgun and fired twice at my father. One reloaded the gun, the other two ran in the direction my father had taken. The man who reloaded the gun ran off in that direction also, then I heard another shot. I begged the men in the car to spare my life.

"A while later, the other three returned. They all talked in low tones behind the car.

"Finally, they came around and told me, 'All right, nigger, we're going to let you go.'

"One of them told me to get out of the car; another said, 'I'll tell him when to get out.'

"Noble Thompson asked me 'You don't want to get beat up any more, do you?'

"I answered, 'I sure don't.'

"He said, 'If this comes up again, you had better not know anything about it.'

"They told me that they gave me ten days to get off the place and clear off my tenants. I had two tenants, Willie Huff, and A. B. Robinson, who worked for me. And also an old man, S. B. Moton, who had no other place to stay.

"When they put me out of the car, I was bloody, ragged and half-blinded. I went to my sister's house and told what had happened.

"The news spread. Church meetings broke up and we all went down to where my father lay in the thickets. That was about 1 o'clock p. m.

"When we got to the thickets, we saw my father dead, lying half on his side. He had been shot three times in the back and some one said his arm was broken. Nearly all of his teeth had been knocked out, and his tongue was cut out.

"Some one went and got Constable George Hazelwood. The constable went and got the high sheriff.

"They held an inquest and gave the verdict that my father had met his death at the hands of unknown parties."

NEW YORK TIMES
July 27, 1946

GEORGIA MOB MASSACRES TWO NEGROES AND WIVES

MONROE, Ga., July 26—Two young Negroes, one a veteran just returned from the war, and their wives were lined up last night near a secluded road and shot dead by an unmasked band of twenty white men.

The ghastly details of the multiple lynching were told

238

today by Loy Harrison, a well-to-do white farmer who had just hired the Negroes to work on his farm. Harrison was bringing the Negroes to his farm when his car was waylaid by the mob eight miles from Monroe. Questioning of one of the Negroes by the mob indicated, Harrison said, that he was suspected of having stabbed his former employer, a white man. The Negroes, Roger Malcolm and George Dorsey, both 27, were removed from the car and led down a side road.

The women, who were sisters and who had just recently married Malcolm and Dorsey, began to scream. Then a mob member said that one of the women had recognized him.

"Get those damned women, too," the mob leader shouted.

Several of the men then came back and dragged the shrieking women from the automobile. A few moments later Mr. Harrison heard the shots—many of them and the mob dispersed.

The grotesquely sprawled bodies were found in a clump of bushes beside a little-used sideroad, the upper parts of the bodies scarcely recognizable from the mass of bullet holes.

Dorsey's mother, Monia Williams, said that her son had just been discharged after five years in the Army and that she had received his discharge button in the mail just this week.

The lynching was the first in the nation in nearly a year and was the first multiple lynching since two 14-year-old Negro boys were hanged by a Mississippi mob in October, 1942. For Georgia it was the first lynching of more than one person since 1918 when ten Negroes were lynched in Brooks County.

NEW YORK TIMES
July 29, 1946

RELATIVES SHUN FUNERAL OF NEGROES LYNCHED IN GA.

MONROE, Ga., July 28—Close relatives of two of the four Negroes killed by a white mob here Thursday failed

239

to appear at funeral services today and friends voice the belief that they were "too frightened" to appear.

EDITORIAL FROM THE WASHINGTON POST
January 2, 1954

END OF LYNCHING

One of the best year-end news items has come out of Tuskegee Institute. For two successive years the Nation has had no lynching. At least for the present the blot that had so long stained the American record and poisoned the relations between the white and colored races has been lifted. While Tuskegee will continue to compile lynching statistics, its president, Dr. L. H. Foster, reports realistically that its annual report on this subject has had its significance as a yardstick of race relations.

The current report will be especially gratifying to those who have believed that the states, themselves, under the impact of an aroused public opinion, could wipe out this especially heinous type of crime. To be sure, there are still would-be lynchers in the South and in other parts of the country. Lynchings were prevented last year in Alabama, New York and Arizona. But law enforcement is always a matter of eternal vigilance. There is good reason to believe that, having wiped out this offense to American civilization, the states will continue to maintain their new record.

WASHINGTON POST-TIMES-HERALD
September 1, 1955

15-YEAR-OLD IS LYNCHED; WOLF-WHISTLED AT WHITE

GREENWOOD, Miss., Aug. 31—The body of a 15-year-old Chicago Negro who had disappeared after he allegedly made "fresh" remarks to a white woman was found floating in the Tallahatchie River today. He had been shot through the head. Two white men, one of them the husband of the woman allegedly insulted by the boy, earlier had been charged with kidnaping the victim, Emmett Till, from the home of his relatives here.

In New York, Roy Wilkins, executive secretary of the National Association for the Advancement of Colored People, branded the slaying a "lynching."

A 125-pound cotton-gin blower had been tied to the boy's neck to make his body sink but his feet floated to the surface, leading to the discovery. A coroner's jury ruled that death was due to the gunshot in the temple. In addition to the bullet wound, the top of Till's head was smashed, the medical examination disclosed.

Leflore County authorities had charged Roy Bryant, a white storekeeper in the nearby Money community, and his half-brother, W. J. Milan, with kidnapping Till. Sheriff George Smith said the boy was abducted because of the allegedly insulting remarks made to Mrs. Bryant in the Bryants' country store the night before.

Bryant and Milan, however, told police they released the boy unharmed after Mrs. Bryant told them he was "not the one" who had made offensive remarks to her.

The Bryants were said to have become offended when Till, who had visited the store with other teen-agers, spoke to Mrs. Bryant and waved "good-by."

Some bystanders said that Till had sounded the two notes of the wolf whistle at Mrs. Bryant.

While the NAACP called on the Government and Gov. Hugh White to take quick action in the case, the Governor said at Jackson he had not heard from anyone about the Till boy's death. Referring to the NAACP, he said: "They're in the press all the time, that gang."

ATLANTA CONSTITUTION
September 22, 1955

WITNESS ACCUSES TWO MEN OF TILL KIDNAP-SLAYING

SUMNER, Miss., Sept. 21—Moses Wright, 64-year-old Negro sharecropper, took the witness stand today and pointed out two Mississippi white men as the kidnappers of his slain nephew, 14-year-old Emmett Louis Till of Chicago.

In the dramatic setting of a Deep South courtroom packed with Negroes and whites occupying segregated sections, the elderly cotton farmer twice rose from the witness chair and singled out the defendants, Roy Bryant, 24, and his half brother, J. W. Milam, 36, with the words "There he is, that's the man."

Today marked the beginning of testimony by witnesses in the case of the Till kidnap-slaying.

Dressed in black trousers, white shirt, white suspenders and dark blue tie with light blue stripes, Wright settled in the witness chair and pulled nervously at long fingers which he alternately cupped to his mouth or waved in the air to illustrate his words.

Throughout his testimony, the witness was called "Uncle Mose" by the prosecution attorneys, and simply "Mose" by the defense lawyers. In turn, Wright answered the prosecution with "yes sir," and the defense examiners with "that's right, that's right."

With few preliminaries, Wright launched into the story of the kidnaping, which reportedly took place about 2 a.m., Aug. 28, a Sunday. He said he was sleeping with his wife, Elizabeth, in one room and that Emmett Till was sleeping in another room with Wright's son, Simeon, 10.

The witness said he was awakened by someone at the door shouting, "Preacher, preacher." Wright is known as "Preacher" in the neighborhood of Money, a small farming community in adjoining Leflore County, some three miles west of Wright's cabin home.

Wright said he went to the door and a man's voice said, "I want to talk with you, I'm Mr. Bryant." He said he opened the door and a man entered with a pistol in his right hand and a flashlight in his left. Wright said he did not turn on the lights of his house and that it was dark at the time.

He said the man with the pistol and flashlight, subsequently identified by Wright as Milam, said, "I want that boy who dirty-talked at Money."

It had been alleged that Emmett Till "wolf-whistled" and made some "ugly remarks" to Bryant's 21-year-old wife, Carolyn, while she was alone on Aug. 25, in a grocery store her husband owns at Money.

Wright described how two men went with him to Till's

bed while a third man remained on the cabin porch with his head "bent like he was hiding." Asked if the man with the bowed head was "a Negro," Wright said "he acted like he was a colored man."

Wright said the man with the flashlight directed Till to dress and accompany the intruder. He said that on the way out of the cabin, Mrs. Wright said, "We will pay you if you let the boy go," and that one of the men said, "You get back in that bed and I'll want to hear those springs."

Wright said the three men and the boy went outside to a nearby tree. He said he heard "what seems like a little voice, lighter than a man's," say something and then the group drove toward Money in a car.

Wright said he stood at a screen door for about 20 minutes but Emmett never returned. He said he took his car to get some gasoline and drove away from his home with his wife.

The witness said he next saw Emmett on Aug. 31, when the youth's body, with head bludgeoned and shot, was recovered from a river in Tallahachie County.

Wright said he was taken to the river side by a deputy sheriff of Leflore County and that he identified the body as that of his nephew. He said he was wearing a large silver ring which had belonged to Emmett's father killed in World War II.

BIRMINGHAM (ALABAMA) WORLD
September 27, 1955

TWO CLEARED IN TILL CASE

SUMNER, Miss., Sept. 24—Since before the turn of the twentieth century no white man in Mississippi has been given the death penalty for killing a Negro and here Friday evening the state's approximately 65 year record was kept intact when an all white Tallahatchie county jury found Roy Bryant and J. W. Milam, the defendants in the nationwide publicized "wolf whistle" trial, not guilty.

MONTGOMERY ADVERTISER

April 26, 1959

4,733 MOB ACTION VICTIMS SINCE '82, TUSKEGEE REPORTS

TUSKEGEE, Ala., Apr. 25—While lynchings have about reached the vanishing point in recent years, Tuskegee Institute records show 4,733 persons have died from mob action since 1882.

Except for 1955, when three lynchings were reported in Mississippi, none has been recorded at Tuskegee since 1951. In 1945, 1947, and 1951 only one case per year was reported.

The most recent case reported by the institute as a lynching was that of Emmett Till, 14, a Negro who was beaten, shot to death and thrown into a river at Greenwood, Miss., Aug. 28, 1955. He was accused of making ugly remarks to or whistling at a white woman. Two white men were acquitted of his death after a trial which attracted international attention.

For a period of 65 years ending in 1947 at least one lynching was reported each year.

The most for any year was 231 in 1892.

From 1882 to 1901, lynchings averaged more than 150 a year.

Since 1924 lynchings have been on a marked decline, never more than 30 cases which occurred in 1926.

Among the incidents other than the Till case since 1944 are these:

George W. Lee, 51, Negro, shot to death May 7, 1955, at Bezoni, Humphreys County, Miss., after he refused to withdraw his name from voting list.

Lamar D. Smith, 63, Negro, shot down on lawn of Lincoln County Courthouse at Brookhaven, Miss., Aug. 6, 1955. Smith had been encouraging others of his race to qualify as voters.

MONTGOMERY ADVERTISER
June 7, 1959

WHEN IS MURDER LYNCHING

The recent mob murder of a rape suspect who was taken from a Mississippi jail raises a serious question of definitions:

What exactly is a lynching?

Tuskegee Institute, an all-Negro Alabama college, has become the authority on lynchings in the United States and is most frequently quoted by newspapers as listing just what killing is and what is not a lynching.

Tuskegee, which says that Mississippi has had four lynchings since 1952, gives this definition of it:

"There must be legal evidence that a person was killed. That person must have met death illegally. A group of three or more persons must have participated in the killing. The group must have acted under the pretext of service to justice, race or tradition."

BIRMINGHAM (ALABAMA) NEWS
March 8, 1960

NEGRO IS HANGED BY HEELS, K'S ARE CUT INTO HIS BODY

HOUSTON, Tex., Mar. 8—Four masked white youths hung a Negro man from a tree by his heels last night and carved two series of KKK's into his chest and stomach after beating him with chains, allegedly in reprisal for recent sit-in demonstrations by Negro students at Texas Southern University.

Felton Turner, 27-year-old unemployed awning worker told police that he was walking near his home in a Negro section at 10:15 last night when a car with four masked white youths pulled up, grabbed him and forced him to come with them. They drove to a wooded area where he was tied and hung from a tree by his heels. The youths beat him with chains, cut off his clothes and, with knives, slashed K's about three inches high into his stomach and chest.

One of the white youths said the wounds were in reprisal for sit-ins at lunch counters in Houston by Texas Southern University Negro students. A group of students from the all-Negro university staged their first sit-in Friday at a lunch counter in a supermarket. The sit-ins spread to a drugstore Saturday and a third store yesterday.

Police Lt. Breckenridge Porter said Turner's wounds could not have been self-inflicted.

BIRMINGHAM (ALABAMA) NEWS
May 22, 1961

BRICKS, PELLETS, GAS BOMBS FLY IN MONTGOMERY RIOTING

MONTGOMERY, Ala., May 22—Thugs bounced the car several times, then rolled it on its left side and finally all the way over.

A cheer went up from the mob, nearly 1500 strong.

"Let's burn the nigger-lover's car!" a woman screamed.

A dirty man in overalls tossed a lighted match and darted back into the crowd. Flames, and the roar of the mob, leaped high in the night.

A pickup truck loaded with concrete blocks pulled up. "Come on, boys," the driver shouted. "Here's you some ammunition!"

Man after man grabbed the blocks, broke them and ran off in different directions. As more U. S. marshals arrived, their cars were bombarded with the bricks and rocks. Negroes passing in cars were hit.

A band of whites moved toward the church. They began throwing their ammunition through the stained-glass windows.

The marshals formed a "wall of men" and advanced toward the mob. A tear-gas bomb was thrown into its midst. A teen-aged boy threw it back.

Another tear gas bomb was thrown. It struck a woman

in the back. She fell and was walked over by part of the mob trying to escape the gas.

A third bomb bounced along the street, onto a parking lot and underneath a car. Two small children in the car screamed for their parents as the choking gas poured in through open windows.

A photographer attempting to make pictures of the violence was mobbed. When last seen he was being dragged into the crowd by eight or nine men.

More Negroes in passing cars were stoned. Women were screaming, "go home, you dirty niggers."

City police moved into the mob when it became evident the marshals had lost control. Firemen turned stinging streams of water on the crowds.

The water split the mob into several small bands. The bands began running down the streets tossing bottles and stones through the windows of Negro homes.

Negroes watching the fracas from their porches were dragged into their yards, beaten and kicked.

An enraged Negro man ran across his porch to the bannister and fired a shotgun into the fleeing mob.

Pellets from the shotgun whistled above the heads of the crowds.

Highway patrolmen began arriving en masse on the scene. Sheriff's deputies were close behind. Civil defense workers with dogs moved into the riot area.

This was Sunday night in Montgomery.

For a second straight day, the mob was there. Curses, obscenities and yells were there.

There was one great difference between Sunday and Saturday.

The mob didn't win last night. It was finally run off.

Its ugliness, unruliness and threats toward a church full of Negroes didn't reach Saturday's velocity.

Make no mistake . . . terror gripped the capital.

But there to fight back were U. S. marshals, police, highway patrolmen—and finally National Guardsmen.

The situation began forming about 3 p.m. in a six-block area around the Negro First Baptist Church where the Rev. Ralph D. Abernathy is pastor.

The Rev. Martin Luther King and Negro integrationists, had called a press conference there. A few people were milling around outside.

247

But by 5 p.m. 50 to 60 cars had parked in the area, and several hundred people—Negro and white—had gathered. Negroes began arriving in the area in cars and pickup trucks. Whites walked onto the scene or drove up in carloads.

Between 7 and 8 p.m., marshals converged on the neighborhood and the park across from the church. They came in cars, pickup trucks and mail trucks.

Crowds jeered their arrival.

"Here come the nigger lovers," a woman screamed. "How much is the NAACP paying you to protect them dirty niggers?"

A man, his wife and two small children pushed through the crowd for a ringside view.

About 8:25 p.m., a group of white men, encouraged by screaming women, began bouncing a late model sedan in which some marshals had ridden.

Marshals dispersed them, however, so a larger force picked out another car. It belonged to a white minister who was inside the Negro church.

This one they turned over and set on fire.

The mob's momentum increased. It got the concrete-block ammunition.

A fire truck screamed into the area. Firemen failed at first to extinguish the blaze. A cheer went up.

A woman on the corner screamed to passing white motorists:

"Get out and fight with us if you are white!"

But when the mob advanced on the church—where the Negroes were in near panic—lawmen stopped them.

The mob didn't fight tear gas, riot guns and officers who finally meant business.

Firemen sprayed streams of water powerful enough to knock down a man.

Then arrived the highway patrolmen, sheriff's deputies, and also Civil Defense workers with dogs.

Cars were being turned over and set on fire in different parts of the city. Gang fights between Negroes and whites were being reported all over Montgomery.

Large crowds were reported gathering in the downtown area. It was reported hoodlums were smashing windows out of the Holiday Inn Motel.

The radio continuously announced beatings of Negroes by bands of whites. A house was reported set on fire by a band of white men.

At the scene of the house fire, someone had tossed a "Molotov cocktail" onto the roof of a house owned by James Peek, of 3886 Maclamar Rd.

Peek said it is the Ku Klux Klan's way of getting even with him for killing a Klansman two years ago.

Peek was armed with a machine gun.

Across town, a group of Negroes attempted to integrate the Municipal Airport cafeteria. They were turned out by sheriff's deputies, who told them, "The law is back on our side now."

Back at the first Baptist Church, Maj. Gen. Henry V. Graham had arrived.

He briskly greeted Mann and conferred about how to deploy National Guard troops which were en route to the church.

A city motorcycle scout roared into the crowd of lawmen and reported Negroes in the Negro federal housing project near the church were shooting at arriving guardsmen.

Graham rushed several blocks to the scene and quickly put a riot squad into action. The soldiers routed the snipers at bayonet point.

A group of Negro ministers left the church to go into the housing project area and urge Negroes to stay in their homes.

Inside the church, Martin Luther King told the Negroes the lawmen would be coming into the church soon to harass and arrest the "freedom riders."

A state official, acting on orders from Gov. John Patterson, abandoned plans to arrest the riders for ignoring a court injunction prohibiting them from riding buses in the integrated manner.

Gen. Graham ordered the Negroes in the church to remain inside until it was safe for them to return home.

At 3 a.m. they were finally escorted to their homes by National Guardsmen.

A motorcycle scout rode through the gasoline and water near the smoldering car. He skidded out of control and went smashing to the pavement. The motorcycle rolled on for several yards, then fell.

As the main body of the mob split up and left the area

249

in small bands, a highway patrolman spotted a small paper sack being lowered by a rope from the belfry of the church.

U. S. Marshal W. W. Williams, of Macon, Ga., rushed into the church and across the street into the park. There he opened it and what he feared was a bomb turned out to be a bag of rocks.

As the mob scattered, News Photographer Norman Dean revealed his camera and began taking pictures.

State officials poured into the area by carloads. A state official grimly informed Public Safety Director Floyd Mann that Montgomery had been placed under martial law.

"The governor has just called for 100 armed guardsmen," the official said, "and they'll be coming in within the next half hour."

Mann, who had been on the scene since arrival of the first Highway Patrol units, shoved his way through the crowd of lawmen to inform his superior officers of the new turn of events.

A U. S. marshall failed to recognize Mann and attempted to stop him. We listened as Mann tongue-lashed him and blamed him and his companions for the riot.

Atty. Gen. MacDonald Gallion, when asked to comment on the situation, also blamed federal intervention.

"We expected as much," Gallion said, "when those marshalls moved in and increased tension by catering to the Negro agitators."

MONTGOMERY ADVERTISER

May 23, 1961

WHITE GIRL CHEERS ON CROWD OF TEEN RIOTERS

A robust blonde-haired white girl appeared to hold the emotions of a teen-age mob in the palm of her hand Sunday night in front of the Negro First Baptist Church.

The self-styled cheerleader, dressed in pedal-pushers and a low-necked blouse, stood in front of a crowd of about 75 persons a block from the church, hurling taunts and jeers at every passing car.

Her "followers" chanted "amen" every time she directed an attack at a passing group. When she was quiet those behind her rested waiting for new direction which was never too long in coming.

The group was composed mostly of older teen-agers although some grown men, ranging in age from 30 to 60, were seen in the ranks.

Although the unidentified girl never resorted to profanity her high-pitched voice was able to direct the group's attention to both whites and Negroes coming into the area.

When a carload of whites passed by she shouted, "Park your car and get out. We need you."

Shortly after that a group of Negroes came by and she dared them to get out of their car. The group behind her echoed, "Yeah, yeah, yeah."

Most of the boys in the crowd were dressed in unbuttoned shirts and blue jeans. Many had ducktail haircuts. Some of the girls were attired in tight shorts and low-cut blouses. This led one spectator to note that this looked more like a rock 'n roll convention than a Ku Klux Klan gathering.

The blame for Sunday night's riot was laid squarely on the shoulders of teen-agers, by law enforcement officers. Police on the scene said that most of them were from Montgomery.

At a press conference Monday, James Hardman, an Alcohol and Tobacco Tax Division agent from Jacksonville, Fla. said, "They were dressed like teen-agers but they certainly didn't act like kids."

Police have not yet identified the girl.

NEW YORK TIMES
May 27, 1961

ATTORNEY GENERAL FORESEES A NEGRO AS U. S. PRESIDENT

WASHINGTON, May 26—Attorney General Robert F. Kennedy, in a broadcast to the world over the Voice of America, today acknowledged the United States' imperfections in the areas of equal rights for Negroes. He said, however, that progress was being made in that area so rapidly that "There's no question that in the next thirty or forty years a Negro can achieve the position . . . of President of the United States."

A PARTIAL LISTING OF APPROXIMATELY 5,000 NEGOES LYNCHED IN UNITED STATES SINCE 1859

ALABAMA: Abernathy, Duke, Oct. 30, 1900. Henry Abrama, Montgomery, Nov. 29, 1897. Reddrick Adams, Seale, Apr. 12, 1896. J. M. Alexander, Tuskegee, June 13, 1895. Albert Anderson, Sept. 13, 1898. James Anderson, Taylor Ferry, Oct. 10, 1896. John Anderson, Lafayette, Oct. 2, 1898. Paul Archer, Carrolton, Sept. 15, 1893. Lewis Balaam, Jackson, Sept. 4, 1909. Andy Beard, Kennedy, Mar. 18, 1897. Bud Beard, Carrolton, Dec. 17, 1897. Ed Bell, Selma, Aug. 7, 1904. Charles Bentley, Leeds, Aug. 2, 1901. Berney, Wetumpka, Nov. 18, 1912. William Bird, Sheffield, Nov. 11, 1918. Scott Bishop, Marbury, Dec. 20, 1902. Thomas Black, Tuscumbia, Apr. 22, 1894. John Bonner, Kennedy, Dec. 16, 1897. Louis Bonner, Kennedy, Dec. 16, 1897. Calvin Brown, Specific locality unknown, July 6, 1891. John Brown, Childersburg, Oct. 1, 1891. Robert Brown, Specific locality unknown, July 6, 1891. William Brown, Rienzi, Apr. 29, 1906. Thomas Browne, Point Clear, June 26, 1895. John Brownlee, Oxford, July 19, 1894. Richard Burton, Boyds, Jan. 28, 1916. Eben Calhoun, Pittsview, Apr. 29, 1907. John Calloway, Calhoun County, Mar. 21, 1898. Wiley Campbell, June 25, 1902. William Cantor, Childersburg, May 16, 1892. Carson, Selma, Jan. 3, 1913. Walter Carter, Nov. 30, 1903. Walter Clayton, Bay Minett, Apr. 6, 1908. Thomas Clinton, Specific locality unknown, Nov. 30, 1903. Zeb Colley, Greenville, Apr. 21, 1895. Isaac Cook, Montgomery, Aug. 12, 1890. Azariah Curtis, Butler, Dec. 7, 1912. Cyat, Henry, Oct. 10, 1896. James Daniel, Goose County, July 20, 1897. Davenport, Leighton, Jan. 24, 1909. Bud Davis, Moulton, Mar. 6, 1901. George Davis, Inverness, Apr. 19, 1892. Phillip Davis, Specific locality unknown, Nov. 30, 1903. Daniel Dawson, Tyler, Mar. 19, 1895. Robert Dawson, Selma, May 6, 1901. Mary Deane, Greenville, Apr. 21, 1895. Herman Deeley, Taylorsville, Jan. 18, 1915. John Dell, Montgomery, Oct. 9, 1910. Noah Dickson, Walnut Grove, May 22, 1889. Andrew Diggs, Scottsboro, June 24, 1903. Moses Dossett, Prichard Station, Sept. 22, 1907. Daniel Dove, Specific locality unknown, Oct. 20, 1906. Manuel Dunegan, Chilton County, Apr. 15, 1895. Dan Edwards, Selma, June 24, 1893. Roxie Elliott, Centerville, Apr. 15, 1891. Holland English, Bakerhill, Apr. 2, 1894. Emma Fair, Carrolton, Sept. 15, 1893. John Fitch, Specific locality unknown, Sept. 27, 1896. James Fox, Specific locality unknown, Aug. 10, 1915. Amanda Franks, Jefferson, May 12, 1897. James Freeman, Columbus City, May 31, 1895. Joseph Giohen, Berlin, Dec. 8, 1893. Alice Green, Greenville, Apr. 21, 1895. Martha Green, Greenville, Apr. 21, 1895. Frank Griffin, Stanton, Mar. 31, 1890. Zachioli Grohan, Whistler, Apr. 2, 1891. Neal Guinn, Haynesville, Aug. 5, 1931. Caines Hall, Kingston, May 1, 1904. Cleveland Harding, Florence, Mar. 24, 1907. George Harris, Limestone, June 16, 1901. Samuel Harris, Salem, Nov. 3, 1902. John Hayden, Lamar County, June 1, 1897. O'Dee Henderson, Fairfield, May 9, 1940. Alexander Herman, Courtland, July 16, 1901. Poe Hibbler, Pickens County, July 23, 1917. George Hoes, Butler, May 8, 1892. Joseph Holman, Tyler, Mar. 19, 1895. Robert Holman, Tyler, Mar. 19, 1895. Paul Hull, Carrolton, Sept. 15, 1893. Charles Humphries, Lee County, Mar. 18, 1900. Charles Hunt, Brantley, Aug. 17, 1899. William Hunter, Selma, Aug. 1, 1896. James Jackson, Bibb County, Jan. 31, 1897. "Kid" Jackson, Hope Hull, Aug. 17, 1915. Oliver Jackson, Montgomery, Mar. 29, 1894. Solomon Jackson, Wetumpka, June 17, 1898. William Jackson, Wetumpka, June 17, 1898. Joseph James, Woodstock, Dec. 22, 1896. Jerry Johnson, North Birmingham, Sept. 3, 1907. Sidney Johnson, Coaling, July 12, 1898. Tony Johnson, Tuscumbia, Apr. 22, 1894. Wes Johnson, Headland, Feb. 2, 1937. Burrell Jones, Monroeville, Oct. 13, 1892. John Jones, Anniston, July 13, 1890. Jon Jones, Altoona, July 1, 1904. Moses Jones, Monroeville, Oct. 13, 1892. William Jones, Fort Deposit, Dec. 19, 1914. Joshua Balaam, Jackson, Sept. 4, 1909. John Kellog, Blanche, Feb. 20, 1898. Oliver Latt, Tunnel Springs, Aug. 23, 1905. William Lewis, Lamison, Apr. 14, 1894. John Lipsey, Pickensville, Aug. 27, 1907. Eliza Lowe, Henry County, Aug. 1, 1891. Willis Lowe, Henry County, Aug. 1, 1891. Henry Lucas, Vinegar Bend, Nov. 2, 1907. Horace Maples, Huntsville, Sept. 7, 1904. John Marritt, Pickens

County, Mar. 26, 1897. Jesse Matson, Calera, May 26, 1910. "Dic" Mayes, Selma, May 6, 1901. Ed Mayes, Selma, May 6, 1901. Louis McAdams, Wilsonville, Jan. 3, 1901. Tobe McGrady, Perote, Oct. 5, 1895. Marshal McGregor, Banks, Jan. 5, 1899. George Meadows, Pratt Mines, Jan. 15, 1889. Henry McKenny, Dothan, July 3, 1910. William Miller, Brighton, Aug. 6, 1908. Benjamin Minty, Berlin, Dec. 8, 1893. Clinton Montgomery, Magnolia, Dec. 20, 1909. Isadore Moreley, Selma, Aug. 1, 1896. Robert Moseley, Dolimite, Nov. 14, 1894. Robert Moseley, Huntsville, Mar. 22, 1890. Ernest Murphy, Daleville, June 27, 1893. James Nance, Jefferson, May 13, 1897. Ed Onlu, Eufala, Apr. 14, 1893. Leon Orr, Specific locality unknown, June 20, 1896. Allen Parker, New Monroesville, Oct. 30, 1892. Henry Paters, Prichard, Oct. 6, 1906. Pedigrie, Andalusia, Feb. 20, 1906. John Pennington, Enterprise, Aug. 7, 1901. Iver Peterson, Eufaula, Feb. 12, 1911. Jack Pharr, Claiborne, Aug. 30, 1897. Edward Plowly, Pine Apple, Mar. 14, 1905. William Plowly, Pine Apple, Mar. 14, 1905. Ephreim Pope, Lamison, June 22, 1904. Ray Porter, Clanton, Aug. 21, 1891. William Pournay, Chestnut, Sept. 3, 1901. James Powell, Specific locality unknown, June 5, 1895. Jesse Powell, Letohatchee, July 23, 1917. William Powell, Letochatchee, July 23, 1917. Edward Prater, Clay County, July 8, 1892. Fred Quigleton, Talledaga, Nov. 3, 1907. Randall, Winfield, Apr. 25, 1891. John Rattler, Greenville, Apr. 21, 1895. Camp Reese, Wetumpka, June 17, 1893. Frank Reeves, Butler County, May 30, 1901. William Reynolds, Tuscumbia, Apr. 6, 1902. Bunkie Richardson, Gadsden, Feb. 11, 1906. Grant Richardson, Centerville, Oct. 9, 1910. Albert Roberts, Inverness, Apr. 19, 1892. Douglass Robertson, Mobile, Jan. 22, 1909. Esau Robinson, Emelle, July 4, 1930. Richard Robinson, Prichard Station, Oct. 6, 1906. Ray Rolston, Anniston, Nov. 24, 1909. Berry Rowder, Childersburg, May 16, 1892. James Rowder, Childersburg, May 16, 1892. Henry Russell, Hope Hull, Aug. 17, 1915. Newt Saunders, Opp, Nov. 30, 1907. Mack Segars, Brantley, Dec. 28, 1893. Jerido Shivers, Coffee County, May 19, 1895. Ruben Sims, Little River, Apr. 16, 1904. Albert Sloss, Courtland, Nov. 2, 1899. Edwin Smith, Wetumpka, Jan. 4, 1915. John Smith, Scottsboro, Mar. 20, 1897. William Smith, Bessemer, Nov. 2, 1912. William Smith, Wetumpka, Jan. 4, 1915. James Speaks, Riverton, July 21, 1897. Louis Spier, Wetumpka, June 17, 1898. John Steele, Birmingham, Sept. 27, 1889. Stover, Habelle, Oct. 21, 1908. Abram Sumroll, Vinegar Bend, Nov. 2, 1907. Terrill, Elba, July 16, 1897. Thomas, Birmingham, Apr. 25, 1909. James Thomas, Blossburg, July 9, 1897. Jesse Thompson, Wetumpka, June 17, 1898. Jesse Thornton, Crenshaw County, June 22, 1940. Winfield Townsend, Eclectic, Oct. 2, 1900. Jesse Underwood, Tuscumbia, July 26, 1891. Sam Verge, Specific locality unknown, Aug. 5, 1912. William Wallace, Axis, Aug. 1, 1910. William Wardley, Irondale, Dec. 7, 1896. Wiley Webb, Selma, Feb. 14, 1892. Lemuel Weeks, Pickensville, July 1, 1916. William Westmoreland, Montgomery, June 24, 1896. Molly White, Jefferson, May 12, 1897. George Whiteside, Sheffield, Nov. 12, 1918. Robert Wilkins, Berlin, Dec. 8, 1893. Ella Williams, Henry County, Aug. 1, 1891. James Williams, Pickens County, Jan. 19, 1893. Jerry Williams, Inverness, Apr. 19, 1892. John Williams, Tuscumbia, Apr. 22, 1894. William Williams, Henry County, Aug. 1, 1891. William Williams, Inverness, Apr. 19, 1892. William Williams, South Side, May 11, 1901. Bud Wilson, Tuscaloosa, Dec. 27, 1889. Bush Withers, Sanford, Oct. 4, 1910. John Womack, Redlevel, May 22, 1918. Sam Wright, Helena, Oct. 15, 1891. Charles Young, Specific locality unknown, Nov. 15, 1903. Charles Young, Clayton, Mar. 29, 1914. William Ziegler, Specific locality unknown, Mar. 24, 1902. Two Unknown Negroes, Montevallo, Sept. 2, 1889. Unknown Negro, Brantley, Apr. 2, 1890. Two Unknown Negroes, Georgiana, Sept. 29, 1891. Unknown Negro, Riverton, July 25, 1890. Unknown Negro, Macon County, Mar. 10, 1892. Two Unknown Negroes, Monroeville, Oct. 13, 1892. Two Unknown Negroes, Sylvan, Feb. 13, 1892. Unknown Negro, Jasper, July 5, 1892. Two Unknown Negroes, Specific locality unknown, Dec. 10, 1893. Unknown Negro, Brierfield, July 17, 1893. Unknown Negro, Centerville, Sept. 6, 1893. Four Unknown Negroes, Selma, Dec. 12, 1893. Two Unknown Negroes, Selma, Apr. 5, 1894. Unknown Negro, Specific locality unknown, Oct. 12, 1896. Unknown Negro, Toadvine, Oct. 14, 1896. Unknown Negro, Excel, Sept. 2, 1897. Unknown Negro, Lafayette, Oct. 23, 1898. Unknown Negro, Geneva, May 7, 1900. Three Unknown Negroes, Opp, Dec. 6, 1901, Unknown Negro, Leeda, May 11, 1901. Unknown Negro, Hartford, Mar. 26, 1907. Unknown Negro, Midway, Jan. 4, 1907. Unknown Negro, Bolivar, Feb. 1, 1909. Unknown Negro, McFall, Oct. 8, 1910. Unknown Negro, Clayton, Aug. 30, 1911. Unknown Negro, Union Springs, Apr. 2, 1911. Unknown Negro, Cuba, Dec. 20, 1912. Unknown Negro, Dothan, Feb. 19, 1912. Unknown Negro, Kilgore,

Aug. 28, 1913. Unknown Negro, Hope Hull, Aug. 17, 1915. Unknown Negro, Greeley, Jan. 10, 1917. Unknown Negro, Reform, July 16, 1917.

ARKANSAS: Albert Aikens, Pine Bluff, May 24, 1909. Henry Allen, Brinkley, Jan. 6, 1893. William Anderson, Pillar, July 8, 1906. Robert Austin, Marion, Mar. 19, 1910. Robert Austin, Marion, Mar. 19, 1910. Andrew Avery, Garland City, July 31, 1917. Henry Beavers, Wilmar, Feb. 9, 1892. James Bailey, Beebe, July 7, 1891. George Baily, Devill's Bluff, Dec. 20, 1909. Eugene Baker, Monticello, July 30, 1892. Abe Bailey, St. Charles, Mar. 26, 1904. Mack Baldwin, St. Charles, Mar. 26, 1904. Wm. Baldwin, St. Charles, Mar. 26, 1904. John Barrett, Askew, Apr. 20, 1905. Peter Berryman, Mena, Feb. 20, 1901. H. Blackburn, Argenta, Oct. 7, 1906. Joseph Blakely, Portland, May 30, 1909. Jacob Bowers, Carlisle, Sept. 12, 1915. Bowles, Gordon, Aug. 23, 1892. Hamp Brisco & Son, Specific locality unknown, Feb. 10, 1892. Mrs. Brisco, Specific locality unknown, Feb. 10, 1892. John Brodie, Lee County, June 12, 1900. William Brooks, Palestine, May 23, 1894. Frank Brown, Conway, Sept. 22, 1905. Henry Bruce, Gulch County, Feb. 9, 1894. William Caldwell, Osceola, Sept. 11, 1895. James Calton, Elmarth, Feb. 7, 1906. Henry Capus, Magnolia, June 22, 1894. Allen Carter, Synne, Aug. 4, 1892. Perry Carter, St. Charles, Mar. 26, 1904. Ed Coy, Texarkana, Feb. 20, 1892. Jim Crazy, Milton, Dec. 9, 1896. Henry Crobyson, McGehee, Sept. 22, 1894. Daval, Reader, Jan. 8, 1898. Alfred Davis, Lonoke County, Jan. 5, 1894. Anthony Davis, Texarkana, Oct. 8, 1906. Chich Davis, Wilmot, July 24, 1899. Howard Davis, Newport, Oct. 28, 1914. Arthur Dean, Augusta, Sept. 9, 1911. Willie Dees, Osceola, May 1, 1899. Frank Dodd, DeWitt, Aug. 9, 1916. Robert Donnelly, Union Township, July 2, 1892. General Duckett, Little River County, Mar. 22, 1899. Glenco Days, Crossett, Feb. 19, 1904. Albert England, Wynne, Nov. 4, 1895. Garrett Flood, St. Charles, Mar. 26, 1904. Randall Flood, St. Charles, Mar. 26, 1904. Monroe Franklin, Russellville, Aug. 20, 1912. Newton Gaines, Specific locality unknown, Dec. 6, 1898. Samuel Gates, England, Sept. 13, 1917. John Gilbert, July 22, 1903. Felix Gilman, Prescott, May 27, 1916. Edwin Goodwin, Little River County, Mar. 23, 1899. Henry Griffin, St. Charles, Mar. 26, 1904. Walter Griffin, St. Charles, Mar. 26, 1904. Godfrey Gould, Clarendon, July 31, 1898. Goode Gray, Rison, July 1, 1898. Robert Greenwood, Cross County, Dec. 7, 1893. Nat Hadley, Durdon, Nov. 20, 1891. Loy Haley, Hope, June 15, 1915. W. H. Harkin, Clinton, Apr. 18, 1899. George Harris, Varner, Feb. 23, 1892. Gulbert Harris, Pine Bluff, Feb. 14, 1892. Harrison, Champagnolle, Sept. 20, 1892. Levi Hayden, Texarkana, June 3, 1898. Hellem, Luxora, Sept., 1903. "Doc" Henderson, Bearden, May 9, 1893. James Henry, Little Rock, May 13, 1892. Hilliard, Hope, Jan. 18, 1909. Aaron Hinton, St. Charles, Mar. 26, 1904. William Hunter, Star City, June 14, 1910. Huntley, Reader, Jan. 8, 1898. Aaron Jimerson, Ashdown, Aug. 9, 1917. Alexander Johnson, Monticello, July 14, 1898. Armstead Johnson, Pine Bluff, June 13, 1889. Henry Johnson, Lake Village, Nov. 3, 1903. Killis Johnston, St. Charles, Mar. 26, 1904. Benjamin Jones, Little River County, Mar. 23, 1899. Henry Jones, Hamburg, June 25, 1891. James Jones, Specific locality unknown, Aug. 22, 1895. Joseph Jones, Little River County, Mar. 23, 1899. "Judge" Jones, Pine Bluff, Mar. 25, 1910. Moses Jones, Little River County, Mar. 23, 1899. Newton Jones, Boxley, Nov. 29, 1893. Robert Jordon, Camden, Aug. 10, 1892. John Kelly, Pine Bluff, Feb. 14, 1892. Lee Key, Knoxville, May 12, 1901. Frank King, Little Rock, June 20, 1895. Joseph King, Little River County, Mar. 23, 1899. William Larkin, Camden, Feb. 14, 1890. Charles Lewis, Hope, Oct. 20, 1911. Lightfoot, Newport, Dec. 7, 1892. Nathan Lucey, Forrest City, Oct. 16, 1911. William Madison, St. Charles, Mar. 26, 1904. Castle Manse, Clarendon, Aug. 9, 1898. Edward McCollum, Sheridan, Oct. 6, 1903. Horace McCoy, Foreman, Mar. 10, 1902. "Dock" McLane, Ashdown, May 14, 1910. Allen Mitchell, Earle, June 13, 1918. Laura Mitchell, Specific locality unknown, Apr. 5, 1910. Julian Moseley, Arkansas City, July 14, 1892. Nat Mullens, Earle, June 17, 1900. Charles Mulligan, Conway, Aug. 30, 1891. Washington Mussay, Augusta, Dec. 5, 1907. A. M. Neely, Forest City, May 19, 1889. Nelson, Varner, Nov. 14, 1893. Lee Newton, Specific locality unknown, Aug. 1, 1902. William Norman, Hot Springs, June 19, 1913. Presley Oates, Specific locality unknown, May 20, 1897. William Patrick, Forrest, Dec. 3, 1915. Henry Phillips, Osceola, Nov. 15, 1897. Thomas Parker, Kendall, Oct. 15, 1897. Frank Pride, Specific locality unknown, Apr. 5, 1910. Sam Powell, Huttig, July 6, 1910. Ben Patterson, Hackette, Oct. 1, 1891. Edward Peyton, Marianna, Oct. 1, 1891. William Rice, Specific locality unknown, Nov. 8, 1891. Frank Robertson, Bradley, Mar. 20, 1903. Dean Reynolds, Specific locality unknown, Jan. 15, 1889. J. E. Robinson, Texarkana, Mar. 8, 1889. Willis Robinson, Newport,

Dec. 18, 1918. Dennis Ricord, Clarendon, Aug. 9, 1898. James Ried, Monticello, July 14, 1898. Charles Richards, Marion, Mar. 19, 1910. Paul Scroggs, Brinkley, Jan. 6, 1893. Charles Stewart, Morrillton, May 21, 1892. John Stewart, Bearden, May 9, 1893. William Saunders, Clarendon, Aug. 9, 1898; James Smith, Proctor, Feb. 8, 1917. Lee Simms, Little Rock, Sept. 5, 1913. Sanford, Lewis, Mar. 23, 1912. Charles Smith, St. Charles, Mar. 26, 1904. James Smith, St. Charles, Mar. 26, 1904. John Thomas, Osceola, Sept. 11, 1895. Flannegan Thornton, Morrillton, Apr. 19, 1893. Alexander Thompson, Gurdon, Apr. 23, 1903. John Turner, Warren, Apr. 6, 1903. White Vetton, Spring Hill, Jan. 4, 1905. John Wallace, Jefferson Springs, May 31, 1893. Washington, McGehee, Sept. 22, 1894. Luke Washington, McGehee, Sept. 22, 1894. D. L. Watson, Hamilton, Sept. 16, 1897. Rilla Weaver, Clarendon, Aug. 9, 1898. Robert Weaver, Specific locality unknown, May 30, 1890. Elijah Wells, Wynne, Nov. 20, 1902. Edward Williams, Baxter, Aug. 26, 1897. Ernest Williams, Parkdale, June 20, 1908. John Williams, Plummersville, July 5, 1912. Hog Wilson, Stephens, Sept. 3, 1902. James Woodman, Specific locality unknown, July 6, 1905. William Wyatt, Rison, Aug. 24, 1897. Charles Young, Forrest City, Oct. 20, 1902. Unknown Negro, Turner, Jan. 1, 1890. Unknown Negro, Newton County, Dec. 14, 1891. Unknown Negro, Wynne, July 2, 1892. Unknown Negro, Marche, Mar. 6, 1894. Two Unknown Negroes, Hampton, July 14, 1895. Unknown Negro, Specific locality unknown, Sept. 19, 1895. Unknown Negro, Pine Bluff, Dec. 17, 1896. Unknown Negro, Robroy, Sept. 5, 1897. Two Unknown Negroes, Reader, Jan. 8, 1898. Unknown Negro, Marcella, Mar. 15, 1898. Unknown Negro, Sherrill, Jan. 1, 1898. Unknown Negro, Little River County, Mar. 23, 1899. Unknown Negro, Arkadelphia, Dec. 21, 1900. Unknown Negro, West Point, May 26, 1900. Unknown Negro, Specific locality unknown, July 22, 1903. Two Unknown Negroes, Stephens, Aug. 31, 1904. One Unknown Negro, Crossett, Sept. 5, 1904. Unknown Negro, Hot Springs, Nov. 29, 1906. Unknown Negro, Junction City, July 12, 1906. Two Negro Women, Stamps, Mar. 20, 1907. Unknown Negro, Stuttgart, Aug. 9, 1916. Unknown Negro, Specific locality unknown, Oct. 8, 1917.

CALIFORNIA: Calvin Kunblern, Pueblo, May 22, 1900. Henry Planz, San Jose, Nov. 11, 1889. Washington H. Wallace, La Junta, Mar. 25, 1902.

DELAWARE: George White, Wilmington, June 12, 1903.

FLORIDA: Adams, Lake Butler, July 18, 1903. David Alexander, Pensacola, Apr. 5, 1909. Charles Anderson, Perry, Sept. 26, 1909. Richardson Anderson, Ocala, Jan. 28, 1916. John Archer, Ocala, Nov. 19, 1912. Sam Arline, Tampa, Apr. 15, 1912. Walter Austin, Arcadia, Feb. 18, 1892. Washington Bradley, Bronson, Sept. 6, 1904. Galvin Baker, Marianna, Mar. 5, 1911. John Bapes, Mulberry, Aug. 21, 1906. James Barco, Panasoffkee, June 29, 1900. Lee Barley, De Land, Sept. 29, 1891. Isaac Barrett, Orange Dale, June 5, 1897. Robert Bennet, Lake City, July 4, 1895. John Black, Specific locality unknown, July 27, 1906. Henry Boggs, Ft. White, Nov. 9, 1893. Hattie Bowman, Graceville, Sept. 2, 1910. John Brooks, Ellaville, May 19, 1895. J. T. Burgis, Palatka, May 29, 1894. Champion, Gainesville, Feb. 18, 1891. Edward Christian, Graceville, Sept. 2, 1910. Jumbo Clark, High Springs, Jan. 15, 1904. Denniss Cobb, Arcadia, May 30, 1892. William Collins, Mayo, June 9, 1895. Alfred Daniels, Gainesville, Nov. 28, 1896. James Davis, Inverness, June 8, 1906. Robert Davis, Mulberry, June 27, 1900. Bert Dennis, Newberry, Aug. 19, 1916. James Dennis, Newberry, Aug. 19, 1916. Mary Dennis, Newberry, Aug. 19, 1916. James Denson, Madison, Jan. 7, 1901. James Denson's Stepson, Madison, Jan. 7, 1901. Samuel Echols, Ellaville, May 19, 1895. Henry Edwards, Juliette, Mar. 5, 1897. Sam Ellis, Tampa, Mar. 7, 1910. Wade Ellis, Tampa, Mar. 7, 1910. William English, Bradentown, July 4, 1912. J. C. Evans, Milton, Oct. 4, 1937. John Evans, St. Petersburg, Nov. 14, 1914. Andy Ford, Gainesville, Aug. 25, 1891. S. G. Garner, Kissimmee, Mar. 29, 1917. James Gilmore, Juliette, Mar. 15, 1897. Henry Gordon, Mulberry, May 20, 1903. Crane Green, Pine Barren, July 21, 1903. Jack Green, Juliette, Mar. 5, 1897. Charles Griffen, Specific locality unknown, June 22, 1891. Charles Harris, De Land, Sept. 23, 1896. Cellos Harrison, Marianna, June 16, 1943. John Haskins, Newberry, Aug. 19, 1916. Richard Hawkins, Tallahassee, July 20, 1937. Henry Henson, Micanopy, Jan. 12, 1892. Green Jackson, Ft. White, July 18, 1890. Henry Jackson, Miami, May 22, 1918. William Jackson, Ocala, Dec. 4, 1894. Anthony Johnson, De Land, Sept. 23, 1896. Charles Jones, MacClenny, May 7, 1896. Sam Jones, Juliette, Mar. 5, 1897. Frank Jordan, Inverness, May 17, 1906. Harry Jordon Alachua, Jan. 13, 1896. William Kaneker, Apalachicola, June 7, 1892. Dan Kennedy,

Mulberry, May 3, 1903. Robert Larkins, Ocalm, July 12, 1893. West Lawrence, Pensacola, Nov. 22, 1899. William Leach, Dade City, Aug. 6, 1915. Jackson Lewis, Tampa, Dec. 5, 1903. Samuel Lewis, Specific locality unknown, Aug. 18, 1895. Richard Lowe, Mayo, Nov. 26, 1910. Charles Martin, Madison, Feb. 1, 1899. Robert Matthews, Gull Point, Nov. 26, 1910. Henry McDuffie, Orlando, July 8, 1892. Sam McIntosh, Kathleen, July 9, 1910. Wash Melton, Juliette, Mar. 5, 1897. James Miley, Juliette, Mar. 15, 1897. Otis Miller, Juliette, Mar. 15, 1897. Maik Morris, Tallahassee, June 6, 1909. H. Murphy, Atlon, Sept. 14, 1912. Jacob Nader, Lakeland, Feb. 13, 1909. Preech Nellis, Ocala, Nov. 14, 1912. Robert Matthews, June 11, 1910. Andrew McHenry, Newberry, Aug. 19, 1916. Norman McKinney, Dennellon, Jan. 16, 1901. H. M. Owens, Trenton, July 23, 1915. Jesse James Payne, Madison, Oct. 12, 1945. Doc Peters, Cottondale, July 1, 1905. Charles Pitman, Greenville, Feb. 2, 1908. Ernest Ponder, Tallahassee, July 20, 1937. Benjamin Price, Specific locality unknown, Oct. 5, 1908. Hicks Price, Starke, Nov. 25, 1897. Manny Price, Newberry, Sept. 1, 1902. Otis Price, Perry, Aug. 9, 1938. Amos Randall, Mulberry, May 20, 1903. William Rawles, Specific locality unknown, Apr. 2, 1895. William Reagin, Specific locality unknown, July 27, 1906. William Reed, Kissimmee, Feb. 28, 1915. John Richards, Sparr, Feb. 17, 1915. Fred Rochelle, Bartow, May 30, 1901. George Rose, Specific locality unknown, May 13, 1894. John Sanders, Sneads, June 10, 1900. Robert Scruggs, Newberry, Sept. 1, 1902. Leander Shaw, Pensacola, July 29, 1908. Simmons Simpson, Marianna, Mar. 29, 1890. James Smith, Starke, Sept. 14, 1894. John Smith, Arcadia, Apr. 10, 1909. Otea Smith, Julietta, Mar. 5, 1897. Roscoe Smith, Yellow River, July 6, 1913. Samuel Smith, Greenville, Jan. 9, 1894. Charles Smoke, Blountstown, Aug. 28, 1931. Richard Smoke, Blountstown, Aug. 28, 1931. Lee Snell, Daytona Beach, Apr. 20, 1939. Pierce Taylor, Tallahassee, Jan. 25, 1897. Henry Thomas, Parish, Mar. 9, 1903. Jack Thomas, Live Oak, June 27, 1900. Kid Tempers, Blountstown, July 10, 1913. Shepherd Trent, Punta Gorda, June 25, 1917. John Van Brunt, De Land, Apr. 20, 1896. A. C. Williams, Quincy, May 13, 1911. Alonzo Williams, San Antonio, Aug. 1, 1902. Arthur Williams, Wellborne, Nov. 6, 1898. Daniel Williams, Specific locality unknown, Dec. 11, 1890. Jacob Williams, Madison County, July 6, 1896. James Williams, Specific locality unknown, May 25, 1892. Sam Williams, Dade City, Feb. 8, 1901. Patrock Wills, Quincy, Jan. 26, 1893. Melvin Womack, Winter Garden, Mar. 31, 1951. William Wright, Dade City, Feb. 8, 1901. Charles Willis, Ocala, Jan. 14, 1894. Nim Young, Ocala, May 15, 1894. Stella Young, Newberry, Aug. 10, 1916. Two Unknown Negroes, Live Oak, Dec. 15, 1891. Unknown Negro, Fort White, June 17, 1891. Unknown Negro, Specific locality unknown, Dec. 15, 1891. Unknown Negro, Waldo, Sept. 7, 1892. Unknown Negro, Specific locality unknown, May 25, 1892. Three Unknown Negroes, Lake City Junction, Nov. 14, 1893. Unknown Negro, Marion County, Dec. 17, 1894. Three Unknown Negroes, Bartow, May 30, 1895. Two Unknown Negroes, Mayo, June 11, 1895. Unknown Negro, Apalachicola, Aug. 20, 1897. Two Unknown Negroes, Dunellon, June 13, 1899. Unknown Negro, Dunellon, June 13, 1899. Unknown Negro, Dunellon, June 13, 1899. Unknown Negro, Jasper, Aug. 9, 1899. Two Unknown Negroes, Brooksville, May 14, 1900. Unknown Negro, Jennings, Mar. 11, 1900. Unknown Negro, Sneads, June 10, 1900. Unknown Negro, Chipley, Sept. 7, 1901. Unknown Negro, Bluff Springs, July 28, 1902. Unknown Negro, Mulberry, May 20, 1904. Unknown Negro, Madison, Nov. 9, 1906. Unknown Negro, Arcadia, June 15, 1909. Unknown Negro, Duval County, May 9, 1909. Four Unknown Negroes, Bonifay, Aug. 2, 1910. Two Unknown Negroes, Bonifay, July 30, 1910. Unknown Negro, Tampa, Mar. 8, 1910. Six Unknown Negroes, Lake City, May 21, 1911. Unknown Negro, Bonifay, July 7, 1913. Unknown Negro, Quincy, Aug., 1918.

GEORGIA: Simon Adams, Columbus, June 9, 1900. Daniel Ahren, Greensboro, Apr. 6, 1894. Albert Aikens, Lincolnton, May 24, 1909. Joseph Allen, Moultrie, Mar. 24, 1898. Rich Allen, Watkinsville, June 29, 1905. Thomas Allen, Monroe, June 30, 1911. Walter Allen, Rome, Apr. 1, 1902. James Anderson, Specific locality unknown, Dec. 6, 1898. Simon Anderson, Wellston, July 31, 1909. Wiley Annett, Newton, June 24, 1903. John Anthony, Lincolnton, Nov. 16, 1889. Lon J. Aycock, Watkinsville, June 29, 1905. Albert Baker, Waycross, June 27, 1908. Jesse Barker, Monticello, Jan. 15, 1915. Samuel Barker, Monticello, Jan. 15, 1915. John Barley, Marietta, Mar. 18, 1900. William Barnes, Montezuma, Nov. 8, 1910. John Belin, Specific locality unknown, Feb. 1, 1898. John Bigley, Palmetto, Mar. 16, 1899. Henry Bingham, Palmetto, Mar. 16, 1899. George L. Bivins, Leesburg, Feb. 11, 1899. Samuel Bland, Eastman, Dec. 20, 1915. Harrison Boone, Sparta, Sept. 26,

1896. Ann Bostwick, Specific locality unknown, June 25, 1912. George Brannan, Specific locality unknown, Jan. 27, 1897. Allen Brooks, Berryville, Apr. 3, 1900. John Brosin, Monticello, Aug. 31, 1902. Benjamin Brown, Tallapoosa, Oct. 23, 1902. Edward Brown, Palmetto, Mar. 16, 1899. Nathan Brown, Rochelle, Sept. 20, 1914. Washington Brown, Athens, Feb. 28, 1890. Thomas Brownlee, Butts County, May 2, 1895. Daniel Buck, Bluffton, July 1, 1891. Homer Burk, Cochran, Mar. 21, 1912. George Burton, Digbey, Sept. 11, 1898. Murray Burton, Ellaville, Apr. 8, 1911. James Caleaway, Liberty Hill, Oct. 24, 1900. John Calhoun, Barnesville, May 25, 1918. Austin Callaway, La Grange, Sept. 8, 1940. Lewis Capt, Lumpkin, May 18, 1897. Floyd Carmichael, Lakewood, July 31, 1906. Bud Catlen, Palmetto, Mar. 16, 1899. William Cato, Statesboro, Aug. 16, 1904. Samuel Chandler, Monroe, July 2, 1895. Andrew Chapwan, Specific locality unknown, Oct. 11, 1911. Eula Charles, Monticello, Jan. 15, 1915. B. Clark, Sopertown, Aug. 27, 1909. Benjamin Clark, Tarrytown, Aug. 27, 1909. David Clark, Odum, June 16, 1899. John William Clark, Cartersville, Oct. 1, 1930. Edward Claus, Eastman, June 14, 1903. Linton Clinton, Meigs, Mar. 1, 1917. James Cobb, Cordele, May 23, 1918. George Coldhand, Colquitt County, Jan. 9, 1895. Thomas Coley Goldsboro, Jan. 9, 1908. Collins, Athens, Feb. 10, 1894. Robert Collins, Oglethorpe, Feb. 15, 1894. Mary Connell, Leary's, Oct. 4, 1916. William Cornaker, Talbotton, June 22, 1909. Bud Cosby, Fayetteville, Feb. 7, 1918. T. Z. Cotton, Columbus, Aug. 13, 1912. John Crutchfield, Hamilton, Jan. 22, 1912. A. B. Culberson, Evans, Feb. 4, 1915. John Cummings, Appling, May 15, 1904. Robertson Curry, Hawkinsville, Mar. 6, 1908. Mitchell Daniel, Leesburg, Apr. 27, 1899. Ed Dansy, Willacoochee, Feb. 7, 1918. Peter Davis, Ft. Gaines, Aug. 29, 1911. Warren Dean, Specific locality unknown, July 17, 1893. Claxton Dekle, Metter, Dec. 15, 1917. George Dorsey and wife, Mae, Monroe, July 25, 1946. John Dukes, Arabi, July 9, 1938. John Duncan, Spring Place, Oct. 1, 1889. Robert Edwards, Cummings, Sept. 10, 1912. Claude Elder, Watkinsville, June 29, 1905. Frank Erle, Vidalia, July 25, 1901. Henry Etheridge, Jackson, Apr. 26, 1912. Spencer Evans, Crawfordville, Mar. 22, 1918. Robert Evarts, Apr. 26, 1894. William Fambro, Griffin, Feb. 24, 1903. William Ferguson, Adel, Dec. 19, 1893. Gus Fish-Head, Safford, July 23, 1899. Peter Flambe, Cochran, July 21, 1915. George Foot, Leesburg, Feb. 11, 1899. Charles Forsythe, Jeffersonville, Jan. 22, 1897. Joseph Fowler, Blakely, Mar. 2, 1909. Fayette Franklin, Mitchell County, June 28, 1894. Charles Frazier, Brooks County, Dec. 23, 1894. George Fuller, Marion County, Dec. 28, 1900. Armor Gibson, Forsyth, Mar. 14, 1895. Charles Gibson, Mason, Sept. 12, 1897. John Gilham Macon, Sept. 3, 1918. Jacob Glover, Monticello, Dec. 6, 1898. James Glover, Specific locality unknown, Aug. 22, 1904. Welcome Golden, Waycross, Dec. 16, 1891. Augustus Goodman, Bainbridge, Oct. 29, 1905. John Goosby, Specific locality unknown, Oct. 24, 1899. David Goosenby, Atlanta, Sept. 19, 1894. Kennedy Gordon, Portal, Apr. 15, 1901. Benjamin Gorman, Specific locality unknown, June 1, 1903. George Grant, Darien, Sept. 8, 1930. Alonzo Green and his son, Wayside, Oct. 21, 1915. Andrew Green, Lovett, Aug. 23, 1897. King Green, Gum Branch, July 20, 1909. William Grouslsby, Elberton, Apr. 29, 1901. James Guer, Liberty Hill, Oct. 24, 1900. Sidney Gust, Specific locality unknown, Jan. 5, 1897. Charles Hale, Lawrenceville, Apr. 7, 1911. Robert Hall, Newton, Jan. 30, 1943. Albert Hamilton, Cordele, Jan. 30, 1912. Balam Hancock, Gibson, Nov. 25, 1895. William Hardee, Nicols, May 12, 1896. Frank Hardeman, Willaston, Oct. 19, 1900. Joseph Hardy, Talbotton, June 22, 1909. James Harmon, Social Circle, July 11, 1890. Charles Harris, Dearing, May 7, 1907. George Harris, Dublin, June 18, 1895. Harvin Harris, Macon, Feb. 12, 1916. Robert Harris, Watkinsville, June 29, 1905. William Harris, Colquitt County, Aug. 12, 1895. John Harvard, Cochran, Dec. 1, 1909. Belle Hathaway, Hamilton, Jan. 22, 1912. Will Head, Brooks & Lowndes Counties, May 17, 1918. Eugene Hemming, Hamilton, Jan. 22, 1912. Anthony Henderson, Unadilla, Jan. 9, 1897. Louis Henderson, Blakely, Aug. 3, 1899. John Henry, Hawkinsville, Mar. 6, 1908. George Herbert, Cowen, July 2, 1907. Samuel Hevens, Toccoa, June 14, 1915. Caleb Hill, Jr., Irwinton, May 30, 1949. Lee Hill, Wrightsville, Feb. 7, 1903. Thomas Hill, Spring Place, Mar. 1, 1893. Jordan Hines, Molena, June 27, 1900. Lucius Holt, Concord, Dec. 2, 1893. William Holt, Leesburg, Feb. 11, 1899. William Hopkins, New Bainbridge, May 29, 1903. William Hopps, Jesup, Dec. 26, 1889. Samuel Hose, Newman, Apr. 25, 1899. Benjamin Howard, Josselin, Aug. 25, 1892. Peter Hudson, Cuthbert, Sept. 26, 1916. Tip Hutson, Palmetto, Mar. 16, 1899. James Irwin, Ocilla, Feb. 1, 1930. Jackson, Cochran, July 21, 1915. Charles Jackson, Amboy, Apr. 15, 1910. Peter Jackson, Jesup, Dec. 26, 1889. Lenny Jefferson, Metcalf, June 11, 1900. Lewis Jefferson, Homersville, Nov. 4, 1895. Edward Jenkins, Clayton, Oct. 22,

1893. John Jessy, Forsyth, Aug. 30, 1892. Collins Johnson, Sale City, Nov. 17, 1917. D. C. Johnson, Sale City, Nov. 17, 1917. Frank Johnson, Specific locality unknown, Oct. 2, 1897. Henry Johnson, Valdosta, May 10, 1901. Sydney Johnson, Brooks & Lowndes Counties, May 17, 1918. Washington Johnson, Safford, July 23, 1899. William Johnson, Specific locality unknown, Jan. 22, 1911. Marshall Jones, Douglas, May 4, 1900. Owen Jones, Pulaski, Nov. 1, 1890. Robert Jones, Augusta, Feb. 25, 1911. Solomon Jones, Forrest, Aug. 1, 1899. Dawson Jordan, Ellaville, Apr. 8, 1911. Wesley King, Specific locality unknown, Feb. 21, 1891. Robert Kingut, Waycross, Dec. 14, 1891. William Kirkland, Thomasville, Sept. 25, 1930. Dewey Lake, Sylvester, Jan. 21, 1916. Felix Lake, Sylvester, Jan. 21, 1916. Frank Lake, Sylvester, Jan. 21, 1916. Major Lake, Sylvester, Jan. 21, 1916. Lee Lawrence, Jasper County, Nov. 8, 1894. Rodium Leamon, Sylvester, Jan. 21, 1916. Rufus Lesuere, Thomaston, Aug. 17, 1904. Lewis, Valdosta, Aug. 21, 1916. Thomas Linton, Specific locality unknown, May 22, 1899. Charles Lokie, Tifton, Aug. 7, 1908. Martin Love, Tunnell Hill, July 11, 1889. Terry Lovelace, Manchester, Oct. 19, 1911. Robert Lovett, Morgan, Aug. 15, 1913. Dan Lumpkin, Columbus County, Feb. 20, 1910. Charles Mack, Safford, July 25, 1899. Charles Mack, Swainsboro, Sept. 26, 1891. Roger Malcolm and wife, Dorothy, Monroe, July 25, 1946. Robert Mallard, Lyons, Nov. 20, 1948. Samuel Martin, Wrightsville, Mar. 24, 1890. Sebastian McBride, Portal, Aug. 30, 1904. Arthur McCauley, Specific locality unknown, July 28, 1902. William McClue, Clem, Aug. 11, 1899. Jess McCortele, Cartersville, Feb. 25, 1916. Garfield McCoy, Newton, June 24, 1903. William McGroff, Baconton, July 11, 1911. George McKinney, Newton, June 24, 1903. John McLeod Swainsboro, May 18, 1911. John Meadows, Carmel, Aug. 8, 1898. Edward Merriweather, Monticello, Nov. 23, 1898. William Miles, Columbus, June 1, 1896. Charles Miller, Culloden, Sept. 10, 1906. Henry Milner, Griffin, Oct. 15, 1896. S. S. Mincey, Ailey, July 29, 1930. Lacy Mitchell, Thomas County, Sept. 28, 1930. Rufus Moncrief, Whitehall, Sept. 18, 1917. John Moody, Bryan County, Mar. 2, 1901. John Moore, Hamilton, Jan. 22, 1912. Joseph Moore, Crawfordsville, May 22, 1911. William Moore, Jesup, Oct. 12, 1889. Anderson Moreland, Forsythe, June 11, 1892. Peter Morris, Arlington, Jan. 23, 1915. Ephrim Muchlea, Hazelhurst, May 23, 1893. Joe Nowling, Pelham, Mar. 28, 1917. Richard Olliver, Donaldsonville, May 27, 1898. Owen Opietress, Forsythe, June 18, 1894. William Owens, Jesup, Aug. 29, 1891. Samuel Owensby, Hogansville, May 5, 1913. Edward Pearson, Swainsboro, July 11, 1906. Banjo Peavey, Fort Valley, June 8, 1903. George Penner, Elberton, June 13, 1890. Rich Perry, Marion County, June 10, 1890. Charles Pickett, Ellaville, Apr. 8, 1911. Samuel Pike, Brooks County, Dec. 23, 1894. Jesse Poke, Eastman, June 10, 1890. Polasco, Valdosta, Oct. 31, 1890. Charles Powell, Macon, Feb. 4, 1912. Warren Powers, East Point, Sept. 4, 1889. Sandy Price, Watkinsville, June 29, 1905. George Prince, Elbert County, June 10, 1890. Ike Radney, Colquitt, Aug. 11, 1918. Andrew Rainey, Bainbridge, Apr. 23, 1903. Evan Ralent, Specific locality unknown, July 27, 1910. William Reed, Bainbridge, May 25, 1937. Albert Reese, Cuthbert, June 25, 1909. Sandy Reeves, Waycross, Sept. 24, 1918. Sylvester Rhodes, Collins, Mar. 5, 1894. Eugene Rice, Brooks & Lowndes Counties, May 17, 1918. John Riggins, Bainbridge, Aug. 17, 1915. Hollis Riles, Bainbridge, Sept. 3, 1949. Chime Riley, Brooks & Lowndes Counties, May 17, 1918. Andrew Roberts, Waycross, June 28, 1890. Albert Royal, Amboy, Apr. 15, 1910. George Read, Rome, Jan. 3, 1901. Paul Reedd, Statesboro, Aug. 16, 1904. Charles Robertson, Allendaletown, Mar. 2, 1895. Lewis Robinson, Watkinsville, June 29, 1905. Rich Robinson, Watkinsville, June 29, 1905. Albert Rogers and Son, Statesboro, Aug. 17, 1904. Joshua Ruff, Gibson, Nov. 18, 1897. Louis Sammin, Sufford, July 23, 1899. Robert Sapp, Blakeley, May 6, 1941. Simon Schuman, Brooks & Lowndes Counties, May 17, 1918. Ben Scott, Echols County, Sept. 2, 1897. Scott, Rebecca, Aug. 28, 1904. George Scott, Russellville, June 26, 1898. Thomas Seabright, Bainbridge, Oct. 8, 1905. John Shake, Specific locality unknown, July 28, 1913. Caesar Sheffield, Valdosta, Apr. 16, 1915. Barry Sherard, Brooks County, Dec. 23, 1894. Harris Sherman, Shellman, Mar. 13, 1901. Moxie Shuler, Bainbridge, Sept. 29, 1916. Hurbert Simmons, Neal, Nov. 20, 1904. John Simmons, Cairo, Nov. 19, 1890. Jesse Slayton, Columbus, June 1, 1896. Benjamin Smith, Swainsboro, May 21, 1911. Charles Smith, Sandersville, Oct. 7, 1916. Neal Smith, Specific locality unknown, Oct. 4, 1895. Serborn Smith, Covington, May 21, 1892. Jesse Staten, Quitman, Nov. 16, 1917. William Stewart, Eastman, Dec. 20, 1915. Elijah Strickland, Palmetto, Apr. 25, 1899. Elijah Sturgis, Cuthbert, Sept. 26, 1916. Virgie Swanson, Greenville, Aug. 25, 1913. John Sweeney, Tarrytown, Aug. 27, 1909. James Tabor, Alamo, Apr. 11, 1910. Samuel Taylor, Brooks County, Dec. 23, 1894. Calvin Thomas, Specific locality unknown, Dec. 25, 1893. George Thomas, Ft. Gaines, Sept. 22, 1908. John Thomas, Midville, Nov. 10, 1889. Arthur Thompson, Arlington, June 1, 1904. Gilbert Thompson, Statesboro, Feb. 24, 1908. Sterling Thompson, Campbell County, Jan. 3, 1901. Will Thompson, Brooks & Lowndes Counties, May 17, 1918. John Towne, Damascus, Sept. 5, 1908. Jack Troy, Talbotton, Sept. 21, 1904. Hayes Turner, Brooks & Lowndes Counties, May 17, 1918. Mary Turner, Brooks & Lowndes Counties, May 17, 1918. John Vease, Augusta, Feb. 25, 1911. Daniel Walker, Washington, Oct. 28, 1911. Jack Walker, Gay, Aug. 18, 1905. John Walker, Montezuma, Nov. 8, 1910. John Ware, Royston, Sept. 18, 1904. John Warren, Donald, Dec. 21, 1911. Lem Warren, Terrell County, Sept. 16, 1896. Foser Watts, Monroe, June 31, 1911. Moses Weaver, Tifton, Oct. 12, 1904. Isaac Webb, Goldsboro, Jan. 9, 1908. Grant Welly, Thomasville, Sept. 8, 1900. Allen West, Abbeville, Feb. 26, 1891. William West, Apr. 14, 1892. Henry White, Durand, Sept. 21, 1916. Henry White, Younker, Oct. 11, 1908. William White, Jeffersonville, Jan. 22, 1897. Alex Whitney, Harlem, May 13, 1900. Walter Wilkins, Waycross, June 27, 1908. John Wilks, Byron, Oct. 27, 1907. Williams, Odum, June 16, 1899. Alonzo Williams, Oboopee, July 29, 1903. Charles Williams, Specific locality unknown, Oct. 7, 1896. Chesbley Williams, Cordele, Nov. 30, 1912. Jesse Williams, Eastman, Sept. 8, 1892. John Williams, Fowistown, Sept. 7, 1898. John Williams, Waynesboro, Oct. 24, 1890. Oscar Williams, Griffin, July 23, 1897. Vance Williams, Louieville, Aug. 25, 1908. William Willis, Grovetown, May 14, 1900. Charles Wilson, Albany, May 27, 1910. James Wilson, Dalton, Oct. 26, 1892. John Wise, Pembroke, July 28, 1902. William Womack, Eastman, May 14, 1906. Frank Wosten, Homer, Oct. 12, 1890. Rolley Wyatt, Specific locality unknown, Feb. 19, 1909. Yarborough, Americus, Oct. 5, 1912. Gene Yerly, Watkinsville, June 29, 1905. Harry Young, Specific locality unknown, Apr. 22, 1902. Richard Young, Savannah, Mar. 29, 1902. Unknown Negro, Rome, Dec. 3, 1889. Unknown Negro, Irwinville, July 1, 1889. Two Unknown Negroes, Barton County, Oct. 31, 1890. Unknown Negro, Camak, Dec. 15, 1891. Five Unknown Negroes, Lithonia, Apr. 5, 1892. Three Unknown Negroes, Clarksville, May 17, 1892. Unknown Negro, Jesup, July 21, 1892. Unknown Negro, Hazelhurst, May 23, 1893. Three Unknown Negroes, Brooks County, Dec. 23, 1894. Unknown Negro, Blackshear, June 13, 1894. Unknown Negro, Miller County, May 22, 1894. Unknown Negro, Americus, Aug. 20, 1898. Two Unknown Negroes, Safford, July 23, 1899. Unknown Negro, Jackson, Nov. 23, 1899. Unknown Negro, Leesburg, July 25, 1899. Unknown Negro, Ty Ty, Sept. 14, 1899. Unknown Negro, Allentown, Nov. 1, 1901. Unknown Negro, Georgetown, June 29, 1901. Unknown Negro, Quitman, Jan. 5, 1901. Unknown Negro, Randolph County, Mar. 18, 1901. Unknown Negro, Ways Station, Aug. 10, 1901. Unknown Negro, Cordele, Oct. 16, 1903. Unknown Negro, Whighald, Sept., 1903. Five Unknown Negroes, Reidsville, May 21, 1907. Unknown Negro, Hickox, June 27, 1908. Unknown Negro, Statesboro, Feb. 17, 1908. Unknown Negro, Valdosta, Feb. 26, 1908. Unknown Negro, Barnett, July 1, 1909. Two Unknown Negroes, Clark County, Sept. 6, 1910. Unknown Negro, Cairo, July 31, 1910. Unknown Negro, Vidalia, Mar. 2, 1910. Unknown Negro, Dublin, Oct. 5, 1911. Two Unknown Negroes, Cornelia, Mar. 4, 1913. Unknown Negro, Americus, June 21, 1913. Two Unknown Negroes, Gordon, Sept. 29, 1916. Three Unknown Negroes, Brooks & Lowndes Counties, May 17, 1918.

ILLINOIS: Edward Brown, Specific locality unknown, Sept. 4, 1902. Scott Burton, Springfield, Aug. 15, 1908. Sam Bush, Decatur, June 3, 1893. Allen Butler, Lawrenceville, July 14, 1893. George Donigan, Springfield, Aug. 16, 1908. Woodford Hughes, Specific locality unknown, Feb. 26, 1902. William Jones, Cairo, Nov. 3, 1909. I. D. Mayfield, Danville, July 23, 1903. Edward Person, Paris, Oct. 12, 1942. Robert P. Praeger, Collinsville, Apr. 4, 1918. F. W. Stewart, Iacon, Nov. 7, 1898. Joseph Strands, Johnston City, June 10, 1915. Hallery Willis, Camp Ellis, Nov. 7, 1943. Peter Willis, Sarsaw, July 20, 1889. David Wyatt, Bellville, June 6, 1903. Unknown Negro, Thebes, Apr. 26, 1903. Two Unknown Negroes, Tamms, Sept. 12, 1913.

INDIANA: James Dillard, Sullivan, Nov. 20, 1902. Thomas Henderson, Rockport, Dec. 16, 1900. James Jennings, Specific locality unknown, May 22, 1891. Eli Ladd, Blountsville, Feb. 8, 1890. John Rollo, Bonneville, Dec. 17, 1900. Bud Rowland, Rockport, Dec. 16, 1900. Thomas Shipp, Marion, Aug. 7, 1930. Abraham Smith, Marion, Aug. 7, 1930. Henry Smith, Specific locality unknown, Nov. 18, 1890. George Ward, Terre Haute, Feb. 26, 1901.

IOWA: William Heffen, Moscow, Aug. 5, 1901. George Smith, Specific locality unknown, Jan. 15, 1889. Unknown Negro, Mitchelville, Jan. 18, 1896.

KANSAS: Dan Adams, Salina, Apr. 20, 1893. Fred Alexander, Leavenworth, Jan. 15, 1901. Richard Fisher, Hiawatha, Sept. 9, 1889. Montgomery Godley, Pittsburg, Dec. 25, 1902. Doctor Herman, Topeka, May 13, 1901. Jeff Luggle, Cherokee, Apr. 24, 1894. George Mills, Weir, Oct. 30, 1899. James Thompson, Larned, Sept. 14, 1889. Commodore True, Hiawatha, Nov. 29, 1892. Charles Williams, Galena, Apr. 25, 1899. John Wilson, Leavenworth, Aug. 21, 1893.

KENTUCKY: Richard Allen, Mayfield, Feb. 23, 1898. Henry Alley, Hillside, Nov. 13, 1914. William Arkinson, McKinney, Sept. 2, 1893. Ernest Baker, Cadiz, Jan. 22, 1906. Arch Bauer, Tompkinsville, Oct. 2, 1898. Leon Beard, Normandy, July 7, 1905. Arthur Bell, Princeton, June 4, 1915. Thomas Blambard, Fulton, Apr. 10, 1902. James Bond, Guthrie, Dec. 19, 1892. Mark Brown, Shelbyville, July 20, 1891. Thomas Brown, Nicholasville, Feb. 6, 1902. Marshall Boston, Frankfort, Aug. 14, 1894. Ephraim Brinkley, Madison, July 22, 1897. Raymond Brushrod, Hainesville, Sept. 26, 1897. Ellis Buckner, Henderson, Nov. 26, 1915. Joe Bumpass, Hickman, Aug. 30, 1904. William Butcher, Hickman, Sept. 2, 1895. Gams Calls, Glasgow, June 16, 1898. William Clifford, Maple Grove, Aug. 16, 1907. Richard Coleman, Maysville, Dec. 6, 1899. Ernest Dewley, Brandenburg, Apr. 30, 1902. Elijah Drake, Madrid Bend, Mar. 20, 1902. James Dudley, Georgetown, Aug. 28, 1891. Bell Duly, Fulton, Feb. 15, 1902. Jumbo Fields, Shelbyville, Oct. 2, 1901. George Finley, Mayfield, Dec. 22, 1896. Clarence Garnett, Shelbyville, Oct. 2, 1901. Lee Gibson, Owenton, Jan. 28, 1892. Henry Givens, Nebo, Dec. 16, 1893. Caleb Godly, Bowling Green, June 24, 1894. John Grange, Franklin, July 25, 1891. Willis Griffey, Princeton, Oct. 15, 1894. M. G. Gumble, Jellico Mines, Jan. 21, 1894. Archie Haines, Mason County, June 20, 1894. Burt Haines, Mason County, June 21, 1894. William Haines, Mason County, June 20, 1894. Thomas Hall, Kevil, Oct. 9, 1903. Ernest Harris, Wickliff, Sept. 12, 1901. John Henderson, Midway, Aug. 17, 1890. Brock Henley, Paducah, Oct. 16, 1916. Charles Hill, Paducah, June 10, 1892. Thomas Holmes, Mayfield, Feb. 23, 1898. Alfred Holt, Owensboro, Dec. 26, 1896. Frank Howard, Wickliff, Sept. 12, 1901. Marion Howard, Scottsville, July 16, 1894. Robert Huggard, Winchester, July 15, 1895. Ernest Humphreys, Princeton, Oct. 2, 1890. Doc Jones, Owensboro, Dec. 19, 1889. Robert Jones, Russellville, Aug. 1, 1908. Thomas Jones, Russellville, Aug. 1, 1908. Virgil Jones, Russellville, Aug. 1, 1908. James Kelly, Paris, July 23, 1889. Frank Leavell, Elkton, Oct. 12, 1905. Charles Lewis, Hickman, Dec. 16, 1918. Harrison Lewis, Springfield, Aug. 26, 1895. Daniel Malone, Covington, July 23, 1889. Fomit Martin, Monticello, Feb. 17, 1896. James Mays, Spyfield, Jan. 11, 1902. Lee McDaniels, Oaks Crossing, July 29, 1892. Jacob McDowell, Providence, May 31, 1908. Judge McNeal, Cadiz, Sept. 1, 1893. Charles Miller, Bardwell, July 7, 1893. Samuel Moody, Auburn, Apr. 18, 1890. Edward Moorman, Guston, Jan. 12, 1893. Richard Moorman, Guston, Jan. 12, 1893. Logan Murphy, Mt. Sterling, Aug. 16, 1892. Robert Morton, Rickford, Feb. 4, 1897. Gabe Nalls, Blackford, Nov. 8, 1894. Ulyssess Nalls, Blackford, Nov. 8, 1894. Austin Porter, Grayson, June 8, 1892. Lewis Radford, Guthrie, Jan. 24, 1904. George Ray, Gensonton, Apr. 26, 1895. Sam Reed, Wickliff, Sept. 12, 1901. Joseph Richardson, Leitchfield, Sept. 26, 1913. Joseph Riley, Russellville, Aug. 1, 1908. William Sanders, Mayville, Mar. 12, 1917. Robert Shaw, Waitman, May 22, 1905. William Skapp, Old Union, Apr. 16, 1891. Mollie Smith, Trigg County, July 1, 1895. James Stewart, Madrid Bend, Mar. 20, 1902. James Stone, Mayfield, Dec. 21, 1896. Leonard Taylor, Newcastle, Aug. 28, 1893. Marie Thompson, Lebanon Junction, June 14, 1904. James Thornhill, Paducah, Oct. 16, 1916. Joseph Thornton, Wickliffe, May 20, 1889. John Turner, Greensburg, Dec. 9, 1889. Len Tye, Hariem, Mar. 2, 1894. William Tyler, Carlisle, July 26, 1894. Charles Walton, Morganfield, Aug. 18, 1893. Fraten Warfield, Elliston, Oct. 18, 1900. John Wilcoxson, Edmonton, Sept. 2, 1892. Thomas White, Aurora, Sept. 14, 1896. Nick Willis, Lebanon, June 1, 1892. George Wilson, Meyers, Aug. 15, 1897. Unknown Negro, Bowling Green, Dec. 28, 1892. Unknown Negro, Paducah, Aug. 19, 1893. Two Unknown Negroes, Henderson, Nov. 21, 1895. Unknown Negro, Calvert, Nov. 25, 1895. Unknown Negro, Fulton, May 11, 1896. Unknown Negro, Rock Springs, Mar. 8, 1897. Unknown Negro, Specific locality unknown, July 17, 1904. Ten Unknown Negroes, Rochester, Nov. 13, 1914.

261

LOUISIANA: Charles Alexander, Plaquemine, Dec. 13, 1897. James Alexander, Plaquemine, Dec. 13, 1897. Ernest Allums, Specific locality unknown, May 3, 1912. Edward Ames, Allentown, Apr. 22, 1900. Thomas J. Amos, Cheneyville, Sept. 1, 1900. Emile Antoine, Grand Prairie, July 30, 1909. Aps Ard, Greensburg, Oct. 1, 1909. William Bell, Amite, Apr. 2, 1898. Ovide Belzaire, Youngsville, July 24, 1895. Oliver Bibb, Winona, Feb. 20, 1902. George Bickham, Ponchatonia, Sept. 21, 1900. Douglas Bolte, Quarantine, Oct. 15, 1897. Nathaniel Bowman, Ponchatonia, Sept. 21, 1900. Felton Brigman, Rodessa, May 4, 1901. Henry Brooks, Shreveport, May 11, 1917. Echo Brown, Amite City, Aug. 9, 1899. Jerry Burke, Clio, Dec. 22, 1896. Wood Burke, Benton, Nov. 28, 1912. Dennis Burrel, New Orleans, May 6, 1898. Walter Byrd, Winnsboro, Sept. 15, 1911. "Norm" Cadore, Baton Rouge, Dec. 28, 1912. James Carr, Millview, Dec. 27, 1903. William Carr, Pisquemine, Mar. 18, 1906. Camp Claxton, Tallulah, Apr. 27, 1892. Thell Claxton, Tallulah, Apr. 27, 1892. George Clayton, Mangham, June 18, 1918. Seth Cobb, Devail Bluff, June 12, 1900. Thomas Collins, Bunkie, July 16, 1915. James Comeaux, Jennings, Aug. 27, 1913. "Cotton," Carrolle, Mar. 28, 1906. Joseph Craddvels, Taylor Town, Nov. 2, 1903. Jack Davis, Baldwin, July 24, 1897. William Davis, Blanchard, Mar. 5, 1901. J. H. Day, Monroe, June 14, 1892. Joseph Dazzele, St. Bernard, May 19, 1896. Ely Denton, Rayville, Mar. 14, 1910. "Dic" Dickson, Minden, June 5, 1901. Anton Domingo, Lafayette, Nov. 29, 1906. Ralph Dorans, Ruby, June 28, 1907. Nicholas Dublano, Loreauville, May 13, 1902. Mond Dunley, Minden, July 13, 1896. Frank Dupree, Forest Hill, June 12, 1903. Munroe Durden, Sylvester, Dec. 2, 1914. Silas Ealy, Bossiers City, May 3, 1907. Warren Eaton, Monroe, Oct. 22, 1913. Charles Elliott, Ponchatonia, Sept. 21, 1900. James Estes, Delhi, Nov. 20, 1909. Felician Francis, New Orleans, Sept. 26, 1895. Gilbert Francis, St. Joseph, Feb. 29, 1896. George Franklin, Homer, Apr. 1, 1902. Washington Furran, Monroe, Oct. 2, 1897. Henry Gardner, Monroe, Mar. 15, 1907. Joseph Gifford, Floyd, Oct. 27, 1909. Isaac Glover, Springfield, Sept. 14, 1910. John Gordon, Specific locality unknown, Aug. 10, 1897. Edward Gray, St. Peter, June 14, 1899. Charles Griffin, Munroe, Aug. 7, 1914. Presto Griffin, Munroe, Aug. 7, 1914. Bub Hall, Bastrop, Aug. 7, 1918. Edward Hamilton, Shreveport, May 12, 1914. Louis Hamilton, Bossier Point, Oct. 9, 1896. Jess Hammett, Vivian, Aug. 29, 1916. Andrew Harris, Bethany, Aug. 3, 1908. Henry Harris, Lena, May 15, 1900. Jack Harris, Concordia, June 24, 1903. William Harris, New Orleans, Mar. 9, 1898. Scott Harvey, Tallulah, Apr. 27, 1892. Alexander Hawkins, Gretna, Sept. 24, 1896. James Heard, Benton, Nov. 28, 1912. Hearn, Benton, Dec. 6, 1898. Nicholas Hector, New Iberia, Oct. 12, 1908. Bread Henderson, Mooringsport, Dec. 11, 1914. Alex Hill, Floyd, Oct. 27, 1909. Henry Hill, Mangham, Sept. 8, 1909. Henry Holmes, Munroe, Aug. 7, 1914. Emma Hooper, Hammond, Mar. 1, 1917. Jim Hudson, Benton, Jan. 26, 1918. John Hugerly, Allentown, Apr. 22, 1900. Charles Jackson, Redwood, May 15, 1897. Mathias Jackson, Alexandria, June 28, 1907. Thomas Jackson, Blanchard, May 13, 1906. Thomas Jackson, St. Peter, Feb. 17, 1901. Mark Jacobs, Beinville, June 10, 1892. Frank James, Bayou Sara, July 15, 1896. Silas Jimmerson, Benton, Nov. 28, 1912. Fred Johnson, New Orleans, Oct. 12, 1917. Grant Johnson, Alden Bridge, May 4, 1901. Gus Johnson, Amite City, Jan. 19, 1897. Henry Johnson, Echo, June 1, 1907. Nubry Johnson, Baton Rouge, Oct. 19, 1900. Sam Johnson, Grand Cane, Sept. 25, 1912. Archie Joiner, Amite City, Jan. 19, 1897. George Jones, St. Charles, July 16, 1899. Jim Jones, Rayville, Feb. 26, 1918. John C. Jones, Minden, Aug. 8, 1946. George Kenny, Taylor Town, Oct. 16, 1903. Fred Kilbourne, Clinton, Apr. 17, 1907. George King, New Orleans, Dec. 23, 1892. Joseph Lamb, Francisville, Nov. 26, 1902. Cornelius Lee, Plaquemine, Feb. 7, 1903. Columbus Lewis, Lincoln, Apr. 26, 1898. Jim Lewis, Rayville, Feb. 26, 1918. Tobe Lewis, Sylvester Station, Dec. 2, 1914. Watkins Lewis, Shreveport, Dec. 12, 1914. Oscar Livingston, Point a la Hache, Aug. 2, 1931. Bird Love, Raybille, Mar. 16, 1896. James McCauley, Monroe, Sept. 16, 1896. Vance McClure, New Iberia, July 26, 1892. Jerry McCly, Tallulah, Apr. 27, 1892. Isaac McGee, Homer, July 27, 1896. Kane McKnight, Sylvester Station, Dec. 3, 1914. George McNerl, Monroe, Mar. 16, 1918. John Miles, Specific locality unknown, Sept. 19, 1908. Thomas Miles, Shreveport, Apr. 9, 1912. Robert Mitchell, Oak Grove, Feb. 5, 1908. William Moeley, Winona, Sept. 8, 1902. F. C. Moland, Bossier, June 20, 1901. Joseph Momas, Luling, Jan. 26, 1903. Charles Morrell, Edgard, Nov. 17, 1898. Patrick Morris, New Orleans, Jan. 12, 1896. William Morris, Balltown, Oct. 12, 1901. William Nixon, Delhi, Nov. 8, 1911. William Oliver, Jefferson, Oct. 1, 1897. Wiltzie Page, Bienville, Feb. 24, 1906. Andrew Pigge, New Orleans, Mar. 9, 1898. Frank Piper, Alexandria Rapides County, May 8, 1904. Isaac Pizer, Shreveport, Mar. 23, 1896. James Porter, Minden, July 13, 1896. Laura

Porter, Monroe, Aug. 25, 1910. Oval Poulson, Opelousas, Jan. 20, 1911. Will Powell, Rayville, Feb. 26, 1918. Sam Poydrass, Lake Charles, Dec. 7, 1901. Henry Rachel, Shreveport, Nov. 27, 1909. Courtney Rendrick, Monroe, July 13, 1896. John Richards, Monroe, Mar. 16, 1918. R. T. Rogers, Tallulah, May 28, 1906. Isiah Rollins, Ponchatonia, Sept. 21, 1900. Romeo, Slidell, Aug. 19, 1914. Daniel Rout, Amite, July 29, 1917. Jerry Rout, Amite, July 29, 1917. Marvel Ruffin, Edgard, July 10, 1917. Louis Senegal, Carenero, Mar. 24, 1896. Alfred Shaufilet, Calhoun, Aug. 26, 1906. Scott Sherman, Morehouse Parish, Dec. 28, 1892. Man Singleton, Grant Point, Aug. 11, 1899. A. L. Smart, Monroe, Jan. 10, 1896. Prophet Smith, Bossier, June 20, 1901. William Smith, Hammond, Sept. 22, 1895. Walter Starkes, Baldwin, June 12, 1896. Charles Strauss, Bunkie, Apr. 16, 1907. William Street, Doyline, June 3, 1898. Jennis Sturs, Shreveport, July 26, 1903. U. G. Tally, McNary, May 25, 1916. Miles Taylor, Claibourne, July 24, 1911. Joseph Thomas, Plaquemine, Dec. 13, 1897. Louis Thomas, Girard, July 15, 1901. Onexzime Thomas, Grand Prairie, July 30, 1909. Atticus Thompson, Forest, July 13, 1897. Frank Thompson, Shreveport, Nov. 24, 1901. Thomas Underwood, Monroe, June 4, 1892. Thomas Vital, Fenton, Feb. 21, 1901. Link Waggoner, Minden, Sept. 9, 1892. Charles Washington, Mooringsport, Dec. 11, 1914. William Way, Monroe, Aug. 24, 1909. Hiram Weightman, Franklin, Aug. 5, 1896. Sam West, East Louisiana, Sept. 1, 1901. Edward White, Hudson, June 28, 1892. George Whitney, Ethel, May 8, 1906. Lamb Whittle, Concordia, June 24, 1903. Clyde Williams, Monroe, Apr. 22, 1918. Coat Williams, Pine Grove, May 15, 1892. Ernest Williams, Blanchard, Dec. 16, 1913. Frank Williams, Blanchard, Dec. 16, 1913. Flint Williams, Monroe, Mar. 15, 1907. Gus Williams, Amite City, Jan. 19, 1897. Monsie Williams, Tangipahoa, Nov. 26, 1905. R. C. Williams, Ruston, Oct. 13, 1938. Robert Williams, Concordia Parish, Sept. 14, 1892. James Wilson, Gibsland, June 10, 1907. Thomas Wilson, Batchelor, June 1, 1905. John Woodward, Vidalia, Mar. 10, 1902. Unknown Negro, Bossier, May 21, 1896. Unknown Negro, White Castle, Jan. 17, 1897. Unknown Negro, Oak Ridge, June 15, 1898. Unknown Negro, Jones, Dec. 13, 1899. Unknown Negro, Lindsay, July 27, 1899. Unknown Negro, Crowley, July 19, 1901. Unkown Negro, Doylands, Jan. 24, 1901. Two Unknown Negroes, West Carrol, Jan. 26, 1902. Unknown Negro, Calcasieur, Oct. 17, 1902. Unknown Negro, Victoria, Apr. 10, 1902. Unknown Negro, Iros, Aug. 12, 1905. Unknown Negro, Mer Rouge, Dec. 13, 1907. Three Unknown Negroes, Jonesville, July 18, 1908. Unknown Negro, Morehouse, Aug. 15, 1909. Unknown Negro, Delhi, Apr. 25, 1912. Unknown Negro, Munroe, Aug. 9, 1914. Unknown Negro, St. James, May 7, 1914. Unknown Negro, Conshama, Aug. 26, 1915. Unknown Negro, Grand Bayou, Aug. 21, 1915.

MARYLAND: Asbury Green, Centerville, May 12, 1891.

MISSISSIPPI: Sloan Allen, West, Dec. 23, 1893. Samuel Adams, Pass Christian, Nov. 5, 1903. Washington Adams, Columbus, June 10, 1938. Thomas Allen, McGee, Mar. 11, 1899. Wood Ambrose, Prentiss, June 11, 1906. Alex Anderson, Grenada, Mar. 20, 1898. Moses Anderson, Brookfield, Apr. 6, 1899. Askew, Mississippi City, June 10, 1900. Gloster Barnes, Vicksburg, Oct. 23, 1900. Rufus Beagley, Jackson, Nov. 15, 1893. Henry Bell, Greenwood, Jan. 23, 1907. Terry Bell, Terry, Mar. 20, 1895. Robert Betat, Bluff Creek, Mar. 20, 1895. Jack Betts, Corinth, Aug. 13, 1900. Thomas Bowen, Brook Haven, June 29, 1895. Willia Boyd, Silver City, Mar. 23, 1899. William Bradford, Chunky, June 16, 1911. Simon Brooks, Sardis, June 11, 1899. Frank Brown, Tunica, Sept. 14, 1900. Jeff Brown, West Point, Mar. 20, 1916. William Brown, Tunica, Sept. 14, 1900. Walter Brownlee, Hinchcliff, Oct. 15, 1913. Robert Bryant, Vicksburg, May 3, 1903. Thomas Burns, Hernando, Nov. 3, 1914. John Burr, Wesson, Apr. 5, 1908. Charles Burwell, Meridian, July 28, 1895. Robby Buskin, Houston, Feb. 9, 1909. Louisa Carter, Jackson, Nov. 15, 1893. William Carter, Winston County, Dec. 26, 1894. William Chandler, Abbeyville, June 19, 1895. Clark, Trail Lake, June 3, 1904. Andrew Clark, Shubuta, Dec. 21, 1918. Major Clark, Shubuta, Dec. 21, 1918. Thomas Clark, Corinth, Sept. 28, 1902. Thomas Clayton, Hernando, Mar. 10, 1900. Sam Cole, Pea Ridge, Jan. 7, 1898. Alex Coleman, Starkesville, Apr. 3, 1912. Mimms Collier, Steenston, Nov. 18, 1896. James Cooper, Hemlock, May 27, 1897. Spencer Costello, Flora, Jan. 7, 1895. Thomas Crompton, Centerville, Oct. 25, 1906. Harry Crosby, Louisville, Sept. 21, 1913. James Crosby, Tutwiler, Mar. 4, 1900. Henry Crower, Hernando, Oct. 6, 1897. Elmer Curl, Mastadon, June 12, 1910. Joseph Dailey, Comorant, July 14, 1914. Frank Davis, Lula, Oct. 11, 1908. Joseph Davis, Lula, Oct. 11, 1908. Dee Dawson, Hickory, Oct. 10,

1908. R. W. Dawson, Natchez, June 17, 1895. Robert Dennis, Greenville, June 4, 1903. Bill Dukes, Natchez, Aug. 15, 1918. Sterling Dunham, Europa, June 26, 1904. William Edward, Deep Creek Bridge, Mar. 27, 1900. G. W. Edd, Macon, May 7, 1912. Jesse Evans, Edwards, Apr. 16, 1897. Zed Floyd, Tunica, Sept. 12, 1900. Lee Fox, Yazoo City, June 9, 1907. William Fuller, Hickory, Oct. 10, 1908. Rid George, Hattiesburg, Aug. 4, 1905. Charles German, Belen, Oct. 29, 1907. Neeley Giles, Sucarnoochee, Jan. 15, 1912. Pary Giliam, Aberdeen, June 28, 1897. George Gordon, Albin, May 1, 1900. Joseph Gordon, Greenwood, Mar. 12, 1909. Wesley Gould, Leland, July 12, 1898. Ernest Green, Quitman, Oct. 12, 1942. James Green, Boyle, Dec. 11, 1905. Tom Green, Rolling Fork, July 6, 1938. Alfred Grizzard, Tiptonville, June 21, 1889. Haines, Belen, Apr. 3, 1897. Mann Hamilton, Starkesville, Feb. 14, 1912. Lewis Harkhead, Amite County, July 6, 1894. Burke Harris, Cleveland, Mar. 19, 1904. David Harris, Rosedale, Apr. 23, 1930. Henry Harris, Glendora, July 19, 1905. William Harris, Glendora, July 25, 1905. Mose Hart, Corinth, May 20, 1903. Stanley Hayes, Brandon, July 26, 1899. Van Haynes, Columbia, June 2, 1917. W. A. Healey, Jackson, Nov. 15, 1893. Pratt Hempton, Columbia, June 2, 1917. Peter Henderson, Itta Bena, Jan. 20, 1897. A. Hicks, Rocky Springs, May 7, 1894. Alexander Hill, Brookville, Feb. 10, 1915. Richard Hill, Philadelphia, Sept. 1, 1901. Eli Hilson, Brookhaven, Dec. 24, 1903. "Jet" Hinks, Lee County, Nov. 8, 1906. Samuel Hinson, Cushtusha, May 16, 1900. William Hodges, Union, Nov. 2, 1908. Luther Holbert and his wife, Doddsville, Feb. 7, 1904. John Hollins, Drew, Jan. 10, 1903. T. W. Hollinshead, Mar. 28, 1897. Hood, Amite County, July 6, 1894. James Hopkins, Glendora, Dec. 27, 1897. Alma House, Shubuta, Dec. 21, 1918. Maggie House, Shubuta, Dec. 21, 1918. Pat Husband, McHenry, Dec. 16, 1907. Fred Isham, Macon, Feb. 18, 1901. Henry Isham, Macon, Feb. 18, 1901. Benjamin Jackson, Jackson, Nov. 15, 1893. Benjamin Jackson, Quincy, Nov. 8, 1893. Mahala Jackson, Jackson, Nov. 15, 1893. W. J. Jackson, Hernando, Oct. 15, 1908. Forest Jameson, Brookfield, Apr. 6, 1899. William Jackson, Tunica, Oct. 11, 1907. John James, Woodville, Oct. 10, 1905. William James, Tallahatchie County, Sept. 14, 1905. Cato Jarrett, Stouts Crossing, July 7, 1903. Abe Johnson, Yazoo City, June 8, 1907. Charles Johnson, Walnut Grove, Aug. 17, 1902. Edward Johnson, Vicksburg, Jan. 20, 1915. Elijah Johnson, Vicksburg, Mar. 29, 1931. Frank Johnson, Hickory, Oct. 10, 1908. Harry Johnson, Yazoo City, June 8, 1907. Thomas Johnson, Hattiesburg, July 25, 1895. Jones, Braxton, June 28, 1910. Charles Jones, Yazoo City, Sept. 20, 1908. Charles Jones, Weason, Dec. 10, 1897. George Jones, Mayersville, Sept., 1903. James Jones, Macon, Jan. 1, 1898. Walter Jones, Harriston, Sept. 28, 1913. William Jones, Harriston, Sept. 28, 1913. William Jones, Lake Cormorant, Mar. 6, 1898. George Kincaid, Cleveland, June 12, 1903. Charles Lang, Quitman, Oct. 12, 1942. Henry Leidy, Biloxi, Nov. 10, 1908. Lewis, Gulfport, Dec. 20, 1900. Edward Lewis, Hattiesburg, Aug. 4, 1905. George Linton, Brookhaven, June 28, 1894. Pigg Lockett, Scooba, Sept. 10, 1930. Joseph Luflore, St. Anne, Oct. 21, 1899. James Martin, Bolton, Dec. 23, 1899. Warner Matthews, Ocean Springs, Feb. 1, 1901. Harvey Mayberry, Teysela, Apr. 3, 1898. Mayfield, Trail Lake, June 4, 1904. Henry McAfee, Brownsville, Apr. 19, 1900. William McAlpin, Smith County, Oct. 27, 1903. Belfield McCray, Carrolton, Aug. 1, 1901. Betsy McCray, Carrolton, Aug. 1, 1901. Ida McCray, Carrolton, Aug. 1, 1901. Jchn McDaniel, Smithdale, Aug. 4, 1902. "Bootjack" McDaniels, Winona, Apr. 13, 1937. John McDowell, Rankin County, Sept. 19, 1905. Wilder McGowan, Wiggins, Nov. 21, 1938. Johnson McQuirk, Love Station, Feb. 16, 1914. Leon McTatie, Lexington, July 22, 1946. Meyer, Carrollton, Oct. 27, 1907. Mayshe Miller, Aberdeen, Oct. 25, 1914. Otto Mitchell, Durant, June 15, 1910. William Mitchell, Sardis, July 16, 1915. Pierce Moberly, Meridian, June 25, 1905. Horace Montgomery, Specific locality unknown, Apr. 11, 1909. David Moore, Tunica, Sept. 14, 1900. "Judge" Moseley, Lockhart, Nov. 7, 1911. John M. Moses, Crystal Springs, June 25, 1897. Horace Muller, Cookamie County, May 13, 1902. Ready Murdock, Yazoo City, June 4, 1894. Allen Myers, Rankin County, July 20, 1894. Allen Nance, Greenwood, Oct. 6, 1916. Henry Noark, Hattiesburg, July 25, 1894. William Ody, Clayton, July 15, 1902. Thomas O'Neill, Meridian, Apr. 19, 1910. William Otis, Rawles Springs, Sept. 20, 1899. Mack Charles Parker, Poplarville, Apr. 24, 1959. Daniel Patrick, Scranton, June 20, 1899. William Patterson, Westville, July .19, 1898. Lawson Patton, Oxford, Sept. 8, 1908. Dago Pete, Tutwiler, June 3, 1900. Sam Petty, Leland, Feb. 24, 1914. Theodore Picket, Jackson, July 6, 1895. Eli Pigatt, Brookhaven, Feb. 10, 1908. David Poe, Van Cleave, Mar. 10, 1908. Augustus Pond, Tupelo, July 7, 1894. George Pond, Fulton, July 6, 1894. William Price, Carrolton, Aug. 4, 1901. Thomas Ranston, Van Cleave, Mar. 10, 1908.

Henry Ratcliff, Gloster, May 1, 1900. C. C. Reed, Silver City, Mar. 23, 1899. Alt Rees, Rosetta, Sept. 1, 1905. Bush Riley, Tallula, Jan. 14, 1904. George Robinson, Raymond, Aug. 15, 1930. George Robinson, Tunica, Oct. 11, 1907. William Robinson, Greenville, Aug. 17, 1909. William Robinson, Lambert, June 27, 1913. Joe Rodgers, Canton, May 8, 1939. Fayette Sawyer, Cleveland, Mar. 19, 1904. Saybrick, Fishers Ferry, Mar. 30, 1894. James Sellers, Pittsboro, July 28, 1897. Rev. Isaac Simmons, Liberty, Mar. 26, 1944. David Simms, Coahoma, Nov. 22, 1905. Sam Simms, Jackson, May 8, 1906. James Shoots, Tunica, Oct. 11, 1907. Claud Singleton, Poplarville, Apr. 20, 1918. Frank Smith, Newton, Nov. 11, 1893. Henry Smith, Clinton, May 29, 1894. William Stern, Rosemeath, Sept. 6, 1899. Frederick Sullivan, Byhalia, Nov. 24, 1914. Mrs. Frederick Sullivan, Byhalia, Nov. 25, 1914. Henry Sykes, Van Vleet, Oct. 23, 1907. John Taylor, Aberdeen, Nov. 12, 1915. Andrew Thomas, Scranton, July 18, 1895. Henry Thomas, Bolar, Jan. 21, 1889. Luke Thomas, Biloxi, June 15, 1894. Nicholas Thompson, Armory, Sept. 1, 1910. Emmett Till, Monez, Aug. 28, 1955. Samuel Towner, Alligator, July 15, 1913. Roosevelt Townes, Winona, Apr. 13, 1937. Andrew Trice, Olive Branch, July 20, 1907. Jesse Tucker, Houston, July 10, 1904. Van Horne, Trail Lake, June 3, 1904. Mulloch Walker, Corinth, Aug. 11, 1898. Thomas Waller, Brookhaven, Dec. 16, 1897. Howard Wash, Laurel, Oct. 17, 1942. Sam Washington, Vicksburg, July 29, 1907. James Watts, Pea Ridge, Jan. 7, 1898. Willie Webb, Drew, Feb. 23, 1913. Frank West, Bolton, Dec. 23, 1899. White, Tallahatchie County, Dec. 6, 1898. Holly White, Scooba, Sept. 10, 1930. Steve Wiley, Inverness, Mar. 22, 1931. Andrew Williams, Houston, Feb. 7, 1913. John Williams, Ittababa, Aug. 28, 1908. Lewis Williams, Hewitt Springs, June 9, 1894. Will Williams, Centerville, Sept., 1903. William Williams, Hamburg, Oct. 16, 1897. "Pink" Willis, Poplarville, Jan. 16, 1909. Minor Wilson, Silver City, Mar. 23, 1899. William Wilson, Port Gibson, Aug. 11, 1899. Malachi Wright, Houston, July 9, 1949. Moses York, Tunica, Apr. 16, 1900. Henry Young, Lake Cormorant, Aug. 4, 1905. Perry Young, Winona, June 27, 1896. Wes Young, Valley Park, Dec. 5, 1906. John Youngblood, Summit, Nov. 20, 1902. George Younger, Columbus, May 23, 1906. Unknown Negro, Fannin, Dec. 23, 1893. Unknown Negro, Biloxi, July 14, 1894. Unknown Negro Woman, Simpson County, July 24, 1894. Unknown Negro, Rodney, May 23, 1895. Unknown Negro, Simpson County, Sept. 2, 1895. Unknown Negro, Sunnyside, Oct. 21, 1896. Two Unknown Negroes, Vardaman, Jan. 10, 1897. Unknown Negro, Vicksburg, Apr. 10, 1897. Three Unknown Negroes, Meridian, Nov. 27, 1898. Unknown Negro, Pushington, July 24, 1899. Unknown Negro, Amity County, May 7, 1900. Two Unknown Negroes, Arcadia, Dec. 19, 1900. Unknown Negro, Perry County, Nov. 4, 1901. Unknown Negro, Darling, Nov. 1, 1902. Two Unknown Negroes, Cross Roads, July 20, 1902. Unknown Negro, Estabutchie, Oct. 20, 1902. Unknown Negro, Summit, Nov. 20, 1902. Unknown Negro, Hattiesburg, Oct. 29, 1903. Unknown Negro Woman, Smith County, June 8, 1903. Four Unknown Negroes, Smith County, June 8, 1903. Unknown Negro, Woodville, May 28, 1903. Three Unknown Negroes, Doddsville, Feb. 7, 1904. Unknown Negro, O'Neil. May 24, 1904. Unknown Negro, Saucier, Mar. 17, 1904. Unknown Negro, Specific locality unknown, July 9, 1904. Unknown Negro, Benoit, Jan. 4, 1905. Unknown Negro, Helm Station, Mar. 5, 1905. Unknown Negro, Basin, Oct. 6, 1906. Unknown Negro, De Kalb, June 30, 1906. Two Unknown Negroes, Laurel, Sept. 7, 1906. Unknown Negro, Penola, Jan. 17, 1906. Unknown Negro, Brookhaven, Jan. 2, 1908. Two Unknown Negroes, Commerce, Jan. 28, 1908. Two Jenkins Brothers, Van Cleave, Mar. 10, 1908. Four Unknown Negroes, Kemper County, Oct. 28, 1909. Unknown Negro, Greenville, May 7, 1912. Unknown Negro, Jackson, Dec. 17, 1912. Unknown Negro, Drew, Jan. 30, 1913. Two Unknown Negroes, Clarksdale, Oct. 11, 1915. Unknown Negro, DeKalb, July 11, 1915. Unknown Negro, Cedar Bluffs, June 28, 1915. Unknown Negro, Louisville, May 15, 1915.

MISSOURI: William Allen, Springfield, Apr. 15, 1906. Frank Embree, Steinmetz, July 23, 1899. Fayette Chandler, St. Charles, Apr. 3, 1916. Mrs. Paralee Collins, West Plains, June 17, 1914. Robert Coleman, Charleston, July 3, 1910. J. C. Collins, Mondak, Apr. 5, 1913. James Copeland, Springfield, Apr. 14, 1906. John Buckner, Valley Park, Jan. 17, 1894. Erastus Brown, Villa Ridge, July 10, 1897. George Burke, Columbia, Sept. 17, 1889. Mundee Chowagee, Marshall, Apr. 28, 1900. Andy Clark, Leeper, Jan. 21, 1903. Henry Darley, Liberty, May 4, 1900. Emmett Divens, Fulton, Aug. 15, 1895. Harry Duncan, Springfield, Apr. 4, 1906. Sam Field, Charleston, July 3, 1910. Harry Gates, Lexington, Aug. 12, 1902. Thomas Gilyard, Joplin, Apr. 15, 1903. French Godley, Pierce City, Aug. 19, 1901. William

Godley, Pierce City, Aug. 19, 1901. Raymond Gunn, Maryville, Jan. 12, 1931. Peter Hampton, Pierce City, Aug. 20, 1901. Thomas Hayden, Fayette, Nov. 1, 1899. Ulyssess Haydon, Monett, June 29, 1894. Robert Hepler, Nevada, Jan. 22, 1892. William Henderson, Jackson, Oct. 11, 1895. John Hughes, Moberly, Feb. 18, 1893. George Johnson, Platte City, Aug. 1, 1909. Joseph Johnson, Hillers Creek, July 2, 1894. Isaac Kollins, West Plains, June 17, 1914. Rudd Lane, Louisiana, Sept. 1, 1915. D. Malone, Caruthersville, May 3, 1903. Richard Mayes, Springfield, Feb. 21, 1893. Arthur McNeal, Richmond, Mar. 2, 1901. W. J. Mooneyhon, Caruthersville, May 3, 1903. Robert Pettigrew, Belmont, May 12, 1905. A. B. Richardson, Caruthersville, Oct. 11, 1911. Dallas Shields, Fayette, Mar. 19, 1914. Nelson Simpson, Neelyville, Jan. 3, 1901. David Sims, Clarkton, Apr. 27, 1892. Benjamin Smith, La Plata, Aug. 3, 1889. Thomas Smith, Polar Bluff, Sept. 3, 1890. Samuel Sykes, Hayti, Jan. 3, 1916. George Tracy, Kingston, Feb. 17, 1895. Olli Truxton, Glasgow, Jan. 20, 1891. Ward, Galena, Feb. 2, 1898. Henry Williams, Macon, June 30, 1898. W. F. Williams, Mt. Pleasant, Feb. 21, 1915. Benjamin Woods, Caruthersville, Oct. 11, 1911. Cleo Wright, Sikeston, Jan. 25, 1942. Louis Wright, New Madrid, Feb. 17, 1902. Oliver Wright, Higbee, Mar. 26, 1902. Curtin Young, Clarkville, June 6, 1898. Sam Young, Clarkville, June 6, 1898. Unknown Negro, Verona, Jan. 22, 1894. Unknown Negro, New Madrid, Nov. 29, 1898. Unknown Negro, New Madrid, May 30, 1910.

NEBRASKA: Joseph Coe, Omaha, Oct. 9, 1891. George Hurst, Neely, Feb. 2, 1894.

NEW MEXICO: Arthur Woodward, Silver City, Sept. 2, 1905. Talcum Woodward, Silver City, Sept. 2, 1905.

NEW YORK: Robert Lewis, Port Jervis, June 2, 1892.

NORTH CAROLINA: Peter Bazemore, Lewiston, Mar. 26, 1918. Robert Berrier, Lexington, Oct. 25, 1889. Mack Bess, Nearland, Sept. 8, 1891. Joseph Black, Kingston, Apr. 5, 1916. David Boone, Morganton, Sept. 11, 1889. J. A. Burris, Albemarle, June 12, 1892. Robert Charmers, Cranberry, Apr. 22, 1896. Jack Dillingham, Salisbury, Aug. 6, 1906. Kinch Freeman, Winton, Dec. 24, 1890. Harrison Gillespie, Salisbury, June 11, 1902. John Gillespie, Salisbury, Aug. 6, 1906. Nease Gillespie, Salisbury, Aug. 6, 1906. William Harris, Asheville, Nov. 15, 1906. Luke Hough, Wadesborough, Aug. 21, 1901. Thomas Johnson, Concord, Mar. 29, 1897. Henry Jones, Harps Cross, Jan. 11, 1899. Thomas Jones, Seven Springs, Aug. 25, 1902. Joseph Kiser, Concord, May 29, 1897. Isaac Lincoln, Ft. Madison, June 2, 1893. Joseph McNeely, Charlotte, Aug. 26, 1913. Robert Melker, Cherryville, Apr. 13, 1941. John Moore, Clark, Aug. 27, 1905. Oliver Moore, Tarboro, Aug. 19, 1930. Lyman Purdee, Elizabethtown, May 3, 1892. Hezekiah Rankin, Asheville, Sept. 25, 1891. George Ratcliffe, Clyde, Mar. 4, 1900. John Richards, Goldsboro, Jan. 12, 1916. George Ritter, Carthage, Mar. 22, 1900. John Sigmond, Stanley Creek, Sept. 9, 1889. Frank Stack, Morganton, Sept. 11, 1889. George Taylor, Rolesville, Nov. 5, 1918. James Walker, Washington, Mar. 25, 1902. Nathan Willis, Town Creek, Nov. 27, 1897. James Wilson, Wendell, Jan. 27, 1914. Thomas Whitson, Asheville, Feb. 24, 1893. Wilson Whitson, Asheville, Feb. 24, 1893. Unknown Negro, Pocket Township, Jan. 6, 1893. Two Unknown Negroes, Pitt County, May 11, 1899. Unknown Negro, Forest City, Sept. 1, 1900. Unknown Negro, Seaboard, May 19, 1904. Unknown Negro, Pine Level, Jan. 12, 1908. Unknown Negro, Charlotte, May 26, 1910. Unknown Negro, Pelham, Oct. 8, 1910.

OHIO: Noah Anderson, New Richmond, Aug. 21, 1895. Henry Corbin, Oxford, Jan. 14, 1892. Richard Dixon, Springfield, Mar. 7, 1904. Charles Mitchell, Urbana, June 4, 1897. Seymour Neville, Rushsylvania, Apr. 15, 1894. Roscoe Parker, West Union, Jan. 12, 1894. Unknown Negro, Millersburg, Apr. 1, 1892. Unknown Negro, Cleveland, June 27, 1911.

OKLAHOMA: Henry Argo, Chickasha, May 31, 1930. Father Bailey, Oklahoma City, July 16, 1907. Edward Berry, Shawnee, Aug. 6, 1915. William Campbell, Pond Creek, May 25, 1901. Peter Carter, Purcell, Aug. 24, 1911. Henry Conly, Holdenville, June 16, 1917. Cora, Guthrie, Dec. 21, 1892. John Cudjo, Wewoka, Nov. 4, 1913. Benjamin Dickerson, Noble, Jan. 27, 1914. Carl Dudley, Lawton, Apr. 9, 1916. John Foreman, Nowata, Sept. 29, 1916. Sanders Franklin, Paul's Valley, Aug. 14, 1913. James Garden, Muskogee, Dec. 24, 1907. Peter Johnson, Edmond, Oct. 1, 1898. L. Magill,

Madill, June 29, 1918. Oscar Martin, Idabel, Apr. 3. 1916. B. S. Morris, Watonga, Sept. 16, 1896. Laura Nelson and Son, Okemah, May 25, 1911. Powell, Nowata, Sept. 29, 1916. Henry Ralston, Paul's Valley, Aug. 14, 1913. Marie Scott, Wagoner County, Mar. 31, 1914. Sylvester Shennien, Wilburton, June 26, 1909. Dennis Simmons, Anadarko, June 13, 1913. Edward Suddeth, Cometa, Oct. 22, 1911. Samuel Turner, Muldrow, Jan. 1, 1912. Bud Walker, Mannford Creek, Dec. 6, 1911. Dr. E. B. Ward, Norman, May 9, 1915. George Washington, Wagoner, Sept. 4, 1915. Crockett Williams, Eufaula, Aug. 7, 1914. James Williams, Colbert, Mar. 31, 1907. In Ki Wish, Specific locality unknown, Sept. 16, 1894. Unknown Negro, Woodward, Mar. 3, 1891. Unknown Negro, Lincoln, Sept. 26, 1894. Unknown Negro, Chickasha, July 2, 1906. Unknown Negro, Choctaw Nation, May 23, 1906. Unknown Negro, Mannford, Nov. 15, 1910. Unknown Negro, Durant, Aug. 18, 1911. Unknown Negro, Wagoner County, Jan. 2, 1913.

OREGON: Alonzo Fisher, Mansfield, Sept. 15, 1902. A. J. Hunt, Specific locality unknown, Apr. 24, 1891. W. S. Thompson, Lake View, Aug. 2, 1894. Unknown Negro, July 17, 1914.

PENNSYLVANIA: Dennis Hampton, Barnsley, May 23, 1891. David Pierce, Dunbar, Dec. 13, 1899. Zachariah Walker, Coatesville, Aug. 13, 1911.

SOUTH CAROLINA: Michael Adams, Barnwell, Dec. 28, 1889. Dora Baker, Lake City, Feb. 22, 1898. F. B. Baker, Lake City, Feb. 22, 1898. Hayward Banks, Columbia, May 10, 1893. Peter Bell, Barnwell, Dec. 28, 1889. Walter Best, Fairfax, Feb. 23, 1918. James Black, Ravenals, June 5, 1902. William Black, Barnwell, Jan. 11, 1890. William Blake, Hampton, Dec. 7, 1895. Joseph Bronson, Blacksburg, Mar. 29, 1912. William Brewington, Wadis Station, Jan. 26, 1889. Lawrence Brown, Stilton, Jan. 6, 1897. William Burts, Basket Mills, Feb. 17, 1900. Jesse Butler, Aiken County, July 20, 1903. Andy Caldwell, Ridgewater, June 22, 1889. Rose Carson, Elloree, July 13, 1914. Flute Clark, Little Mountain, Nov. 26, 1910. Benjamin Collins, Phoenix, Nov. 10, 1898. Simon Cooper, Sumter, Jan. 8, 1897. William Cornish, Port Royal, July 21, 1901. Anthony Crawford, Abbeville, Oct. 21, 1916. Jeff Crawford, Bethune, June 2, 1894. Frank Da Loach, Barnwell, Dec. 20, 1905. John Da Loach, Barnwell, Dec. 20, 1905. Tut Danford, Mt. Carmel, May 17, 1889. Jeff Darling, Phoenix, Nov. 9, 1898. Arthur Davis, Florence, Jan. 6, 1909. Jacob Davis, Greenwood, Aug. 23, 1893. Mark Davis, Newberry, Nov. 15, 1906. Robert Davis, Greenwood, Aug. 30, 1906. Alfred Dublin, Olar, Mar. 13, 1912. Richard Dublin, Olar, Mar. 13, 1912. Daniel Dicks, Ellenton, July 18, 1896. Willie Earle, Pickens County, Feb. 17, 1947. Reub Elrod, Piedmont, July 1, 1903. Robert Ethridge, Mont Willing, Aug. 20, 1906. Rose Etheridge, Phoenix, Nov. 9, 1898. Charles Evans, Norway, July 11, 1903. John Fagler, Ross Station, Nov. 28, 1903. Henry Fitts, Norway, Dec. 21, 1912. Hugh Furz, Barnwell, Dec. 28, 1889. Sam Gaillard, Specific locality unknown, May 6, 1893. Harry Gill, Lancaster, June 3, 1894. Eliza Goode, Greenwood, Nov. 18, 1898. James Gray, Golboro, July 23, 1897. Allen Green, Walhalla, Apr. 24, 1930. William Grier, Coward, Dec. 4, 1914. Haines, Thickety, July 14, 1901. Dennis Head, Aiken County, July 20, 1903. Essex Harrison, Phoenix, Nov. 10, 1898. George Hudson, Trenton, June 2, 1907. Moses Hughes, Union, June 14, 1906. David Hunter, Clinton, Jan. 4, 1898. Columbus Jackson, Phoenix, Nov. 9, 1898. Ira Jackson, Piedmont, July 15, 1895. Willis Jackson, Greenville, Oct. 10, 1911. Daniel Jenkins, Union, June 21, 1930. Henry Johnson, Central, Dec. 3, 1890. Hudson Johnson, Barnwell, Dec. 28, 1889. Judge Jones, Barnwell, Dec. 28, 1889. Ripley Johnson, Barnwell, Dec. 28, 1889. Hannah Kearse, Colleton County, Dec. 5, 1895. Isom Kearse, Colleton County, Dec. 5, 1895. Melville Kennedy, Windsor, Feb. 29, 1896. Robert Kennedy, Spartanburg, Nov. 8, 1893. John Ladison, Anderson County, Nov. 24, 1901. Willie Leaphart, Lexington, May 5, 1890. "General" Lee, Dorchester County, Jan. 15, 1904. Richard Lundy, Edgefield, Dec. 10, 1891. Joseph Mackie, Edgefield Court House, Oct. 23, 1898. James Mason, Abbeville County, July 14, 1894. Duncan McFatton, Cheraw, Nov. 18, 1892. Hampton McKenny, Phoenix, Nov. 9, 1898. A. McKnight, Union City, June 28, 1889. Dub Meetze, Lexington County, July 18, 1893. Rafe Monoll, Barnwell, Dec. 28, 1889. Charles Nelson, Jefferson, Nov. 24, 1903. Louis Patrick, Bayne, June 18, 1899. Allen Pendleton, Abbeville, Sept. 20, 1905. Robert J. Phoenix, Barnwell, Dec. 28, 1889. Thomas Price, Westville, Apr. 23, 1896. Richard Puckett, Laurens, Aug. 12, 1913. John Richards, Abbeville, Nov. 24, 1895. Peter Rivers, Olar, Mar. 13, 1812. Charles Robinson, Elko, Jan. 16, 1901. Rufus Salter, West Springs, Jan. 11, 1900. Frank Samuels, Branchville,

June 11, 1909. Allen Seymour, Hampton, Dec. 16, 1914. David Shaw, Gray Court, May 31, 1892. Tuillie Simmons, Branchville, June 11, 1909. W. D. Sims, York, Aug. 24, 1917. Jules Smith, Winnsboro, June 14, 1915. William Spain, St. George, Aug. 22, 1906. William Stokes, Colleton County, June 26, 1895. Luther Sullivan, Edgefield Court House, Oct. 23, 1898. John Taylor, Chesterfield County, July 5, 1904. William Thomas, Newberry, Nov. 23, 1912. Bruce Tisdale, Andrews, Feb. 15, 1941. Sam Turner, Kingstree, Dec. 29, 1897. Thomas Watts, Abbeville, Nov. 24, 1895. Fred Whisonant, Blacksburg, Mar. 29, 1912. Nathan White, Quaker Creek, Nov. 28, 1892. Mrs. Wideman, Troy, Dec. 27, 1902. Oliver Wideman, Troy, Dec. 27, 1902. Cairo Williams, Scranton, June 20, 1904. Drayton Williams, Phoenix, Nov. 9, 1898. Jesse Williams, Phoenix, Nov. 9, 1898. Dillard Wilson, Shiloh, Nov. 24, 1914. Unknown Negro, Berkley County, May 16, 1892. Unknown Negro, Berkley County, May 9, 1892. Unknown Negro, Lancaster, June 3, 1894. Unknown Negro, Landrum, Nov. 29, 1894. Unknown Negro, Lincoln County, July 6, 1896. Unknown Negro, Orangeburg, Jan. 8, 1897. Unknown Negro, Saluda, Feb. 13, 1897. Unknown Negro, Hampton, Oct. 21, 1901. Two Unknown Negroes, Norway, July 1, 1903. Unknown Negro, Waterloo, Sept. 1, 1904. Unknown Negro, Marion County, May 7, 1907. Unknown Negro, Lexington, Jan. 6, 1909.

TENNESSEE: Robert Alexander, Ripley, Jan. 3, 1904. Charles Allen, Mc-Kenzie, Nov. 15, 1896. James Ball, Charlotte, July 7, 1894. Frank Ballard, Jackson, June 1, 1894. Alexander Bell, Mt. Pelia, Oct. 5, 1892. William Bell, Dixon County, July 14, 1894. Luther Billings, Brunswick, Oct. 10, 1905. Dennis Blackwell, Alamo, Aug. 27, 1892. Andy Blount, Chattanooga, Feb. 14, 1893. Green Boman, Shelbyville, Feb. 19, 1912. Joseph Brake, Ripley, Dec. 10, 1903. Thomas Brooks, Somerville, Apr. 28, 1915. Charles Brown, Soddy, Feb. 26, 1897. Curtis Brown, Newburn, Oct. 8, 1902. Robert Bruce, Tiptonville, Sept. 13, 1910. Garfield Burley, Newburn, Oct. 8, 1902. George Call, Lynchburg, Jan. 17, 1899. William Chambers, Bellbuckle, Aug. 11, 1899. Robert Clark, Bristol, June 13, 1891. Samuel Clay, Martin, June 12, 1896. Walter Cole, Morgan County, Jan. 21, 1908. John Collar, Godson, Mar. 21, 1898. Nimrod Cross, Sardis, July 6, 1896. Patrick Crump, White Haven, June 1, 1911. Ballie Crutchfield, Rome, Mar. 16, 1901. John Davis, Lewisburg, Nov. 13, 1902. Thomas Devert, Erwin, May 20, 1918. Samuel M. Donald, Huntingdon, Nov. 19, 1896. Samuel M. Donald, Huntingdon, Nov. 19, 1896. York Douglas, McMinnville, Apr. 17, 1896. L. C. Dumas, Gleason, June 8, 1893. Jeff Ellis, Braden, Oct. 15, 1895. Charles Everett, Manchester, May 19, 1892. George Estes, Hales Point, Oct. 29, 1906. Harrison Fuller, Lexington, Jan. 8, 1896. John Gamble, Pikeville, Oct. 22, 1893. Anderson Ganse, Henning, Jan. 16, 1900. Elmo Garvard, Pulaski, May 8, 1908. Henry Giveney, Ripley, Jan. 9, 1900. Roger Giveney, Ripley, Jan. 9, 1900. Albert Gooden, Covington, Aug. 17, 1937. Lampson Gregory, Bells Depot, Mar. 6, 1894. John Gregson, Union City, Mar. 21, 1913. Walter Grer, Shelbyville, Feb. 19, 1912. Henry Griggard, Goodlettsville, Apr. 28, 1892. Ephriam Groggard, Nashville, Apr. 30, 1892. Ronce Gwyn, Tullahoma, Mar. 8, 1905. Edward Hall, Millington, Sept. 1, 1894. Daniel Hawkins, Millington, Sept. 1, 1894. John Hayes, Millington, Sept. 1, 1894. Joseph Hayne, Jellico, Feb. 26, 1893. Robert Haynes, Millington, Sept. 1, 1894. Frinch Haynie, Hendersonville, Feb. 16, 1891. Thomas Huntley, Cumberland Gap, Mar. 26, 1891. Charles Hurd, Wartburg, Nov. 21, 1895. Charles Jones, Elk Valley, June 24, 1903. Hugh Jones, Middleton, July 14, 1908. Jessie Jones, Jellico, Mar. 19, 1893. Edward Johnson, Chattanooga, Mar. 19, 1906. George Johnson, Murfreesboro, Aug. 28, 1908. Jerry Johnson, Farmington, Sept. 3, 1895. "Doc" King, Fayetteville, Sept. 6, 1895. Fred King, Dyersburg, Feb. 18, 1901. Loeb Landers, Dresden, Aug. 1, 1892. Albert Lawson, Paris, July 20, 1909. William Lewis, Tullahoma, Aug. 25, 1891. Thomas Lillard, Woodbury, July 1, 1892. G. W. Lych, Estill Springs, Feb. 10, 1918. Wyatt Mallory, Springfield, Apr. 29, 1901. Mrs. Martin, Sumner County, Feb. 3, 1892. Martin Mayberry, Bryant Station, Apr. 2, 1891. Walter Mc-Clennon, Huntingdon, Oct. 4, 1901. Calvin McDonnell, Memphis, Mar. 8, 1892. Ozias McGahey, Fayetteville, Nov. 29, 1895. Henry McGreeg, Pioneer, Feb. 11, 1894. Jim McIlheron, Estill Springs, Feb. 12, 1918. Joseph Mitchell, McConnell, Nov. 13, 1891. Joseph Mitchell, Rives, May 27, 1898. Henry Montgomery, Lewisburg, Apr. 18, 1894. Thomas Moss, Memphis, Mar. 8, 1892. David Neal, Shelbyville, Feb. 19, 1912. William Nershbred, Rossville, Aug. 12, 1894. Henry Noles, Winchester, Apr. 25, 1901. Berry Noyes, Lexington, Apr. 22, 1918. James Perry, Knoxville, June 10, 1894. Ell Person, Memphis, May 22, 1917. Quinten Rankin, Walnut Log, Oct. 19, 1908. Logan Reams, Duplex, Sept. 10, 1900. Jesse F. Reed, Specific locality unknown, Dec. 14, 1892. Lewis Rice, Ripley, Mar. 23, 1900. Irwin Roberts, Shady Valley, Dec. 17, 1892. Joseph Robinson, Fayetteville, Nov. 29, 1895. Jacob Samuels, Robertson County, May 27, 1912. Henry Sanders, Lavernia, Mar. 13, 1891. James Scales, Pikeville, Nov. 23, 1944. Bradford Scott, Pinson, Mar. 10, 1891. Ligon Scott, Dyersburg, Dec. 2, 1917. Thomas Seacey, Haywood, Apr. 29. 1904. William Sharp, Tiptonville, Sept. 13, 1910. John Shaw, Lynchburg Jan. 17, 1899. Lawrence Sheppard, Memphis, Aug. 24, 1917. Frank Simpson, Lexington, Jan 8, 1896. Allen Small, Lynchburg, Sept. 1903. John Smart, Chapelton, Nov. 19, 1898. George Smith, Union City, Apr. 17, 1931. Needham Smith, Tipton County, Nov. 10, 1894. Jacob Staples, Heiskell's Station, Feb. 19, 1890. Edward Stevens, Savannah, Nov. 17, 1890. Edward Stineback, Tiptonville, Nov. 24, 1908. Tennes Stineback, Tiptonville, Nov. 24, 1908. Marshall Stineback, Tiptonville, Nov. 24, 1908. William Stuart, Memphis, Mar. 8, 1892. James Sweet, Gallatin, May 25, 1911. Charles Tait, Memphis, Aug. 21, 1893. Harriet Talley, Petersburg, Mar. 20, 1895. R. E. Taylor, Walnut Log, Oct. 19, 1908. William Taylor, Franklin, Apr. 30, 1891. John Telley, Dyersburg, Nov. 7, 1913. William Thomas, Dyersburg, Mar. 10, 1916. Thompson, Dyer, July 5, 1891. Richmond Thurmond, Ripley, Aug. 8, 1898. James Underwood, Decatur, May 12, 1902. Eugene Vancy, Manchester, Oct. 15, 1895. Ben Walling, Decaturville, July 19, 1891. Charles Washington, Mine Lick, June 23, 1898. Green Wells, Specific locality unknown, May 26, 1891. Enless Whitakes, Lynchburg, Feb. 6, 1902. Graham White, Millington, Sept. 1, 1894. William Whitley, Lebanon, Mar. 1, 1916. Williams, Tiptonville, Oct. 3, 1900. Elbert Williams, Brownsville, June 22, 1940. Henry Williams, Gadsen, Mar. 16, 1890. John Williams, Jackson, Sept. 14. 1893. John Williams, Mountain City, Sept. 26, 1898. Warner Williams, Millington, Sept. 1, 1894. Tony Williamson, West Point, July 15, 1897. Heck Willis, Lebanon, May 31, 1892. Wilson, Dresden, Sept. 4, 1915. John Winston, Lafayette, June 8, 1911. Thomas Woodward, Humboldt, Aug. 18, 1890. Unknown Negro, Jellico, Dec. 7, 1892. Unknown Negro, Nashville, Dec. 15, 1892. Unknown Negro, Waynesboro, Mar. 4, 1892. Unknown Negro, Forest Hill, Feb. 11, 1893. Unknown Negro, Parsons, Apr. 25, 1895. Unknown Negro, Trenton, June 30, 1896. Two Unknown Negroes, Webb City, Feb. 17, 1897. Unknown Negro, Newcastle, June 23, 1897. Unknown Negro, South Pittsburg. Sept. 26, 1900. Four Unknown Negroes, Caney Springs, Oct. 7, 1901. Unknown Negro, Lewisburg, Aug. 5, 1903. Unknown Negro, Lewisburg, Aug. 5, 1903. Two Unknown Negroes, Lake County, July 22, 1907. Two Unknown Negroes, Clifton, Dec. 6, 1911. Unknown Negro, Clifton, Dec. 6, 1911. Unknown Negro, Memphis, Feb. 15, 1912.

TEXAS: Anderson, Marshall, Feb. 25, 1913. William Armor, Paris, Sept. 6, 1892. Charles Bealle, Lang, 'an. 1, 1891. Edward Bennett, Hearne, May 12, 1890. William Black, Moscow, Nov. 22, 1891. James Brooks, Orange, Aug. 14, 1889. Gene Brown, Benhur, July 27, 1918. John Brown, Navasota, Aug. 4, 1890. Stephen Brown, Seymour, Aug. 7, 1916. Thomas Brown, Hooks Ferry, June 1, 1890. William Butler, Hickory Creek, Feb. 17, 1893. Bessie Cabaniss. Huntsville, June 4, 1918. Cute Cabaniss, Huntsville, June 4, 1918. Pete Cabaniss, Huntsville, June 4, 1918. Sarah Cabaniss, Huntsville, June 4, 1918. Tenola Cabaniss, Huntsville, June 4, 1918. Thomas Cabaniss, Huntsville, June 4, 1918. Tobe Cook, Bastrop, June 10, 1892. Dan Davis, Tyler, May 25, 1912. Henry Davis, Waco, July 14, 1889. William Davis, Franklin, Sept. 21, 1913. Thomas Dixon, Hempstead. May 5, 1916. George Driggs, Hempstead, Apr. 15 1889. Joseph Durfee, Angleton, Oct. 17, 1914. Henry Gaines, Spurger, June 28, 1892. Richard Galloway, Newton County, June 5, 1913. Simeon Garrette, San Augustine, Apr. 20, 1890. Kirby Goolsie, Beaumont, May 27, 1918. Leo Green, Linden, Oct. 26, 1891. Gilbert Guldry, Orange July 3, 1917. Benjamin Harper, Courtney, June 22, 1917. William Hartfield, Cass County. June 28, 1891. William Hawkins, Cypress, July 30, 1890. Elijah Hays, Reisel, June 23, 1917. Patrick Henry, Nechesville, July 3, 1890. George Hughes, Sherman, May 9, 1930. Mary Jackson, Marshall, Feb. 13, 1912. Stephen Jacobs, Fay, Apr. 20, 1890. Robert Jefferson, Temple, June 29, 1917. Charles Jennings, Beaumont, Sept. 3, 1917. Washington Jess, Waco, May 15, 1916. George Johnson, Honey Grove, May 18, 1930. Joseph Johnson, Bay City, Nov. 5, 1916. Charles Jones, Marshall, Aug. 22, 1917. William Johnson. Henderson, July 22, 1891. Edward Lang, Rice, Aug. 19, 1916. David Lee, Jefferson, Jan. 8, 1914. Jeronimo Lerma, Brownsville, June 20, 1916. George Lewis, Belen, July 26. 1889. George Lindley, Greenville, July 28, 1889. Henry Monson, Paris, Jan. 17, 1913. Abe O'Neal, Buff Lake, Sept. 18, 1918. Robert Perry, Karnach, Feb. 25, 1913. John Ransom, Paris, Sept. 6, 1892. Thomas Rebin, Douglas, Feb. 17, 1891. King Richmond,

Sulphur Springs, Aug. 29, 1915. William Roane, Bryan, June 17, 1930. William Robertson, Navasota, June 7, 1914. Thomas Rowland, Douglas, Feb. 24, 1891. George Saunders, Marshall, Feb. 13, 1912. Charles Sawyer, Galveston, June 25, 1917. Munn Sheppard, Cass County, June 28, 1891. Charles Shipman, Ft. Bend County, Nov. 14, 1918. Bert Smith, Goose Creek, Sept. 21, 1917. Henry Smith, Paris, Jan. 31, 1893. Thomas Smith, Spurger, June 28, 1892. William Spencer, Graceton, Oct. 5, 1916. Richard Stanley, Fullbright, Jan. 23, 1913. William Sullivan, Plantersville, Sept. 23, 1892. Jerry Teel, San Augustine, Apr. 24, 1890. Buck Thomas, Clarksville, Nov. 29, 1916. Willie Vinson, Texarkana, July 13, 1942. John Walker, Paris, Sept. 6, 1892. Williams, Kosse, Apr. 5, 1890. George Williams, Waco, June 14, 1893. William Williams, Hearne, Mar. 13, 1914. Prince Wood, Spurger, June 28, 1892. Andy Young, Red R. County, July 22, 1890. Two Unknown Negroes, Liberty, Feb. 19, 1889. Unknown Negro, Millican, May 17, 1889. Two Unknown Negroes, Mexia, Aug. 14, 1890. Unknown Negro, Anderson, Aug. 8, 1890. Unknown Negro, Antlers, June 28, 1890. Unknown Negro, Cameron Station, Apr. 24, 1890. Unknown Negro, Hedsville, Mar. 27, 1890. Unknown Negro, Livingston, June 20, 1890. Unknown Negro, Thornton, Apr. 5, 1890. Two Unknown Negroes, Burnet, Nov. 13, 1891. Unknown Negro, Paris, Sept. 19, 1892. Unknown Negro, Riesil, Apr. 26, 1892. Unknown Negro, Yarborough, Aug. 31, 1893. Unknown Negro, Beaumont, June 4, 1913. Unknown Negro, Big Sandly, May 9, 1915. Unknown Negro, Elysian Fields, July 23, 1917.

VIRGINIA: Owen Anderson, Leesburg, Nov. 8, 1889. Scott Bailey, Halifax, Apr. 23, 1889. Robert Bland, Petersburg, Nov. 23, 1889. James Carter, Amherst, Apr. 6, 1902. Walter Clark, Danville, Oct. 13, 1917. Charles Craven, Leesburg, July 31, 1902. Andrew Dudley, Greenfield, Aug. 4, 1904. Magruder Fletcher, Tasley, Mar. 14, 1889. John Forbes, Petersburg, June 11, 1889. Wiley Gam, Toms Brook, June 6, 1902. Samuel Garner, Bluefield, Sept. 16, 1889. Henry Henderson, Ingram, Feb. 20, 1905. Elmer Moseley, Sussex County, Jan. 14, 1904. Mach Neal Warren, Nov. 30, 1910. William Page, Lilian, Aug. 17, 1917. Martin Roland, Abingdon, Apr. 3, 1889. Allie Thompson, Culpepper County, Nov. 24, 1918: Walker, Lawrenceville, July 1, 1901. Whitehead, Specific locality unknown, May 19, 1904. Unknown Negro, Halifax County, Mar. 22, 1901. Unknown Negro, Newport News, June 11, 1902. Unknown Negro, Richmond, Aug. 8, 1912. Unknown Negro, Hopeful, Dec. 9, 1915.

WASHINGTON: Alfred Shafford, Gilman, Jan. 7, 1889.

WEST VIRGINIA: William Brooks, Elkins, July 23, 1901. Frank Brown, Madison, Feb. 4, 1903. William Carroll, Waniesdorf, July 25, 1902. John Carter, Hinton, July 24, 1889. Rudolph Clements, Wainesdorf, July 25, 1902. Cornelius Coffee, Keystone, Dec. 5, 1892. Alexander Foote, Princeton, Aug. 13, 1891. Anderson Holliday, Elkhorn, Aug. 2, 1894. Peter Jackson, Elkins, July 25, 1902. Walter Johnson, Bluefield, Sept. 5, 1912. Alexander Jones, Bluefield, Jan. 28, 1896. Edgar Jones, Weston, July 6, 1892. William Lee, Hinton, May 11, 1900. Charles Lewis, Sutton, Nov. 3, 1903. Mills Luther, Mercer County, May 13, 1892. Green McCoy, Hamlin, Oct. 25, 1889. James Smith, Logan County, May 27, 1892. "Red" Smith, Naugatuck, May 15, 1892. John Turner, Fayetteville, Aug. 30, 1889. T. Williams, Glen Jean, Feb. 7, 1902. Unknown Negro, Bramwell, Feb. 1, 1896. Two Unknown Negroes, Waniesdorf, July 25, 1902. Unknown Negro, Huntington, Oct. 14, 1910. Unknown Negro, Welch, Nov. 22, 1917.

WYOMING: J. S. Bedford, Big Horn, Oct. 16, 1892. Wade Hampton, Rick Springs, Dec. 14, 1917. John Martin, Laramie, Aug. 30, 1904. Frank Wigfall, Rawlins, Oct. 2, 1904. Edward Woodson, Green River, Dec. 10, 1918.